"The spirit world, knowing that initiation is both the birthright of each human, and the collective responsibility of community, constantly shape-shifts to gain our individual and collective attention. Mary Trainor~Brigham, recognizing the work of spirit in cinema, asks us to reawaken to the truth residing in our bones - that initiation is essential; it is that which propels us toward maturity and living our purpose."
— **Malidoma Patrice Some**, Ph.D, Author, Initiated Elder of the Dagara Tribe, CDs: *Elemental Ritual* and *Ancestralization: What do we owe the Dead?*

"Wow. Who knew all this stuff was going on in the movies? *Deep Cinema* digs into the celluloid and tries to pull out something basic about human behavior and how we experience it in cinematic storytelling. Makes it tough to go back to the 12-plex and put the mind on automatic."
— **John Sayles**, Writer/Director, *Matewan, Lone Star, Honeydripper*

"A fascinating and expertly-written analysis and a form of true modern shamanism which, unlike other books, does not lead you away into fantasy lands but is firmly rooted in this world. If you love film, you will love this; if you are drawn to shamanism, you will love this; if you suspect that there is more to life than you know... well, read on, find your answers, and begin your own initiation into the world of the real."
— **Ross Heaven**, Author, *Vodou Shaman, Plant Spirit Shamanism*, and *The Sin Eater's Last Confessions*

"This is one of those books I wish I'd written. It concurs with my belief that movies and stories can have a shamanic function, but it also spreads out a comprehensive vision of the ancient and still vibrant indigenous world view. Movie examples, including some overlooked gems, are well selected to illustrate rites of passage and the processes of initiation."
— **Christopher Vogler**, Author, *The Writer's Journey-3rd Edition*

"A bold and engaging book. There is no way to go through it quickly as every page, every sentence, has great wisdom. *Deep Cinema's* understanding and presentation of Huna with all its subtleties is right on. I can see this treasure educating people from the worlds of shamanism and film-making about one another. Mary Trainor~Brigham speaks from the experience of her Aumakua. She has entered the void, journeyed 'between the worlds' and brought back her insights and initiations to help us (the tribe) in our healing."
— **Laura Kealoha Yardley**, Author, *Heart of Huna,* Spiritual Teacher & Practitioner

"Be prepared to be transformed! Ms. Trainor~Brigham invites the reader on a remarkable personal journey into the deeper waters of the impulse and purpose of storytelling across culture. This is a monumental work that inspires filmmakers with its wealth of insights and film examples, celebrating film's 'transformative elixir' of individual and social enlightenment. Brava!"
— **Stuart Voytilla**, Author, *Myth and the Movies*

D1445055

"*Deep Cinema* is a paradigm-shifting work which re-invents dimensions of human story-telling in the light of both ancient and prophetic potential. Mary Trainor~Brigham engages catalytic Cosmic forces through her love and understanding of Initiation. Her book has the power to re-ignite the grace of Indigenous Soul. Film-lovers, filmmakers, practitioners of Shamanic wisdom, all will be replenished by embarking upon the profound and delightful voyage this manifesto provides."

> — **Brian Swimme**, Professor of Cosmology, California Institute of Integral Studies, San Francisco, DVD series: *The Earth's Imagination* and *Canticle to the Cosmos*

"*Deep Cinema: Film as Shamanic Initiation* invites a stimulating rendezvous 'round the projector's rays with the likes of C.G. Jung, Ernest Becker and your author, Mary Trainor~Brigham. As commanding as antediluvian adventures 'round ancestral campfires, this invitation requires no R.S.V.P. Just get hold of this book!"

> — **Richard D. Pepperman**, Author, *Setting Up Your Scenes, The Eye is Quicker*, and *Film School*

"Mary Trainor~Brigham's book, *Deep Cinema*, carries the film viewing experience from mere entertainment to shamanic initiation — something many have felt yet never voiced."

> — **Catherine Ann Jones**, Author, *The Way of Story: the Craft and Soul of Writing*

"A compelling and entertaining book that deserves to be read by anyone serious about films and filmmaking."

> — **Phil Hall**, Contributing Editor, *Film Threat*

"As Director Akira Kurosawa has said, 'All filmmaking is a spiritual quest.' Whether one reads Joseph Campbell on the roots of Mythology, Carl Jung on dreams and symbols, modern Quantum Physicists on the apprehension of consciousness as the ground of being, or travels with a Yaqui Shaman, one thing seems certain: Stories that express a world of archetypes rather than a world of stereotypes are more satisfying and thought provoking. The world behind the world as it were, or the shadows on the cave wall exposed for what they are according to Plato. This is very interesting material that gets to the essence of what makes for Story and through that, what makes for good Film."

> — **Richard La Motte**, Author, *Costume Design 101*

"In *Deep Cinema*, Trainor~Brigham bridges the gap between shamanic traditions and modern cinema, giving us greater insight into indigenous cultures, a deeper understanding of the initiatory process, and a mythological template that will help us understand films in a more profound way and transform our lives in the process. Whether you're a movie lover, a student of spiritual teachings, or a writer looking to go deeper, *Deep Cinema* will help you take it to the next level!"

> — **Derek Rydall**, Screenwriter, Author, *There's No Business Like Soul Business* and *I Could've Written a Better Movie Than That!*

"Trainor~Brigham understands the core sensibilities of these films. She enlarges the possibilities of interpretation by bringing to bear cross-cultural references, enhancing the tales she treats by bringing them into an ever-expanding mythical realm. At the same time she probes the intimate pains and joys of the figures on the screen, always with a respect that deepens their mystery."

> — **Pamela Berger**, Filmmaker, Art Historian specializing in the Middle Ages

"Enigmatic and profoundly illuminating, *Deep Cinema* is perhaps the most holistic view of cinematic creation that you'll ever experience."

> — **Scott Billups**, Author, *Digital Moviemaking 3.0*

DEEP CINEMA
Film as Shamanic Initiation

Mary Trainor ~ Brigham, M.A.

FILM
PN
1995
.T638
2008

Published by Michael Wiese Productions
3940 Laurel Canyon Blvd., # 1111
Studio City, CA 91604
tel. 818.379.8799
fax 818.986.3408
mw@mwp.com
www.mwp.com

Cover Design: Michael Wiese Productions
Cover Art: Didier Junk (www.3d-atelier.eu)
Book Interior Design: Gina Mansfield Design
Editor: Janice Rayner
Illustration (page 15 & 50) : John Murray of Taos (interspecific@yahoo.com)
Illustration (page 4) : from *Vodou Shaman* by Ross Heaven, courtesy of Destiny Books,
        Rochester, VT, 05767 Copyright © 2003 Inner Traditions/Bear
        & Company

Printed by McNaughton & Gunn, Inc., Saline, Michigan
Manufactured in the United States of America

© 2008 Mary Trainor~Brigham

Library of Congress Cataloging-in-Publication Data

Trainor-Brigham, Mary.
 Deep cinema : film as shamanic initiation / by Mary Trainor-Brigham.
    p. cm.
 ISBN 978-1-932907-50-6
 1.   Motion pictures--Psychological aspects. 2.   Motion pictures--Social aspects.
 I. Title.
 PN1995.T638 2008
 791.43'653--dc22
                                2008023948

TABLE OF CONTENTS

ACKNOWLEDGMENTS

In the light of reverence for the Domain Basin of **Nature**, I must begin by thanking the **Atlantic Maritime Coast** for providing both mystic origins and a site of home-coming during the roundabout Walkabout process of writing *Deep Cinema*.

And speaking of Origins, in Eternal love for those who have passed on to the Deep Heavens, I thank my mother, **Charlotte Murphy Trainor**, my father **Stephen Lawrence Trainor**, my mentor and colleague, **Rev. Father Edgar Bourque**, my husband's Ashram Spiritual leader, **Rev. Mother Gayatri Devi**, and **Medicine Man Slow Turtle** of the Wampanoag Nation of Cape Cod.

In keeping with the African adage, *"Go to the waters to dream, go to the mountains to cook your dream,"* I must next thank **Taos Mountain**, its **Sacred Blue Lake**, and all the wild-hearted artists of that New Mexican town who provided camaraderie during the bulk of my writing time. This includes **Marianne and Ron Furedi**, at whose Colbalt Blue Mesa Heaven my husband & I were living when I first contacted filmmaker/publisher **Michael Wiese** with a proposal for this book. I can viscerally recall the gratitude that streamed out from my husband and myself to him for taking a chance on an author who, unlike many in his stable of writers, *didn't* have 25 years of experience in the Industry or teaching at UCLA. But Michael & I did share a birth date (albeit four years apart), and a love of several indelible kindred cultural icons, including **Joseph Campbell & Jean Erdman Campbell**, **Maya Deren & Teiji Ito**, **Pablo Neruda**, **Buckminster Fuller**, **D. H. Lawrence**, and alluring **Mermaidens**, whose Spirits must have endorsed this endeavor: Thank you each and every one!

Also for providing artistic & activist camaraderie during this creative process, I thank **Laura Kealoha Yardley, Ross Heaven, Aunty Margaret Machado, Malidoma Some, Brian Swimme, Chellis Glendinning, Didier Junk, Pamela Adger, John Murray, Shawn LaSala-Kimmel, Rebecca Tzigany & James Bertrand, Lisa Sloan, Linda Grotke, Deb Roberts, Patricia Michaels & James Duran, Sherrye Weinstein, Tami Sanders, Marilyn Jesmain** (aka "Otstach"), **Janelle Sperrow** and her Taos black box theatre students, **Bruce McIntosh** and his Taos MetaTheatre players, **Marc Clopton** and his Newburyport Actor's Studio, and **Donna Keonaona Forman** and her Huna Institute.

Actors I need to thank for their ever-enthralling and/or delightful performances include **Juliet Binoche, Olivier Gourmet, Meryl Streep, Mads Mikkelson, Dominique Sanda, Tantoo Cardinal, Philip Seymour Hoffman, Cliff Curtis, Keisha Castle-Hughes, Javier Bardem, Cate Blanchett, Angelina Jolie, Johnny Depp, Sheila Tousey, David Gulpilil, Tilda Swinton, Irfan Khan, Rachel Weisz, Mamaengaroa Kerr-Bell,** and **Laura Morante.**

Soundtracks which sustained me while writing included **The Sheltering Sky, Solaris, The Last of the Mohicans, The Dancer Upstairs, The Piano, The Messenger, The Mission, The Warrior, Copying Beethoven, Leonard Cohen: I'm Your Man,** and **Whale Rider.**

People who aided me with the pragmatic nuts and bolts of getting *Deep Cinema* done and whom I thank from my heart for your generosity include **Janice ("Janessa") Rayner, Pam Brigham, Mark Brigham, Jim Suokko, Jennifer Pettit, Anne Gagnon & Nancy Askin, Gina Mansfield,** and **Wally Griffin.**

My last and most soulful **Thank You** goes out to my husband and favorite Shamanic Actor, **Ciarán Trainor-Brigham,** who sacrificed creative colleagues and the primordial wonder of Taos to move back East and support me in the final phase of writing this book. Despite his grueling work schedule, he managed to provide me many a nocturnal insight and suggestion which deepened the internal current-flow of my writing, and without which it wouldn't be half the hauntingly beautiful offering that it is. Mega Mahalo, **Beloved!**

DEDICATION

Deep Cinema is dedicated to all of you esteemed readers who will dive into its guidance and emerge with Soulful intent to enrich your lives and enhance this Culture.

It is also dedicated to my Canine Muse, Schizandra, the Spiritual Advisor of the Trainor-Brigham family, who earns that appellation by sheer dint of modeling all the best possible qualities in man, woman or beast. And to my Feline Companion/Secretary, Pomakai, who would lay atop the computer until the copier started up, at which point she'd leap down (in her furry "Pirate boots") to most assiduously oversee the print-out. Mahalo!

Pre-eminently, *Deep Cinema* is dedicated to my Soul's enduring Enchantment, Ciarán Trainor-Brigham:

I want to be for you
An Eternally-fresh glass of water
Such that when you drink from me
You taste clarity, purity, brilliance
And deeper ~ salt,
A tang of seaweed, the residue of briny memories...
And finally
Seismic disturbances
Issuing from the ultimate depths
A bubbling cascade: a Remembrance
Of your Original promise.
I want to be no less than that for you.

INITIATORY INTRODUCTION

"Identity would seem to be a garment with which one covers the nakedness of the self, in which case, it is best that the garment be loose; a little like the robes of the desert, through which one's nakedness can always be felt. This trust in one's nakedness is all that gives one the power to change one's robes."

— James Baldwin

I f you've ever walked into a movie one way, secure in your familiar worldview and self-image, and walked out after the screening feeling radically transformed, then you've experienced the power of film as Initiation.

It happened for me the day I drove into Boston intending to see *Elvira Madigan*, a classically sentimental, star-crossed love story involving an aristocratic military man and his circus acrobat lover. Their tragedy ends in an off-screen double suicide, their Spirits symbolized as innocuous butterflies floating upward above a field of flowers. Or so I'm told. I never did see *Elvira Madigan*. What I did see that day advanced my psyche and my film aesthetic into exhilarating new dimensions. Yet dimensions well within any butterfly's ken: Metamorphosis, Initiation.

Boston is a notoriously difficult city to navigate by car, its streets having evolved from former meandering cow paths, and the task of finding parking there is no mean feat. So when I arrived at the multiplex only to be told that they'd moved *Elvira Madigan* to another of their theaters across town, I was in no way disposed to tackle the requisite journey. Scanning the marquee listings, I saw Bernardo Bertolucci's historical drama, *The Conformist*, and remembered its ad in the past Sunday's *New York Times*. It depicted two European women with 1930s coiffures and attire, one a blonde (Dominique Sanda), the other a brunette (Stefania Sandrelli) dancing the tango together. Intrigued, I was in.

Two hours later I emerged, staggered. Having driven to town to view a predictable update of *Romeo and Juliet*, I beheld instead a shattering exposé of all manner of psycho-social-sexual turmoil: Fascism, dementia, addiction, repressed homosexuality, expressed bisexuality, political exiles, hired assassins, a blind man, a hunchbacked philosophy professor, adulterous lust, murderous betrayal, and a profound personal reckoning.

THE CONFORMIST

Bertolucci's tale is a masterpiece of seduction and suspense, well served by Vittorio Storaro's indelible cinematography. What a turbulent plot! The lead character, Italian Marcello Clerici (Jean-Louis Trintignant) is still very young when drawn into a homoerotic, sado-masochistic cat-and-mouse game, orchestrated by a debauched chauffeur. Its apparently devastating outcome squelches any further sexual experimentation on Marcello's part, compelling him instead on a path of utmost social orthodoxy: *The Conformist*. What begins as understandable remorse and cautionary choices on his part devolves into blinkered cowardice when he finds refuge in serving Mussolini's Fascist state. His role? A hired assassin. His target? Marcello's freethinking, anti-Fascist, former college professor, now exiled in Paris.

Not only does the aging, hunchbacked scholar shame Marcello by reminding him of better philosophical and political options. But the professor's young wife, Anna (Dominique Sanda), in her blatant bisexuality, displays greater erotic authenticity than Marcello has allowed himself to pursue. Hardly conformists, they. But by the time this dark duel between Freedom and Fascism is done, Fascism will have prevailed, and these two bold spirits will be dead. At least Anna rails against her fate, exhibiting none of the fragile, masochistic self-sacrifice of Elvira Madigan. In blatant anguish she pleads with Marcello until his icy betrayal is indubitable, and then does her best to outrun her killers through an elegant copse of wintry trees. Her splattered blood is all the more startling in its ghastly contrast to the stark, snowy landscape. No genteel butterfly symbolism here. Oh no.

At the very end of the film it is disclosed that the inciting incident which drove youthful Marcello into a life of brutal conventionality was, in fact, a cruelly crafted illusion, a seductive hoax on the part of the wily chauffeur. Marcello makes this disorienting discovery while wandering the turbulent, nocturnal streets of Rome during Mussolini's downfall. His dictator's regime failing, his artificial cover of a life — superficial, bourgeois wife, and adorable child — left at home, Marcello settles into a dark alcove of a tunnel, contemplating his true nature. In devastation, he's been brought down to "the bone and rag shop of the heart." By having lived a life of compensation for a disaster which never really happened, he has become as morally hollow as Il Duce's shattering statue.

In this brief scene of ashen reflection, we too can envision an entirely different sequence of life choices for this tragic character, choices which could have provided healing, authenticity, and fulfillment for him. At this finale, triggering an irresistible, imaginative recapitulation, we are in effect given two plots for the price of one. How marvelous — filmmaking that can thunder open our inner dimensions and evoke our participation — Shamanic!

NATIVE INITIATION VS. MODERN ROOTLESSNESS

How was this screening an experience of Initiation for me, you may ask. For far too many people the concept of Initiation conjures images of youthful tribesmen from some exotic locale, like Kenya or New Guinea, trance-dancing in monkey fur and feathers, donning masks carved from trees grown above placentas planted at the Initiates' birth — you get the picture. And it's a wonderful one, but not the whole picture, for Initiation is the birthright of *all* humanity. It compels our Souls' evolution as inevitably as our biological make-up grows our bodies, and it can be evaded only at our peril. The show must go on!

Another common misconception about Initiation is the belief that it refers only to that most dramatic, classic coming-of-age: one's transition from childhood to adulthood. And in most tribal cultures, this once-go-'round is entirely adequate, it being so comprehensive. But with our longer life spans and modern psychological perspectives, Westerners must allow for the need to initiate into many facets of our psyche, such as our Trickster Self, our Spirit Spouse, and our own capacity to eventually Mentor and Initiate others from the vantage point of our accrued knowing. At best, it's a life-long, ongoing round, a progressive deepening and clarifying of that which deserves to endure infinitely, a clarification polished during Eldership: what I call Diamond-Cutting (yang) and Pearl-Spinning (yin).

CORE INITIATION

At its core, classic Initiation facilitates the conscious launching of one's Destiny, helps the Initiate endeavor to fulfill their life purpose. In many tribes, information about an individual's Fate would have been discerned by Shamans (or Medicine Men/Women) before the child was even born. At a pre-ordained stage of pregnancy, the spiritual Elders would gather around the Mother-to-be, drum her into a trance and ask questions of the fetus-Soul, who would supply through the Mother their intended name, sex, and destiny. Tweaking may be in order, as when the unborn's chosen Destiny clashes with their chosen sex; then the Elders would advise.

In other tribes, one's individual purpose is discerned in the Initiate's youth during a period of trial (masculine) or isolation (feminine): embarking on a hunt, a Vision Quest, an extended stay in a Moon Lodge, suspension overnight in the trees, or some other such testing ordeal to expedite remembrance of one's life-mission. At any rate, one does not claim Adulthood until one has made adequate separation from one's biological parents, benefited from 'tribal' Mentors, and secured a clear vision of one's place in the grand scheme of things.

Such essential Self-knowing! Is anything more important, really, than discerning this? How sad that so much of humanity has strayed from the fundamental rite of Initiation; imagine the countless divorces, job burn-outs and midlife crises that could be prevented if it were restored.

Because the tribal, dramatic, ritualistic, storytelling dimensions of Initiation have been partially displaced onto the collective experience of film-viewing, we can exploit the medium to re-introduce this phenomenon into our culture. We can tell stories that prioritize knowing our life-purpose and thus re-weave our connections to the Cosmos and to Nature. This is a key goal of *Deep Cinema*.

In Indigenous tribes, the transition from child to adult is clearly discerned by age-groupings. For non-Native peoples, growth cycles are messier to demark, tending to flow into and over one another like a tide's gradual turning, clogged with psychological and cultural seaweed, flotsam, and jetsam.

This is evident in *The Conformist* where the protagonist's normal development is truncated by a violently decadent, premature seduction. This allows him no authentic differentiation (Initiation), only a desperate patchwork of a life which tragically *appears* whole: work, wife, family, political and church affiliations. And yet it is false, every bit of it, even his role as an assassin is ultimately a passive re-enactment of the chauffeur's operatic drama which shattered his youthful soul. And while Marcello's circumstances appear dramatically unique, the world is actually full of such false adults, such mutant hungry ghosts, such zombies.

THE INITIATORY SPIRAL

Anthropologists who have studied Initiation recognize three universal stages to this profound process: Death, Liminal Space, and Rebirth. This can be condensed down to:

> **Death:** of an outgrown identity;
> **Liminal Space:** navigating the Unknown, risking the Underworld, returning to the mysterious Source, and floating in the fertile Void;
> **Rebirth:** returning with a new identity.

For males, the death is usually a matter of breaking past, *forging beyond*, the well-known familial Domain Basin, proving themselves via some ordeal, and returning to the tribe with new skills. For females, it is a matter of *withdrawal* from family and community into a space of incubation, and re-emergence with a new, possibly prophetic, vision.

In both cases, male and female, the person you are after you "resurrect," as it were, is profoundly other than the one you were before you "died."

DEATH

The day I drove to Boston, I certainly had familiar elements of my youthful identity intact, including a certain faith in what I call the cultural "Domain Basins" which contained and shaped me: family, school, church, culture. Like a fish in a pond, I couldn't perceive life beyond them. While not naïve, my sense of self as a fledgling Woman was obviously unevolved and unignited enough to be lured by the hackneyed romantic tale of a circus acrobat falling tragically in love with an aristocratic military man. (*Their* cultural Domain Basins of family, state, and church were powerfully cruel enough to defeat their love — alas!) What I didn't realize was that I was game for such an oppressive and sappy tale not because it *nurtured* my nature, but because it was a classic story being told to young women in my "tribe," time and time again.

And here is as good a place as any to point out that there are two types of Initiation: that which clones youth into pre-fabricated social roles (conformists), and that which respects that each one of us has a unique Destiny to fulfill. As I intend *Deep Cinema* as a Manifesto for creative vision, I am largely forgoing the former to endorse the latter: coloring both in and outside the lines.

At the time of my auspicious trip to Boston, the part of my psyche in league with Deep Mystery was ripe for its unique growth. The Fates conspired to prolong my search for a parking space, had re-located the screening of *Elvira Madigan* across town, and made me arrive at the multiplex just in time for a movie I'd no (conscious) intention of seeing: *The Conformist*.

My old identity was about to undergo phase one of Initiation: Death. Perhaps it had been dying longer than I knew, with no Tribal Elders keen to point out the unraveling process or assure me that Nature's empowering options awaited me.

LIMINAL SPACE

As for Liminal space, that soulful arena of treading stars between identities, when "the old is out of fashion and the new not yet begun," for me that consisted of:

— Growing disillusionment with female roles this culture encouraged.

— The "masculine" task of leaving home and tribe and driving solo the forty-mile trip to Boston, trancing out to my favorite music in the car.

— The "female" ritual of entering the enclosed, cave-like darkness of the theater, a return to a fertile Void, a Cosmic Womb through an Underworld passage.

— Awaiting the unpredictable imagery of new life to flare onto the wall of the screen, and

— Watching the film itself.

I was smitten by Dominique Sanda's acting throughout, its rare mix of power and translucency. She had Anna's bold, predatory sexuality emerge from a primal core of self-confidence, uneroded by patriarchal cultural mores. She was married to a brilliant, politically radical professor more than twice her age, and a hunchback at that. She pursued a woman whom she desired, right under her husband's doting eyes, with impunity. And she did her utmost to resist her treacherously-dealt brutal death, with a passion. After a cultural diet of wilting Ophelias and tragic Juliets, Anna provided a much-needed implosion of psychic sheet lightning.

Her strengths made watching Marcello's weaknesses bearable, as she was all that he was not. His tragic flaw was denial of his sexual identity: "so far into the closet as to be in Narnia," as they say. He certainly became a despicable character: cowardly, elitist, and destructive. But as the plot discloses his litany of narcissistic wounds, one is amazed he survived at all. Hardly anyone saw him for who he was, hardly any one of the usual formative Domain Basins held him lovingly — not his addictive mother nor his insane father, not the church nor the state. Only his former philosophy professor challenged the best in him to emerge. And, having aligned himself with a totalitarian state, Marcello *had* to kill off that brave mentor, along with his vibrant wife. He had to reduce their passionately determined and glowingly-engaged lives to the rubble of his false one.

One of my theories in *Deep Cinema* is that when human Domain Basins fail us, we have something larger in the Spirit realm to fall back on. That is why this introduction is designated "0" in honor of the mysterious Source, the fertile Void that precedes all else. If we only begin with "I," the masculine number of manifestation, without naming the Void as original Source, then we only have the manifest world to deal with, with no inherent and/or transcendent Spiritual Sources of potential to draw upon.

There was a glimpse of awareness of such transcendence in Marcello's face in the final scene, even as the more feral notes of bitterness played across it. Something true in his nature, maybe just a spark from an extinguished fire, glinted in his eyes. Could it re-ignite? If it did, we know it would come at considerable cost to those sharing the false life he'd created, shattering their manifest world. The Uninitiated are treacherous indeed, and not only to themselves, but to themselves first and foremost. The truth will out.

REBIRTH

I emerged from the theater a different person than I'd entered it, trusting a bi-sexual, liberated, impassioned French radical more than the sorry, pre-dictable suicide I'd come to Boston to see. I learned that if all else fails you — family, church, state — you needn't "conform" out of desperation; you can suck it out of your own thumb: "God bless the child that's got its own."

Seeing Jean-Louis Trintignant's character stripped of all support, deprived of every regulatory ritual of Initiation, ironically initiated me. How? Because I recognized in his circumstances, albeit more dramatic than my own, some measure of my personal deprivation. The solution: seeing how Dominique Sanda's character cultivated a life far richer than *The Conformist's* narrowly-prescribed margins. Her liberated exile helped me realize that some psycho-spiritual safety net prevails beyond familiar horizons, if only we are true enough to ourselves to risk the leap. If only that.

The Conformist gave me permission to take a full measure of my own life: family, church, state, school, and ask how much they'd genuinely supported me, or not. Then I asked what in my life exceeded those social institutions and sustained me, what larger Domain Basins could I initiate into. Two answers sprang simultaneously to mind: Spirituality and Nature.

And then they twined together, like yin and yang snakes from Eden, like the dance of DNA, in an ongoing pulsating appreciation of all the wis-dom I'd ever gleaned from Native lore: teachings from Hawaii, Africa, Tibet, pre-Christian Ireland, North, South and Meso-America, from Australia and

New Zealand, Bali, Madagascar, Sri Lanka, etc. I realized that while the modern world had failed me time and again, the ancient ones had not, nor had the most ancient of them all: Creation, Nature, and the Source itself, the fertile Void, the Dream-Time.

Another facet of my Destiny came clear that day as well. I had always loved movies, ever since the age of eight years when my mother took me to see *The Miracle of Marcellino*. About a decade later, the raw beauty, dark savvy and utmost professional skill that went into telling the tragedy of Marcello, *The Conformist*, sealed my soul with an inner resolve to always have film a central part of my life. And so it has been. I'd been initiated onto a path I have not failed, nor has it failed me. And so it goes.

AND NOW: DEEP CINEMA

Years later, I find that I've long had a foot in both canoes: Indigenous and Western cultures, healing and creativity, the mysterious and the manifest. I've earned a Master's degree in Culture & Spirituality, trained to become an Art Therapist, served as a co-Minister in the Unitarian Universalist Church, and worked in many dimensions of film: as a columnist, via acting, as a member of the Harvard Square Scriptwriters' group, and in documentary film production. Throughout it all, I have continued to pursue my passion for Initiation, and Native wisdom teachings have, in turn, continued to provide my Soul's deepest fulfillment.

As best that I (as a white, Irish-American, educated, middle-class woman) can access it, the Indigenous world-view has become mine. For me, its riches far exceed those of this "End Culture" of modern colonialism, corporate dominion, consumerism, and addiction in which we find ourselves dying, or continuously being invited to die, on the Spirit level. We can and must be wary and resilient, and more than survive: thrive and flourish as dynamic souls, not programmed "sheeple." Deeper cinematic storytelling can invite us onto a more authentic and fulfilling pathway.

As the poet Dylan Thomas wrote, "After the first death, there is no other." Regarding this phenomena, one might clarify, "after the first *conscious* death." Once we begin to recognize Initiation's ongoing invitation to dissolve and reform our identities throughout life: that Death and Re-birth, grief and growth, are two sides of the same coin, our consciousness ignites a vibration of "Everlastingness." Faith is no longer a blind trust in external, man-made laws and dictates; *faith becomes fidelity to the insights you have gained.* Once your knowing is organically, instinctually grounded in your trustworthy gut, it has a chance to perdure.

The time has come, again, that we comprehend the Initiatory, Shamanic world-view as our innate Heritage, trusting that a more practiced participation in it can enrich our lives and culture inestimably.

WARNINGS: MINOR & MAJOR

Minor: Per necessity of comprehensive analysis SPOILERS are strewn throughout *Deep Cinema*. So *do* watch each film before reading my take on it if you don't want premature disclosure.

Major: After reading this book, your expectation for what films can/should deliver will have been beckoned to a radically higher/deeper standard. Indelibly. And that's a good thing. Since all change starts with a new dream, we can join collectively to manifest this one. And manifest it we must. Initiation requires metamorphosing from the paler life chapter of dreaming our dreams to the more vibrantly colored, muscularly-engaged epoch of actually living our true lives. And as our tolerance for "Shallow Cinema" ebbs, so too will its production. No more wading deeper and deeper into ever more shallow waters.

After all, the only sin against Initiation is resistance to it: going back to your old identity as if you hadn't tasted the transformative elixir offered, hadn't glimpsed new inner and outer horizons. I, fortunately, was up for the requisite psychic quantum leap: after experiencing the daring innovation of *The Conformist*, wild horses couldn't drag me back to the saccharine likes of *Elvira Madigan*. Or, better put, Bertolucci's stormy masterpiece provided my consciousness precisely the wild horses required to gallop back to my culturally-programmed inner Elvira and rescue "her" from our otherwise masochistic fate. Indeed, this Sleeping Beauty got an irresistible wake-up call into a Brave New World.

INDIGENOUS RENAISSANCE

Let us return to First Things: yin and yang, Spirit and Nature. In the 1940s there was an international poetry contest based in Spain which had a splendid reward hierarchy: Third Prize was a Silver Rose, Second Prize a Golden Rose, and First Prize a Living Rose. The best creative endeavors exceed the mutant marketplace and belong to all, showing Artists to be indeed facets and forces of Nature.

It is said that the Renaissance occurred when the long-forgotten Classic teachings burst back upon the historical scene, re-emerging in all their glory like spiraling cathedral streams of sunlight, penetrating the Dark Ages. It seems to me that we find ourselves in an equal but opposite circumstance today. Not a Dark Age per se, but a relentlessly Lite one: too much light, too much progress, too much domination, too much yang, too much logos, too much isolation, too much exploitation, too much surface tinniness.

We find ourselves in urgent need of a Renaissance, this time of Indigenous teachings, which lie all about us globally, like a scattering of gems from Eden, unrecognized. We can't afford to destroy one more dimension of one more Native culture. We need to atone via recognition, reverence, reconnection. We can't allow any more holes to ulcerate what anthropologist Wade Davis calls our "Ethnosphere."

Yes, we desperately need a Renaissance of Indigenous wisdom. We need realignment with Great Spirit and Deep Mystery to continue to help them dream, and live, the Multi-verse of which we are a significant part. As Jung wrote in his *Memories*, "The decisive question for man is: Is he related to something Infinite or not? That is the most telling question of each person's life." And do you cultivate the creative means to bring that Infinite gift to bear during your finite time on Earth?

May *Deep Cinema* lovingly aid you in this essential process.

PART I

SHAMANIC TEMPLATES

"When shamans enter non-ordinary reality, the rules of the outer world are suspended. Horses fly, plants talk, fairies and leprechauns abound. Time as we know it is suspended. . . Outer rules of space are equally voided in these non-ordinary worlds."
— Sandra Ingerman, *Soul Retrieval*

If we are to perceive film as a means of Shamanic Initiation, we certainly have to be on the same page in terms of Shamanism *and* Initiation, both vast and engrossing areas of study and potential engagement. The round of Death, Liminal Space, and Rebirth is Initiation at its most fundamental. But what of the Shamanic world-view?

Fundamentally, and cross-culturally, it is usually depicted as consisting of Upper, Lower and Middle Worlds. Non-Indigenous peoples commonly experience ourselves as dwelling in Middle World, the earthy realm of the manifest, that of which we are sentient. Shamans however can trance-journey, on a drum or heartbeat, to Upper World, the realm of Spirit(s), and Lower World, an Underworld sometimes seen as Hellish or purgative, but also depicted as the formative, sustaining realm of Nature, ancestry, totemic animals, etc. We are always comprised of, and participating in, all three dimensions. So while some think of Shamanic Journeying as an out-of-body experience, it can be said to be an excursion into the vaster realms of our expandable consciousness.

Upper and Lower Worlds, Above and Below, Spirit and Nature, are innately and eternally inter-flowing, dancing in sublime rhythms, engaged in a passionate, fertile, Cosmically-enduring marriage. We are the children of these parental realms: Sky and Earth, Yang and Yin, Great Spirit and Deep Mystery. Cosmologist Brian Swimme teaches *"We are the self-reflective capacity of the Universe." Self*-reflective, not 'objective' or 'other than.' And we can, via Initiation, evolve into claiming our chosen/Destined values, and sustaining more and more of our Cosmically-ordained powers. The filmmakers among you need only look to Shakespeare for his inclusion of ghosts, fairies, cross-dressing, shape-shifting, witches, skulls — he got the picture, the whole picture, and nothing less.

CULTURAL GEMS AND GENOCIDE

Let us review, compare, and complement two Shamanic templates: one Haitian and the other Hawaiian, one for its cultural mapping and the other for its psychological comprehension. Although Shamanism is the world's oldest spiritual tradition, preceding all others and still universally extant, I quite purposely chose to illustrate it via these two relatively unknown cultures. Why?

Because the Voudon religion has been so brutally trashed via idiotic depictions in the lowest of low-grade horror flicks, some considerable measure of atonement is due. It also opens a door to coastal West African spiritualities, from the very region where Natives were forced across the sea as slaves (via the gruesome trans-Atlantic Middle Passage) to the Caribbean and Americas. And I personally have found the Hawaiian Spirituality of Huna, or Ka Hana Pono, to be the most satisfyingly congruent with my nature's deepest longings. As the ancient Irish assured us, *"You belong with what you long for."* And I am convinced that anyone would benefit from exposure to their Polynesian wisdom teachings rather than continuing to reduce their culture to mere eye-candy tourist trade.

As for serving the balance of dark and light, of yin and yang, I can't imagine greater polarization, in terms of Western perception, than these two peoples *apparently* illustrate: Haiti has been reduced by the likes of France, America, and hyper-powered economic entities like the World Bank, to being the poorest nation in the Western hemisphere. Even in the capital city of Port au Prince, open sewers, HIV, and sweatshops abound.

Set amidst the detritus of abject poverty, Haiti's Afro-Caribbean-based Voudon tradition is certainly perceived as dark, desperate, and destructive. Meanwhile the former royal kingdom of Hawaii, usurped by colonization and reduced to tourism, is blithely perceived as light and pleasurable, a tropical Paradise. Can't you sense the skewed imbalance? Can there really be no grace or revelation from Haitian slums, no mystery or trouble in Hawaii's paradise? Both lands have been mistreated, misapprehended, and wildly misrepresented in terms of their spiritual subtlety, sophistication, and power.

The blunt truth is, both Nations have been overthrown. Americans pondering the fates of Haiti and Hawaii, you can truly say, "Coups to the right of me, ousters to the left, here I am, stuck in the middle" — with whom? The very perpetrators of these takeovers. See the heartbreaking documentaries *Aristide: The Endless Revolution*, and *Hawaii's Last Queen* for the grim particulars. Because Shamanic endeavors are *real*. And anyone must give the sorry states of these once-sovereign nations (along with those of Native American Indians) profound thought before blithely celebrating Thanksgiving or the Fourth of July.

ISLAND CULTURES

Both are island cultures. This is important in that island-living emphasizes the realms of sky and sea more than that of manifest, solid land. The Sky-realm, the air, is easily associated with the Upper World of Spirit, clarity, inspiration, ideation, freedom, mind-tripping, and vision, while the Sea plunges us into the Lower World realm of mystery, dream, emotion, and sorcery, the repressed and the unknown. Non-native Westerners are encouraged to be most invested in Middle World, with its solid exploitable resources and materialistic endeavors, at the expense of the other two Domains.

For Shamanic cinema, we need to shake up that orientation, risk giving ourselves over once more to the soul-engendering, primordially passionate dance of Cosmos and Nature, even as our Ancestors once did. Just behold the continuing volcanic emergence of Hawaii, the Goddess Pele "making all things new." Such evolutionary potential is encoded in our very

3

DNA, like the entwined yin and yang, earth and water snakes which embrace the center pole of Voudon's ceremonial abodes.

VOUDON SHAMANIC TEMPLATE

Upper World: Realm of the Loa (Gods and Goddesses)
Middle World: Marketplace: Humanity & Nature
Lower World: Ancestral Watery Abyss

All penetrated and connected by a World Tree
(vertical Axis Mundi), embraced by two entwined Snakes.
All surrounded by the Bondye: Supreme Good God.

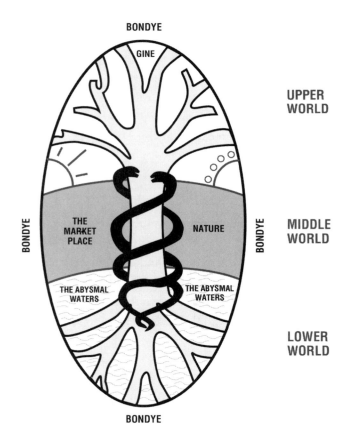

LOWER WORLD: THE WATERY ABYSS

On Haiti's Voudon Cosmic map, the Lower World is known as the Ancestral Abysmal Waters, including a Sacred Island beneath the Sea. It is to this realm that human Souls travel after death in order to adequately shed their mortal coils, and for reckoning. According to Ross Heaven, a white, British Houngan (male Voudon Priest) and the author of *Vodou Shaman, The Haitian Way of Healing and Power*, this provides not an experience of reward or punishment, but more a comprehensive review of one's life.

Any Haitian "final judgment," if you must call it that, is more a measure of the *power* of one's life than its moral rectitude. What matters is one's authentic participation in the Bondye's (Good God's) dappled agenda for our evolution, not the number of merit badges you've earned. One gets the impression with Voudon that if you'd signed on to be the human equivalent of a scorpion, you'd best have had a damn lethal sting. If your job is well done, your Soul can then proceed to become an Ancestor, or even a Loa — an Archetypal Divinity.

Screenwriters, ponder *that* next time you have to create a villain: re-think that deathbed conversion! And don't be afraid to deal directly with this spiritual phenomenon — according to membership statistics addressed in Heaven's *Vodou Shaman*, this is estimated to be the fastest-growing religion on Earth. Once you get past the unseemly misrepresentations, you can see the enthralling allure. If being embraced by the Dalai Lama (which I have been) is being embraced by a wonderfully-compassionate, incarnate God-King, then imagine the thrill of opening yourself to actual possession by a Loa!

"RETIRE MO NAN DLO"

Heaven also explains the fascinating ceremony of *retire mo nan dlo* — "to take the dead out of the water" — when the Soul of the deceased is restored to the Community a year and a day after its bodily demise. The Ancestral Spirit calls out for reunion and is ritually scooped up from the water and installed in a vessel, a clay pot called a *govi*. This is henceforth kept in the Voudon temple, and from here the voice of the dead may speak to the people, offering wisdom and counsel from the Spirit world. Heaven says such counsel is considered invaluable, not only because it comes from a loving and beloved departed Soul, but because that Ancestor is now a walker between worlds.

Over time, as with any Ancestor, remembrance of this person's nature undergoes condensation into fewer and fewer stories, one or two outstanding characteristics. Think of your own family, how one departed member is recalled in terms of their hard-working devotion, another for their humor, another for their graciousness, or courage, yet another as rakish, a roguish black sheep. Some might have been downright vile. Via distillation over time, their Spirit may eventually become a value, an Archetype.

Voudon's Spirit realm — the temple and the abiding emotional frequency of water — together open us to the oceanic liminal space between worlds, and afford Initiatory opportunity. The mysterious image of a Soul *going out to sea and downward* after death invites an entirely different psychic experience than does the pristine image of it ascending upward, evaporating into an abstract, blindingly lit Heaven. This aqueous downward plunge crosses an entirely different threshold, drawing us more into the *complexity*, and unresolved *complexes*, of the unconscious. And isn't this akin to the "possession" we sometimes experience when a blood relative, friend or enemy abruptly dies? We tangle with the angel/daemon of their Spirit, sometimes shedding it and other times resurrecting some dimension of it.

Most significantly, after a mysterious, indeterminable measure of time, some departed Souls reach the outermost regions of the Cosmos, undergo a deepening of their essential nature, and return to their people as Loa.

UPPER WORLD: THE LOA

The Voudon world is surrounded by the "Bondye," the supreme Good God. This unfathomable Entity makes Itself available to humanity by shattering its Love into a veritable plethora of Divinities. These are known as the Loa, whose multitudinous attributes knock the more predictable retinue of Catholic saints right out of the running. Voudon practitioners cultivate a life-long intimacy with this realm, with the aim of further participation in it after Death. I once studied African Dance with the marvelous, New Orleans–born Yoruba Priestess, Louisa Tiesh, who described herself, even in youth-obsessed California, as "an Ancestress of the Future."

Any Archetypal quality you can imagine, virtually any power of Nature, any human attribute you might desire or fear *and then some*, finds its embodiment in the Voudon Parthenon of gods and goddesses. It's truly mind-boggling. Want help with water-based ecological concerns? You can call upon Simbi Dlo, protector of streams, wells and all fresh waters. *Madanm* Lalinn affords enchanting inspiration, imaginative lunar magic. Need to amp up your warrior skills? Make offerings of rum, bullets and blood at the altar of Ogou La Flambo. Want a healing herbal tincture? Let Gran Ibo whisper secret medicinal herbal remedies to you (see *Vodou Visions* by Sallie Ann Glassman).

Surely, if your sense of divinity or sainthood is limited to a dutiful and simplistic idea of goodness, it takes awhile to adjust to a god known as *The First Man's Corpse*, or to Erzulie, the irresistibly languorous *Goddess of Love*. That is until you reflect a bit on the importance of Jesus' corpse, and its resurrection, to the millions of His followers. And until you come to realize that sex and death are arenas of endless amusement for the Loa, who understand how mere mortals grapple with and try to control both. As former humans, these Ancestors have been there/done that, and probably have both fond memories and better understanding than we of these inevitable powers.

In Western terms, the Loa overlap our conception of Archangel and Archetype, if you can allow for an Archangel with a penchant for rum and ribald humor, and an Archetype that can be drummed out of the collective ethers into possession of your very Soul.

FROM LOWER TO UPPER WORLDS

So we have seen the deep Voudon round of human death, submersion, resurrection and possible deepening into the status of Loa. Those who don't qualify for this honor are merely absorbed into the collective dead, *les morts*.

One of the more paradigm-shifting Voudon teachings is this: Even as our individual Souls animate our bodies and minds during this mortal life, so too do the Souls of our former Ancestors, now possibly Loa, comprise the Soul of the Cosmos. As our spirit-animated bodies are far more than a mere collection of cells, minerals, fluids, etc, so too the Heavens are more than dark matter, inanimate star-dust and meteorites, are actually ensouled via the dynamic array that is the Loa. The Spirits of the Milky Way are watching over us, lovingly.

While there are Loa who come close enough for actual possession, others just flash through in greeting, like Haley's Comet. And it is actually important that some keep their distance between human and Divine realms, maintain their Archetypal purity, uphold the moral elegance of the Heavens above the *Sturm und Drang* of human endeavor. This way the best in us can be reminded of our potential Spiritual evolution, and can ongoingly make choices that support it. In the words of the poet e.e. cummings, "I carry your heart, I carry it in my heart. This is the wonder that's keeping the stars apart." We need to individuate in order to relate. And if we are true to our guiding stars, we can actually participate consciously in the living, evolving Cosmic design!

The velvety darkness we perceive in the night heavens is actually suffused with starlight, unseen because (as yet) unreflected. So when next we are deeply roused to "wish upon a star," we'd best prepare ourselves to reflect that which we most deeply desire. As the Haitian proverb goes, "Great Gods cannot ride little horses."

MIDDLE WORLD OF THE MARKETPLACE: HUMANS & NATURE

The Voudon concept of Middle World is where modern Westerners spend most of our time, as if this was all there is. Note that for Haitians the Middle world is divided into two sides: the human Marketplace and its spiritual counterpart, Nature. The teaching here is that our Marketplace should take its cue from Nature, where harmonious give-and-take equals sustainability. For those who wish to create Deep Cinema, it is in this Voudon teaching that we get the most acute warning: what I call the 'mutant Marketplace' has swamped Nature and displaced our grounding. We must strive to reformulate it as creative and inspired.

One way we can bear this distinction in mind is to think of the origins of Wall Street. This raucous, sometimes cut-throat, modern-day signifier of economic fortunes was named after the barricade the Dutch settlers used as a divide from the Indigenous Lenape natives. "Wall Street" is an oxymoron: an "impeding conduit." The flashy LED read-outs of today's stock market, not to mention the sometimes specious elements supporting it (drug traffic), are a far cry from tribal interdependence and generous communal give-aways. And it's certainly a site which continues to separate the "rich" from the "poor."

The difference between an objectified, manipulated, mutant Market and an inspired one, modeled on Nature, cannot be emphasized too strongly. Where Nature is respected, cherished, emulated and embraced, growing participation in its Law becomes the true measure of any Initiated soul. Imagine that a Haitian woman selling you fish is not operating from a mere materialistic perspective but intends that, once consumed, the Spirit of the fish will swim in the waters of your very Soul. Contrast that with grabbing a box of frozen, breaded, dead fillets from a grocery freezer.

Also think respectfully for a moment of what it must mean to the Haitian people to have actually had their Ancestors brought to that most debased and distorted model of the Marketplace, where they were forced on the block and *sold* as slaves. The Haitians' antidote to that horror is to beckon their higher Self, their favorite guardian Loa, to walk with them in the Marketplace, buoyantly bolstering their spirits by reminding them to exchange the best of themselves with the best of others. *Namaste*: the Loa in me recognizes and salutes the Loa in thee. The inspired artist in me applauds yours, and thanks you for having the guts, gospel and verve to stride soulfully into a superficial Exchange where all too often the overpriced clothes have no Emperor.

I am not saying for a naïve minute that the Haitians are able to fully implement this ideal Marketplace unimpeded. Especially now, with many peasants isolated from one another in the hills, fortunate to have even a mule for transportation. After the latest Coup d'Etat on the part of American Marines, ousting democratically-elected President Aristide, the corrupt Haitian military re-emerged with another reign of terror, destroying the peasantry's attempts at Marketplace autonomy. Historically, such fair exchange was meant to supply a level playing field after Revolutions destroyed Feudal systems. But modern Corporate control is up to the same old oppressive tricks.

HOOKING THE HEART

According to the Haitians, a person's smaller self is like a fish that gets hooked in the heart and reeled in throughout life by the love of and for their Greater Self, sitting on a throne beneath the Sea in Lower World. When Death arrives and you are finally reeled in, brought Home, you see none other than yourSelf on that throne, taking the aforementioned underworld measure of fidelity to your Destiny.

These Voudon concepts of smaller and Greater self/head/conscious-ness are vital to Initiation's arc, and could provide an engaging template for movie protagonists. Whether you write, direct, act in (shape-shift) or view a film, do you perceive characters with that kind of heart-hooked commitment to their higher Selves? Or are they, like too many, merely self-deluded slaves to a temporal Marketplace? Ashes to ashes vs. Everlasting.

The Marketplace is always more or less important than we imagine it to be — a tricky entity, in flux, not to be either under or over-estimated. Artists especially need to be reminded to become skilled in matters of marketing, publicity and budgeting, so they don't become intimidated or diminished by foolish compromise in the face of these tasks. Take a lesson from Voudon: don't become enslaved to the Marketplace, but don't be naïve about it either. Do everything in your power to bring your best Self to bear there. Our most important values belong first, not last, or never.

DIVINE HORSEMEN: THE LIVING GODS OF HAITI, POSSESSION

Filmmaker/dancer Maya Deren, in the documentary based on her book of the same title, *Divine Horsemen: The Living Gods of Haiti*, provides rare inti-mate coverage of Voudon serviteurs undergoing possession by their Loa. Her 1947-1951, sometimes grainy, black-and-white footage was edited by Maya's widower, Teiji Ito and his second wife, Cherel Ito, some twenty years after Deren's premature death. As such, and for both better and worse, it displays none of Deren's avant-garde directorial sensibilities, being more of a narrative, educational depiction of Voudon ritual. Yet given the movie industry's usual garish, eye-popping, flaming, blood-splattering, skull-strewn, sensationalistic depictions of Voudon, this uniquely straightforward presentation in itself provides a profound breath of relief.

Illustrated are examples of *Rada* and *Petro* rites, as well as *Congo* partnership ritual and larger-scale, *Mardi Gra* parade celebration. Several key Loa are introduced, and the differences they command are distinctive. Some two dozen of Deren's stills are also available in the bonus material segment of the DVD version of *Divine Horsemen*. These archival prints are actually superior in production values to the film footage, and invaluable for their respectful observation, their handsome composition.

ARTISTS AS TRIBE

Deren herself claims that it was precisely her intuitive and respectful stance as an artist, vs. the more intellectual, analytical posture of anthropologists, that gained her entrée into the deeper dimensions of the Haitian Voudon community. She had "a deliberate discretion, a strong distaste for aggressive inquiry, staring or prying." Rather than systematizing and categorizing her findings objectively, as would a social scientist, Deren "could permit the culture and myth to emerge gradually on its own terms and in its own form."

She attributed this to the sensitivity of being an artist herself: "In a modern industrial culture, the artists constitute, in fact, an 'ethnic group', subject to the full 'Native' treatment. We too are exhibited as touristic curiosities on Monday, extolled as culture on Tuesday, denounced as immoral and unsanitary on Wednesday, reinstated for scientific study on Thursday, feasted for some obscurely stylish reason on Friday, forgotten Saturday, and revisited as picturesque on Sunday." The fact that many filmmakers share Maya Deren's experience of themselves as valuable yet marginalized makes them wonderful Ambassadors on the mission of dialogue between Indigenous and modern Western cultures. It makes them the best of "God's spies," agents for the restoration of Indigenous Soul, and the production of Deep Cinema.

The last word belongs to Maya: "My own ordeal as an 'artist-native' in an industrial culture made it impossible for me to be guilty of similar effronteries towards the Haitian peasants." "Amen" to that. Or, as the Hawaiians say, "Amama." May we resolutely and gratefully take up her standard.

CARIBBEAN INDIGENOUS DISORIENTATION

If modern Westerners are going to endorse more Soulful engagement with Native cultures' world-views (Shamanism, Initiation), we must avoid seeing them through the falsifying lens of exoticism, as if they are radically "other" in terms of humanity. On the other hand, we must respect that they are often radically "other" in terms of values, and in ways from which we can significantly benefit — *viva la difference*!

We must play it as it lays. And from an Indigenous perspective, that's far too often a harrowing matter of enduring wave after wave of disdain, dispossession, and disorientation. A Shamanic world-view has as broad a horizon as the world in which the Shaman lives, including Upper and Lower worlds. From an Indigenous perspective, we are worlds walking through the world, so we must perceive this one as fully as possible.

FROM SHAKESPEARE TO WES CRAVEN

Preparing for director Orson Welles' all-Black-cast Broadway production of *MacBeth*, a Haitian "Witch Doctor" sacrificed goats to use their skins for drums, which became the sacred dwelling-places of the Loa. After a triumphant opening night, the Voudon drummers were led to believe that the play's one negative review was written by a critic who meant them serious harm. And so they drummed up a blood-curdling nocturnal storm to protect the troupe from ill intent. The next day the offending critic contracted a lethal case of pneumonia.

"The Scottish play" is already famous for ill portent, but when true Voudon practitioners are on hand, critics beware!

Shakespeare would have been right at home with such tribal ceremony, having always had a healthy respect for the supernatural. Where would *Hamlet* be without his father's ghost? As for zombification, the Friar in *Romeo and Juliet* assures the lovers that his potion will render their bodily functions so suspended that "No warmth, no breath, shall testify thou livest." And *Henry IV*'s Glendower brags, in terms that invoke Voudon's abode of the Loa (the watery abyss): "I can call Spirits from the vasty deep!" To this, Hotspur coolly replies, "Why, so can I. And so can any man. But will they come when thou dost call for them?"

It's wonderful to have had Maya Deren provide an unadulterated, venerable record of Voudon, a veritable call-and-response between human and Spirit realms. But that caliber depiction is all too rare, and has everything to do with Deren having risked and experienced possession itself, "the White Darkness." Keeping it real is essential. Shamans are pragmatists first and foremost, only multi-dimensionally so. To measure how low the depiction of Voudon films usually sinks, one only need note that one of the far better samples of this genre, *The Serpent and the Rainbow*, was done by Wes Craven, a filmmaker not exactly renown for refined spiritual sensibilities (the *Nightmare on Elm Street* series).

THE SERPENT AND THE RAINBOW: REVERSAL OF FORTUNES

Based on the real-life experiences of the Anthropologist and Botanical scientist Wade Davis, this movie could have brought about a veritable sea-change in how we depict and perceive Voudon. If only it had been more true to the multi-layered book from which it derived! Starting out promisingly enough — actually containing some beautifully rendered rituals and processions — *The Serpent and the Rainbow* finally devolves into an explosive, violent, flaming and bloody morass of the usual comic-book excess that earmarks Zombie flicks. Ho-hum... damn. And that's not the kind of aural/visual abuse you can easily discharge from your nervous system. *All's ill that ends ill.*

Davis' character starts out at a peak of Western accomplishment, well-connected to both an established institute of higher education (Harvard), and a Boston-based pharmaceutical company. Seeking to provide a safer, more effective surgical anesthesia, these powers-that-be send Davis to Haiti on the arrogant mission of obtaining, in an absurdly brief amount of time, the secret formula for Zombification.

So the White man began with confidence that he could grease a few of the Western Hemisphere's poorest Black palms and fly back home with a stupefying substance gleaned from toads and snails and puffer-fish glands. But Haiti shook him down to a more respectful perspective. He peeled through scientific, social, cultural, historical and spiritual layers to the awareness that what he sought to purchase might come at too high a price for the local serviteurs. And that's ultimately most intriguing about this true-life anti-hero: Mission *not* accomplished.

FROM PAGE TO "STAGE"

The written tale is rife with dark irony which never makes it to the screen, such as Davis' visit to the American psycho-pharmacological lab, where large photos of monkeys suffering experimentation struck him as a more gruesome display than any Voudon ritual he'd ever witnessed.

And while the movie depicts a largely peaceful accord between Catholic saints and Voudon Loa, the book includes this astonishing historical tale: a priest actually ordering a military sergeant to shoot a glowing, supernaturally agile apparition of Our Lady, concerned that the locals might espy and start revering her as the Loa of Love, Erzulie. Upon returning home, the priest found his rectory burned to the ground, and he soon afterwards died from a paralytic stroke. The offending soldier was subsequently reduced to madness, wandering alone in a forest near the village. The "vision" transformed into a bird and escaped into the mist of a rainbowed waterfall (more likely the Loa Ayeda Wedo than Erzulie).

The most dismaying apparent compromise made in filming *The Serpent and the Rainbow* is that Davis himself understands, and teaches, what was behind the purposeful proliferation of tacky Zombie tales: they originated as cheesy dime-novel propaganda written by the American military occupying Haiti from 1915-1934. We all know that strongly-armed governments can stir up a witches' brew of Fascism, the likes of which makes Shakespeare's *MacBeth* seem tame. Unfortunately, the aptly-named Wes Craven had a much more narrow viewpoint than did the Bard, ultimately perpetuating the usual diversionary tripe. But to his considerable credit, Wade Davis has sustained concern for our ulcerated Ethnosphere and gone on to support indie film festivals of Indigenous fare.

The Serpent and the Rainbow could have, and should have, shown the truth of Haiti's own rich Heart of Darkness from the Mysterium of the Dark Continent: neither a mere measure of skin color nor an implacable, Walking Dead psychic state, but the sustained and sustaining devotion of the Ancestral Womb-basin, longing to initiate and flood us with Love. If only we dare dance ourselves open to its challenge.

HAWAIIAN SHAMANIC TEMPLATE

Upper Self: *Aumakua*: Divine, Utterly Benevolent Parents. Mana-Loa
Middle Self: *Uhane*: Human Spirit Who Speaks/Hears. Mana-Mana
Lower Self: *Unihipili*: Nature Spirit Who Never Sleeps. Mana

All contained by the precursor Domain of the Loving Void

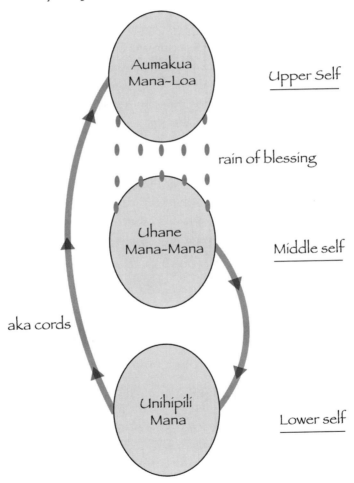

Now let us transition from Caribbean to Pacific in order to encounter the Kahuna, the Mystery-keepers of Hawaii, whose tri-part Shamanic template complements the Haitian's Voudon one, while bringing to bear a more psycho-Spiritual focus, with the Cosmos hula-dancing up through our very bones — *Aloha!*

Situated far from the potentially stodgy traditions of "Old Country" European roots which many mainland Americans share, Hawaiians have a refreshing, sea-breeze-washed belief system strongly invested in helping us create our desired Future. I once undertook a rich intensive of Huna, Hula, and Lomi-lomi, the last being a Hawaiian form of body-work/massage that is very loving, maternal, embracing. The instructor taught us a sensitive, curving stroke that began at the pelvic region and swept diagonally across to the heart and up to the throat. In first caressing the pelvic region, we are invoking the Spirits of the Ancestral Cradle who support us. We then cross the Chalice of the Heart which should always inform our voice. And finally we caress the throat region, encouraging our Human Spirit (Uhane) to find expression.

A well-known Hawaiian chant proclaims; "There is Life in the Word, there is Death in the Word," reminiscent of the Bible's "In the beginning was the Word." Through this full-torsoed, integrative Lomi-lomi stroke, the Ancestral Spirits take a measure of how authentically we are articulating our Destiny. If we are being true, "they are eager to be reborn because we are creating the Future they only dreamed of." Sweet, sweet Aloha.

While there are many and deepening levels to all Hawaiian words, this is but one description of *"Aloha"*: "The shared breath of God." Since Spirit resides in each and every breath, and since the essential Hawaiian Spirit is Love, they teach that you should exhale each breath as if the person(s) you love most in the world would inhale it next. Ahhh. No wonder these islands feel so uniquely alluring.

HUNA: OUR THREE SELVES

The tri-level template of Huna perceives humans as comprised of a Higher Self, *Aumakua*, Middle Self, *Uhane*, and Lower Self, *Unihipili*: our Divine, Human, and Nature spirits. A beloved Mentor of mine, Laura Kealoha Yardley, was first to publish many of this tradition's heretofore hidden teachings in *The Heart of Huna*, supporting the Ancients' prophesy that the time has come to "Let that which is unknown become known."

Energy in the Huna model is known as *mana*. It begins in the Lower Self/Unihipili as just that: "mana," depicted as one watery wave. As it is raised to our middle, Uhane level, that of "the Human Spirit who speaks," it divides into two watery flows, a higher voltage than the originating mana, and is here called "mana mana." At the level of our Higher Self/Aumakua, it is Self as Divine and utterly benevolent Parents with miraculous capacity, three waves or Greatest power, "Mana Loa," which rains down upon us.

Unlike the normal Western, power-over, hierarchical model of living, Indigenous cultures' love for the land allows for an orientation of power, blessings, and revelation coming from Nature, rising *up from below*. For those living in the land of Pele, the Goddess of Volcanoes, how could anyone doubt it? Even the well-known word for Hawaiian dance, *Hula*, means "to raise and spread the light."

As in Voudon, where the human spirits descend to the Undersea realm before ascending to the Loa Sky-realm, so too does the circuitry of Huna go down before it rises. The Middle self, human spirit, cannot access the Higher Self unless its prayers are sent via the physical/emotional Lower self. As one teacher said to me, "If you're not on the ground laughing or crying, you're just not praying."

In other words, prayer in Hawaii is not a mere head trip (Uhane, the rational self). Unless we honor the respectful exchange of charging our prayers with conscious physical effort (ritualized deep breathing) and an authentic emotional "impression," the Lower self just won't be "impressed." Unimpressed, it won't carry our desires to our Higher Self to create them, manifest them, either solo or with the help of others' Aumakua, known as the collective *Po'e Aumakua* (Gathering of Souls). Unless and until we importune change, our Unihipili will continue to re-circulate our encoded emotional states as consistently and repeatedly as it recirculates our blood.

The Unihipili, Nature spirit, is highly respected for its connection to all of Creation, throughout all time. The Unihipili is evolving to become a human spirit even as the more rational, thinking Uhane is evolving to become Aumakua. Although it is considered an impressionable child to our Uhane, this Nature Spirit is certainly a wise enough child. Huna teaches that we should respect the unerring intuitions of the gut as being more reliable than the mind, which can be manipulated and led astray.

THE GUT'S BRAIN

Huna's guidance to trust the gut (Unihipili) is backed up by studies in gastro-neuro-immunology as well. Jordan S. Rubin, who healed himself of Crohn's disease literally at the point of death (*Patient Heal Thyself*) says [emphasis mine]:

"The *gut's brain*, known as the Enteric Nervous System (ENS), is located in sheaths of tissue lining the esophagus, stomach, small intestine and colon. *Considered a single entity*, it is packed with neurons, neurotransmitters and proteins that zap messages between neurons, support cells like those found in the brain. It contains a complex circuitry that *enables it to act independently*, learn, *remember* and, as the saying goes, produce gut feelings." And from Dr. Michael Gershon: "The brain is not the only place in the body that's full of neurotransmitters. *A hundred million neurotransmitters* line the length of the gut, approximately the same number that is found in the brain" (*The Second Brain*). So the next time you feel nauseous, butterflies in your stomach, an intestinal cramp, stop and heed — it could be your Unihipili is trying to get through to you.

HAITIAN AND HAWAIIAN COMPARISON

Aligning Haitian and Hawaiian templates side by side, you can easily identify similarities. Beneath our most familiar Human Middle World/Self is prior Creation, the Past, the Ancestral realm, the processes of which we are largely unconscious but profoundly dependent. And above is our Superconscious or Divine Nature, future potential, the realm of our Aumakua and the Loa, Divinities.

VOUDON	HUNA
Upper World: Spirits	Upper Self: Divine Spirit, Blessing
Middle World: Marketplace	Middle Self: Human Spirit, Speaking
Lower World: Ancestry	Lower Self: Nature Spirit, never sleeps

Comparing these templates we can also easily discern the limitations of Modern, White, Western humankind which too often brings the Human voice (and law and will) to bear on the Marketplace at the cost of an unnerving disregard for the other two Realms.

In fact, in the case of Voudon, only *half* of their Middle zone would be acknowledged: the human side of the Marketplace without respectful regard for Nature's contribution as its harmonious model. Again from the Westerner's perspective, the orientation of the Huna Middle Self is ironically both inflated *and* diminished. Modern "man" often isolates the human self from its grounding in Nature and alignment to its Higher and future state of becoming: Aumakua. So it gets isolated and morphs into a calcified Ego, disproportionately large enough for its own zip code. So, at worst, we depict 'success' as an engorged Ego tooling a mutant Marketplace in service of itself.

OCEANIC INDIGENOUS DISORIENTATION

While Hawaiian culture has not suffered the same blatant cinematic disparagement as has Haitian, neither have its stories been dramatized with any true measure of respect for the Shamanic depths of this once (and future?) Sovereign nation. In the final analysis, the rash of sunny, feel-good, Elvis-in-Hawaii entertainment flicks, supporting the ha'ole-based tourist industry, are just as false to the truth of Huna as Zombie Horror flicks are to Voudon. And while New Zealand is not Hawaii, this scathing depiction of what happens when invaders presume control of Indigenous islands certainly strikes a note applicable to all Polynesian, Oceanic peoples suffering the after-effects of occupation.

A NATIVE DAUGHTER'S RETURN: *ONCE WERE WARRIORS*

Part-Maori director Lee Tamahori took a considerable risk when he choose Alan Duff's novel, *Once Were Warriors*, for adaptation as his first feature film. At a time when New Zealand's Native people were struggling for better social status, this relentlessly searing tale of alcoholism and domestic violence seemed hell-bent on hanging out all their dirty laundry. But Tamahori dared to display the raw reality of "what happens to a Culture after 150 years of Colonialism. How does it survive after being swamped by another Culture?" Thus the plot's harrowing familial oppression holds its own, as well as providing metaphor for the larger Domain Basins of national/cultural oppression. His gamble has proven well worth it, and in ways he couldn't have predicted.

As the Haitian and Hawaiian Shamanic templates teach, we have to go south into the darkness before we ascend to the light. The gold is buried in the shyte. Our deepest treasure is guarded by our greatest fear. Memories from our Nature Spirit re-loop and rule us until they are cleansed (*kala*) by being lifted to a higher vision. Then we must act upon the Inspiration our Higher Self bestows.

As this director avers, "You've got to look at all the skeletons in your closet before you can move on." Yes, the gargoyles at the gate must be dealt with. And the gargoyles of *Once Were Warriors* couldn't be any more menacing and brutal. Yet it triumphs over inestimable travails precisely by willing to look the worst of modern Maori culture squarely in the eye, even an eye swollen shut by domestic violence.

FAMILY EROSION

You know you're in good hands with Tamahori from the get-go. Emerging from a long, seductively-lucrative career doing commercial ads, he opted for **BOLD**, in-your-face, title graphics of the three Alchemical colors found most often in Indigenous art worldwide: Black (yin), White (yang) and Red (passion, fire, blood). The accompanying theme music was inspired by a wailing mix of Jimi Hendrix, Celtic dirge, and Maori welcoming chant. Fabulous.

Once Were Warriors opens with the stock footage, calendar-bright, touristy still of a scenic, picturesque New Zealand mountain. Then the camera pulls back to reveal this to be a billboard above a noisy Auckland highway, beneath which walks Beth Heke (Rena Owen), pushing a shopping cart home from the market. The ideal vs. the real.

While Beth is the heroine of this harrowing tale, Tamahori didn't want her depicted as a Mother Teresa of the ghetto. There's no chance of that. Sexy-tough, she's still hot for her husband of eighteen years, devoted to their five (count 'em!) children, and able to flip the bottle-cap off a pint of cheap brew with seasoned panache.

This mother and her children are our band of modern-day Warriors, and their enemy is found not only (or even always) across racial lines, but actually in their midst. For all their goodness, talent, dreams and promise, this family is being eroded from the inside out by its *pater familias* — "Jake the Muss" (Temuera Morrison), whose alcoholism fuels a hair-trigger temper prone to erupt into violent verbal and physical abuse any nanosecond.

And what abuse! Glad to be out of work and on the dole, Jake Heke celebrates by bringing home a maritime feed of lobster-sized crayfish for wife Beth and their brood. Then he goes to the bar and does what he does best: levels the toughest guy in the joint, and invites all his mates home to 'par-tay' at his place. As he and Beth serenade each other in a boozy haze, the kids huddle together upstairs, wanting to enjoy their parents' romantic interlude, but knowing it will probably devolve into mayhem. And it does, with no stunt doubles to dull the impact. The guests grab their guitars and hastily exit while Jake slams Beth in the face (she spits blood back into his) and into walls, mirrors and finally bed, where it's clear he's about to rape her. Cut to an outdoor early morning scene of dogs scavenging in the garbage. Too perfect.

As pitilessly brutal as was that episode, worse still is the morning after: Beth sits smoking at her kitchen table, her face as distorted as Elephant Man's, and in comes her best mate, to inspect the damage. After a startled expression briefly crosses the face of Maeve (Mere Boynton), she settles into what sounds like an all-too-familiar routine of cheering her brutalized friend. Joking about the consequences of powerful orgasms, she reminds Beth of a woman's lot: "You know the rules, girl — Keep your mouth shut and your legs open."

MUTING THE SPIRIT WHO SPEAKS

"Keep your mouth shut." But remember, Uhane is the Spirit who not only listens but speaks. Our very humanity is measured by our articulation of Nature, Human and Divine Selves. Always look for the characters whose voices prevail, and for those who are silenced. In *Once Were Warriors*, the most articulate one is the adolescent daughter, aptly named Grace (Mamengaroa Kerr-Bell), who keeps a diary which proves pivotal to the plot. Jake finds the diary suspect, denouncing his wife as "too bloody lippy, too bloody smart-mouthed, a bad example for the fucking kids." He then turns on Grace, "Always writing, aren't you? Too fucking smart. You'll end up like your mother here!"

Unfortunately, Grace doesn't live long enough for us to see if she repeats her mother's fate or can fare better. During one of Jake's beer-soaked bashes his friend, "Uncle Bully," (Clifford Curtis) sneaks up to Grace's bed, covers her mouth with one hand and "gently" rapes this virgin beauty. He also blames his victim for having 'seductively' come downstairs in her night-shirt. "It's our little secret, hey Gracie?" Silenced again.

This darkens her world-view, leading her to drug experimentation. She's been warned by her mother and older brother that she'd best prepare for an abusive, controlling fate which is apparently closing in on her. Then one night her father's increasing command makes Grace feel there's no way out, other than transforming the rope from their back-yard swing into a noose.

HOMEWARD BOUND

This is the nadir point. And the turning point that leads Beth back to her traditional roots.

Everything else which distorts their heritage is shown: The temptation to go on welfare rather than work. The huge beer barns built by a vile coalition of the Breweries and the State, who skim hefty revenue and taxes off the ensuing Maori alcoholic plague. The police and social workers doing their best to hold families together. The Christian Church which, in director Tamahori's assessment, " although a very strong and pervasive force, doesn't hold its back end up, lets the Maori people down rather than enhancing their lives, is too duplicitous, so I left it out of the mix."

Well, not entirely: during Grace's nocturnal, rainy, post-rape, Fellini-esque walk through the darker side of town, we're shown a Christian choir decked out in robes singing a rousing, yet preposterous, rendition of "This is the day that the Lord has made." The implication being, if this is the best He can do, maybe He ought to start over.

That's precisely what Beth does: restores herself and her children to her people's Ancestral tradition, moving them back to the family Marae, where Beth and Jake once faced an unconquerable impasse. Beth came from a long line of Chiefs and was the *Puhi*, equivalent of a Princess, in her Tribe when she fell for the ultimate outsider: sexy, singing, punch-swinging Jake. His heritage of self-loathing traced back to an ancestry of slaves, and so these two lovers were not allowed to marry on Beth's familial sacred site.

In the film's finale, Beth reads in her dead daughter's journal of Uncle Bully's sexual violation. Irate, she challenges him at the bar, where Jake chimes in with the only currency he knows: more violence. Although this is *somewhat* cathartic, it's no longer satisfactory for Beth, who denounces her husband of nearly two decades:

"You're still a slave. . . to your fists, to the drink, to yourself. . .
I've found something better, Jake and I'm gonna make damn
sure my kids have it all. Our people once were Warriors. They
were a people with mana, pride. A people with Spirit."

Jake morphs into a caricature of Brando in *Streetcar*, his railing at the night sky blending into a police car's siren wail, much as Beth's anguished howls had blended with the ambulance siren after Grace hanged herself. And, BAM, we're slammed off-screen back into those bold red, black and white graphics, and that indelible Hendrix/Celtic/Maori musical theme. Altogether an unnerving stunner.

TABOO SPACE

It's telling that while the viewers are allowed onto the Marae (courtyard, 'place of encounter') for Gracie's wake, we're not shown the Meeting House itself ('place of Peace'). Other than a moving transitional scene when Beth's face bleeds into that of the *tekoteko* statuary atop the meeting-house, we are not made privy to such artwork as the sacred panels inside.

We witness a brief ceremonial cleansing of the house after Gracie's demise, but aren't told the significance: that this will help her Spirit pass on, so that her siblings won't be haunted in a negative way. We see an Elder silently bless the oldest Heke son with a nose-to-nose greeting, a *honi*, giving approval of his path and signs of Initiation — facial *moku* (tattoos) — approval which Jake could never manage. And although we see that the girlfriends of gang members have the Maori women's lip and chin *moku*, no one explains that this represents the onset of menstrual flow because the voice, like the womb, can either eliminate or give birth: "There is Life in the Word, there is Death in the Word."

When the middle son and his band of brethren from reform school perform a *haka* (Maori dance) at Gracie's wake, we're not given a subtitled translation which would tell us that it denounces violence toward women. Remember the Biblical Walls of Jericho? Well, the vibrational foot-stomping, chest-thumping, tongue-thrusting, low-register chanting of Maori *haka* have been known to bring the palisades of stockaded forts a-tumbling down. You can believe it.

Somehow all of this "not-knowing" on the part of the non-Native audience is fitting, part of keeping the Maori life *kapu*, taboo, unprofaned by voyeurism. It's telling too that so many of the players here have achieved celebrity by modern Western standards (television and opera as well as film) and yet hold their Heritage to be a higher, deeper, and more enduring value.

One out of every three New Zealanders has seen *Once Were Warriors*, making it the country's most popular locally-made feature, besting even *Jurassic Park* and *The Piano*. And, while Tamahori feared that it would engender the same resistance and controversy as did the novel on which it is based, it has instead become a household word in a surprising arena: after the film hit the theaters, there was an upsurge in the number of men seeking help with domestic violence issues, citing "Warrior Troubles."

DANCING IN THE SEA~CAVE

I once attended the wake of a very young girl on the North island of New Zealand. Both her parents were Euro-descendent medical doctors whose clientele were largely Maori. The varying quality and quantity of spiritual care given the family was telling. As mourners arrived, the barefoot Natives lined the entrance walkway to the family's country home softly chanting, dressed in long robes, their heads crowned by green wreaths. A Catholic priest came, said his piece and left soon afterwards. Then a Maori Anglican Minister came, dutifully said his Christian prayers, but also "tramped the house," chanting in the traditional way that released the girl's Spirit from all her toys and clothing in the bedroom she'd shared with her two siblings.

As the child's death had been sudden, violent, and unexpected, I worried for her Spirit's peace. Eventually my concerns were assuaged. A considerable number of Native women remained throughout the night in the large, beautiful, flower-festooned, glassed-in living room hosting the child's small casket at its heart. Some relatives had fallen asleep with their heads in the laps of soothing, chanting Maoris. I approached the eldest, white-haired woman there, whom I'd been told was a female Spiritual leader, and asked how the girl's Soul was faring. She closed her eyes and hummed a bit before opening them, assuring, "She's in the sea-cave between lives, dancing."

Ahhhhh! *"The sea-cave between lives"* ~ the ultimate Liminal space!

THE SHAMANIC ROUND

I truly see the best of actors as Shape-Shifters, soulful spirits who can move between worlds to embody characters of multiple dimensions. They wed the matter of their bodies with the spirit of imagination, giving birth to indelible roles. Young, first-time actress Mamengaroa Kerr-Bell, who brought Grace Heke to life (and death) is, for my money, one such Shamanic player. Roles like hers do not fade at the movie's finale, but go on to resurrect in the hearts of viewers worldwide, pulsing out an SOS for endangered families everywhere, as well as imploring nurturance for the dreams of young artists. Mahalo.

The rule for Deep Cinema is the same as that for Voudon and Huna: "Descent before Ascent," "Submerge before Emerging." Via Negativa and Via Positiva serve Via Creativa. Another way to remember this round is to think that every plot has a Past, Present and Future, only from the Indigenous perspective, not in that order. Instead it starts in Middle World (now), dips into Lower World (past) which contains buried gold and repressed demons, and ascends to Upper World (future), the realm of the gods, divinities, archetypes, ideals, and potential.

Whatever darkness you touch upon, from your repressed Shadow side to Sorcery to true evil, the Underworld, Deep Mystery, velvety sleep, to the Void of all Creation — imagine all of these melding in ribboned strands of darkness. Whatever light you perceive, from your consciousness to logic to blinding dictates, abstractions to true virtue, daylight to the Cosmic heavens, imagine these blending as well. Discretion is required *everywhere*. Demons illumine, gods misbehave. You must realize the dance among worlds is dappled, or be doomed to naive polarization.

I think of "Grasshopper" (David Carradine), a Shaolin Monk on a mission, stealthily watching his prey from the rafters in an episode of *Kung Fu*. The man below cries out in exasperation, "Where do you hail from, Heaven or Hell?" to which our Hero wonderfully replies "Both!" before swinging down for confrontation. It's the answer any true Artist must be able to give. [Note: 'grasshopper' is one translation of 'Unihipili.']

The phrase *Kanawai Kumulipo* is Hawaiian for "Law of Creation." In her booklet on the ancient Hawaiian wisdom teachings known as *Ka Hana Pono*, Connie Rios explains its derivation. The word for Law contains the word *wai* for "water," since for Indigenous peoples, Nature's Laws are indeed refreshing and essential. *Kumulipo*, the word for Creation, contains the word *Kumu* for teacher, a word that also translates to tree: "something that's withstood the test of time, has as much below the surface as above, is firmly grounded in the Earth (the material realm) and also reaches out to the heavens (symbolizing Spirit). And *Lipo* means Deepest Darkness."

When you intend to create *you set this law in motion*, which requires that you first take the Underworld dive in order to energize and retrieve from the Dark all that you've repressed there, all that stands in the way of your righteous creative dream. After they (the skeletons in the closet) have been faced and eliminated, and you're seated upright in your *kapu* (sacred) canoe, the Sea-surrounding depths can be experienced as a fertile void, a loving Womb of gestation, the Source of all Creation.

Part II

A WORLD DESPERATE FOR RE~BALANCE

"A folk tale from Kashmir tells of two Brahmin women who tried to dispense with their alms-giving duties by simply giving alms back and forth to each other. When they died they returned to earth as two wells so poisoned that no one could take water from them."

— from *The Gift* by Lewis Hyde

CORPORATE COLONIALIZATION

The Shamanic Templates clearly show that we should all be walking with our feet in Creation and our heads in Great Spirit/Deep Mystery. We should be ever re-creating ourselves from this marriage of Upper and Lower Worlds, Divine and Natural Selves, Ancestry and Future, Male and Female energy flows (Aumakua), giving birth to something of Everlasting value. This of course requires that we all have access to Nature at her most innately revelatory. And it requires we have the time (freedom and largesse) to vision-quest, moon-lodge, cultivate and maintain our true Spiritual natures. We need to take *time out* to access the timeless, to *space out* in order to tread the stars of the *spaceless*, the liminal realm of Initiatory cycles.

THERE BE DRAGONS: *THE CORPORATION*

Yet there are dark Tricksters in our midst who would rob us of this sacred birthright. There are political and corporate entities (often wed) who are every bit as exploitative as slave owners, only more impersonal about it. To them we are merely facts and figures, potential or actual servants, customers or consumers to increase their profit margins. And, for all they care, we could anonymously live and die beholden to their wily ways. The documentary, *The Corporation*, lists how the diagnostic earmarks of sociopathology apply to many Corporate entities:

— *Callous unconcern for the feelings of others,*
— *Incapacity to maintain enduring relationships,*
— *Reckless disregard for the safety of others,*
— *Deceitfulness: repeated lying and conning of others for profit,*
— *Failure to conform to social norms, and*
— *Incapacity to experience guilt.*

From an interview with Noam Chomsky of MIT we learn that "Corporations were originally associations of people who were chartered by a State to perform some particular function, like a group of people wanting to build a bridge over the Charles River." Mary Zepernick from the Program on Corporations, Law and Democracy, continues, "There were very few chartered corporations in early United States history, and those that existed had clear stipulations on how long they could operate, the amount of capitalization allotted, etc. They couldn't own another corporation. And their shareholders were liable." Corporate permission to even exist was a gift from the people, bestowed only if they determined that the entity would serve the public good.

Howard Zinn, author of *A People's History of the United States*, explains the grotesque, ironic mutation Corporations have undergone to become today's monstrous overlords, the equivalent of Church or King in ages past. The 14th Amendment was passed "to protect newly freed slaves from destruction to their lives, liberty or property." So Corporate heads go to Court, proclaim that their institutions are "persons" deserving of such protection and, incomprehensibly, "the Supreme Court goes along with that." So a Corporation is now "a legal person," yet a person with no soul, no body, no accountability, no moral conscience, just blind passion for the bottom line, the profit margin. And, dark irony, they use the very Amendment designed to protect the rights of former slaves to protect Corporate rights which support the slave-like conditions of sweat shops.

MORE INCLUSIVE VALUES

I once conversed with a woman involved in high-rolling, international monetary trade who said most coolly, "Money is merely data." To which I replied, "and food and rent, fuel, running water, medical care, travel...." She was made a tad uncomfortable by what she surely perceived as my bleeding-heart recitation, and we soon parted company. As T. S. Eliot would say, "Beware the weapons of the weak, the strong have no defense against them." The morally weak. The disingenuous. Because humane options exist, given half a voice (Uhane): see author Riane Eisler's book *The Real Wealth of Nations, Creating a Caring Economy*. With their usual linguistic wisdom, the Hawaiian word for "truth" implies *sheaths of muscle*, many layers, with the speaker (Uhane) having the free will to be as flaccid or toned as they choose.

Indigenous economic values are by nature more womanly by being relational and tribally inclusive. African author/teacher Malidoma Some (whose name translates to: "Friend of the Stranger/Enemy") travels back and forth from the States to his Dagara Village, where he once shared photos of San Francisco's towering insurance buildings with his spiritual Elder. "Insurance" is one of those Western concepts that can jam the gears of Native thinking. If Initiation is an ongoing round of "Death and Rebirth," then how must insurance, with its alleged compensation for loss and death, appear to a Medicine Man? You can imagine: denial at best, dementia at worst.

So Malidoma took his Elder into an African city and showed him a towering insurance building there. The old man observed the busy traffic in and out of the edifice for some time, and then assessed the place: All the enormous externalized power of the superstructure now required that people, mainly young men, run in and out *to hold the building up.* By his sights, young men working alone without an adequate contingent of elders, women and children, could not possibly uphold the place in balance. The insurance building, this epicenter of modern capitalistic endeavor, didn't attract Malidoma's Medicine Man *at all*, who preferred to return to his village where he could access his considerable internal powers to serve others all the days of his life.

ENSLAVEMENT BY ANOTHER NAME: *LIFE AND DEBT*

Stephanie Black's documentary is an exceptionally well-wrought and colorful rendering of what could have been a dry and abstract topic: how the people of Jamaica have been insidiously ground down in the global gears of the very lending institutions which purported to provide them aid.

Assistant Producer Sarah Manley encouraged Ms. Black to film her father, former Prime Minister Michael Manley, early on in the production process, as he was dying of prostate cancer. Included in *Life And Debt* are his last, and very lucid, interviews, providing invaluable history lessons that stand as admonition. Ralph Nader sounded the same warning knell with his description of Globalization as "the subordination of human, environmental and consumer rights." This provides very important insights into a Marketplace which has gone a long way towards separating Native from non-Native populations. But unless you happen to be in the top 2% economic bracket, we're all pretty much in the same boat now. In the lyrics of Leonard Cohen, "Everybody knows the ship is sinking, everybody knows that the Captain lied; Everybody got this broken feeling, like their dog or their Daddy just died."

This current insidious state of affairs makes the archetypal good Navigator, "Captain" Manley's ardent love of his island people all the more attractive. He encourages viewers to look to the origins of modern economic establishments which perpetuate oppressive Colonial strictures and hamper Jamaica's quest for autonomy. As the Second World War drew to a close, the victorious Allies convened to assure themselves future financial security. Meeting in Bretton Woods, New Hampshire, they founded the International Monetary Fund (IMF) to provide themselves short-term loans, and the World Bank, to secure capital for re-building after the War.

At that time, 1944, there were no independent Third World countries per se, only colonialized entities comprising the Empires of a few world powers. *Life and Debt* makes it painfully clear that when Jamaica sought loans to facilitate their full emergence into independence from England, they became trapped in a sinister vortex of ever-increasing debt which is merely a more abstract version of the former Colonialism: slavery and exploitation. It is, impurely and simply, an economic model of dominance.

After unsuccessfully seeking loans from the OPEC nations and Russia, Manley found himself with no option but

— to trust in the International Monetary Fund (IMF), which reduced trade barriers and increased interest rates such that Jamaican farmers suffered;

— to trust in the Inter-American Development Banks which destroyed Jamaica's dairy industry;

— to trust in the World Trade Organization (WTO) which undermined their banana exports; and

— to trust in the World Bank, which created a "Free Zone" of sprawling garment manufacturing barns (sweat shops) which the locals call the Free Slave Zone. 'Nuff said.

One of the director's frustrations is that many Americans find the machinations of global banking institutions too cryptic for their comprehension, even though the U.S.A. often has the largest vote in these organizations. It serves as a none-too-subtle wake-up call to observe Jamaica's impoverished farmers and laid-off sweat-shop workers eloquently articulating a comprehension of global politics far beyond the average American's ken. For those of you with an Astrological bent, I strongly recommend Jessica Murray's *Soul-Sick Nation*, for a lucid explanation of why Americans are so ill-disposed toward facing and questioning their government's more sinister economic policies.

REGGAE RHYTHMS: HELPING THE STATISTICS GO DOWN

Life and Debt uses a number of effective artistic devices to show how the sorcery of Globalization pulled off this dark sleight of hand, perpetuating Old World domination over would-be emerging nations.

Cleverly, a large part of this film's narration comes from Jamaica Kincaid's pithy, politically-subversive book, *A Small Place*, which sardonically describes how modern-day tourism is a variety of Colonial oppression. Black-and-white segments, actually filmed in the present, of banking edifices with British coats of arms, fleshy travelers arriving at the airport, and banana pickers working in primitive conditions, illustrate how little progress has been made. Other savvy choices, such as children watching news of local riots on television, show the infantilized, passive role into which all the Natives have been forced.

The film's spiritual dimensions are embodied in part by local singer Buju Banton, strolling through the shanty towns like a one-man Greek Chorus, singing of injustice. And there is a cluster of Rastafarians, sitting around a bonfire reading scriptural injunctions against usury (excessive interest on loans), with the smoke weaving past their faces giving their recitation primordial power. They are well aware that their farmers, "the backbone of this country," have been crushed. And local economist Dr. Michael Witter describes how devaluation of their dollar has increased debt from $800 million in 1970 to $7 *billion* today. More than 50% of every Jamaican dollar earned goes toward paying off *interest* on loans.

Movie viewers in Brazil, Argentina, and Ghana have all asked director Stephanie Black why she hadn't filmed in their countries, similarly crippled by globalized economics, and she answered, "Because then I wouldn't have had the great Reggae music soundtrack." It does work wonderfully, showing time and again how artistic vision exceeds Corporate greed, how the powers-that-be aren't pulling the wool over these musicians' eyes.

ARTISTS AND OTHER THRESHOLD GUARDIANS

Artists by nature stand at the dual thresholds of past and future, resource and inspiration, the manifest and the dream. This helps them exceed the constrained perspective of the Marketplace which the world banks manipulate so soullessly. As such, the Reggae musicians of *Life and Debt* provide stellar models for Artists everywhere, who know in their Unhihipili that Creativity trumps and exposes any political or social constraints the mutant Marketplace seeks to impose.

So the caliber of an Artist's gift can be consistently "valuable" no matter where along the economic spectrum they reside, from rank poverty to flush celebrity. An Artist knows that true wealth is found in the flow of their unique giftedness, and true poverty in the absence of this Muse. The Marketplace is a secondary (but vital) concern in the life of any Artist, whose gratitude for being truly gifted ignites the impulse to freely gift others with their talent, to "pass it on," as in lovingly strolling and singing through the slums of Kingston. And such Artist's creativity, if authentically realized, will endure. As for the Marketers? "It is easier for a camel to pass through the eye of a needle than for a rich man to enter the Kingdom of Heaven."

Plaintive lyrics from *Time Will Tell* by Bob Marley and the Wailers certainly apply here, "Think you're in Heaven, but you're really in Hell," which is very disorienting to the Shamanic round of descent, reclamation and return. Local poet Mutabaruka's verse, *All My Friends*, could well apply to Manley's disillusionment with the manipulative multi-nationals:

"All my friends are fascists, racists, murderers and thieves,
  All my friends are Church folks, godly people, praying to their sky-god,
  All my friends are Living Dead, trying to escape from themselves..."

Because Michael Manley was one of the first victims of Globalization, his voice serves as a warning to other countries who might be tempted to go down that slippery slope of dependency and debt. He reminds me of a character in an Irish folk tale: a man who's been trapped under a spell warns a midwife (another classic threshold guardian) not to hold onto any gifts given her from the Fairy realm which are not gold or silver, as only these are enduring, unable to be devalued. Riding homeward, she begins to offload the lesser gifts which, upon contact with the earth, explode like bombs and ignite destructive fires. Had she carried them into her Village, it would have indeed been destroyed. Thanks for the warning, Michael.

TRICKSTER/EXCESS

A number of documentary films mention how difficult it is to interview the heads of these multinational Corporations, since their lies and spin are too often transparent. Alice Walker's book, *Now Is the Time to Open Your Heart*, addresses this conundrum:

"The more powerful the powerful appear, the more invisible they become. In the old days it worked differently. It was said that the powerful merged with the Divine, until the Divine was all that one saw. But now the powerful have merged with the Shadow, really with Death, and when you encounter them they are really hard to see. Even for the Shaman."

Indigenous cultures wisely caution that even our gods may occasionally overstep their bounds and require reining in. Maya Deren tells how Ghede, Loa of the Dead, should only be concerned with men's Souls, yet often lets gluttony prompt him to trespass into the domain of Azaka, Loa of Agriculture. Doesn't this remind you of the IMF loaning money to Jamaica, purportedly to aid them, then charging their farmers obscene interest rates?

One way to frame these Corporate inhuman-entities-with-human-rights from a Shamanic perspective, is to understand them as "Tricksters," and not the class of Tricksters that teaches valuable lessons either, but the class to avoid. In American Indian lore, Tricksters are depicted as wily animals, such as Coyote. They are restless, often on the move with no set home, and thus no loyalty to place or tribe. Picture Corporate sweat shops moving from Jamaica to Mexico to Honduras to Haiti to keep the wages most low. They may possess excessive intestines, symbolizing exorbitant appetite (again, usury), or over-sized penises, suggesting a macho need to exert their power over others: nearly 100 nations, from Albania to Zimbabwe, are currently beholden to the IMF.

How to out-trick the Tricksters? <u>Consciousness</u>. We can all call upon the Loa Petwo Ounsi for discernment, whose eyes are aflame from the fires of her calabash Womb (her Holy Grail) to help eliminate any demons who roam Middle World. And we can invoke Azaka to make certain our "crops" flourish free of the Trickster's grasp, returning the Marketplace to Voudon's recommended harmonious alignment with Nature. Amen, *Amama* to that.

Consciousness: Awareness that there are indeed those soulless among us who play by outdated, imperialistic, culturally-destructive rules. They purport to be benevolent, and can thrive only if we remain unaware of their true agenda. The "heroes" and "heroines" of Deep Cinema must see with the Shaman's "Strong Eye" through the chaos into a place of universal, creative, visionary healing, a larger Domain Basin than that generated by these fiends who assail us. Let's globalize that!

RE~ENGAGING INDIGENOUS SOUL

Initiation is the birthright (birth-rite) of each and every one of us, aligning us to a temporal purpose flowing forth from Eternal intent. It means that each and every one of us must seek until we situate ourselves at the center of our own lives (Upper, Lower and Middle Worlds/Selves), and not by any means live enslaved to another's exploitation. That is Hell, pure and simple, and the Toltecs refer to their Altars of Intention as "Exits out of Hell." We must get clear. As author Hermann Hesse sagely advised, *"If you do not yet know your life's work, your current work lies in finding it."*

Begin by grounding. It's far easier to engage Indigenous Soul when you cultivate belonging to place. What would it mean to see films which make simplifying a virtue, eco-tourism a value, pilgrimage to Native cultures a blessing? Or, another option: show people making the effort to discern, and then live, precisely where they'd love to live. Have them putting down roots and abiding in stewardship with the flora and fauna until they are an integral part of their beloved environs: *"I had a farm in Africa...."*

Nature itself, physical locale, should be germane to the plot, a measure of the character's grounding or lack thereof. If the place is shaping the protagonist positively, make that an appreciated value. If it's thwarting them, note that with emotional intensity. Think of the doomed character in *The Dead Girl*, speaking from the upright glass casket of a phone booth, fantasizing to her lover about getting away from the toxic city to pristine Nature and blue skies. Exploited and imperiled, reduced to selling her*self* in the Marketplace, she plaintively longed for enlivening and nurturing Domain Basins. Alas.

And while we're at it, how about making films where people stay Indigenous to their bodies, age naturally and find peace with that? Too often in cinema, grey hair and a softening jaw-line are signs of an isolated psycho Unabomber rather than a Wise Elder. What was the last movie you saw in which older stars went easy on hair dye and Botox? In which the landscape, weather and wildlife truly felt as important as the humans? Yes, it happens, sometimes most skillfully, and provides profoundly satisfying relief.

WHERE AND WHAT DO YOU LOVE?

According to Jungian analyst Helen Luke, money was once minted in the temple of a goddess, Moneta, and thus belongs to the female principle of relationship. Its necessity comes about only when the more basic exchange of bartering fails to suffice. An example would be that of a baker needing the services of a coat maker. Rather than balancing the equation by taking a leather coat and then providing loaves of bread week after week after week, it's easier to exchange an agreed-upon monetary sum.

Money should then be a measure of value, not an imposed obligation. Taxation came about when a monarch became envious of the "common" people's exchanges and decided he wanted a piece of the take. Supposedly taxes serve the public good, the "Commonwealth," but what say do the people really have in this? "Taxation without representation" is all too common. If the will of the people were truly heeded, how rare would wars become?

Helen Luke's perceptions led me to study money minted the world over, to see how different countries design their bills and coins. We speak of "gold" and "silver," but have forgotten their affiliation with Sun and Moon. Usually there is a head of state on one side, but the other side varies enormously, according to the country's values. And while some are cryptic and incomprehensible at first glance, others are quite compellingly beautiful.

Here is a helpful exercise for you, one which you can also imaginatively apply to the characters in any film, to better clarify their values, conflicts, etc.:

If you were the Monarch of your own realm, first of all where would that be? What geographical characteristics would it have? How coastal, mountainous, rural, urban? How large? How populated? As sprawling and ethnically diverse as say, Canada? Or as small and culturally homogenous as Nepal? Really *see* your domain. Then, if your face were on a coin or bill of that realm, as Regent, what would you have on the back to show what you value most? And finally, how many of your personal monetary exchanges truly reflect that value? I've facilitated this exercise in numerous workshops, where the majority of people enthusiastically included elements from Nature.

CULTURAL POST~TRAUMATIC STRESS

But in actuality this value, of Nature, is often ignored. How did this unholy split between humans and Earth come about? Upon any amount of reflection, it seems radically unnatural for entire peoples to be blind to the wonder and awe, the very *sacredness* of the Earth. So why have so, so many chosen the "yee-hah!" path of Cowboys over Indians, isolationism over tribalism, possession over generosity, exploitation over stewardship?

Given that so many blinkered oppressors appear Euro-American, we'd best look back to 15th to 19th-century Europe for an answer to that query. We can stare into the darkness of those times until our eyes burn with awareness that the destruction of land-based, pagan worship was deliberate, prolonged, exacting, and hideously violent: the Inquisition. I assure you this was not some barbaric epoch, but includes the time of Shakespeare. He and other writers preserved the peasants' love of sprites and fairies, nature gods and other such "demonic" entities being systematically condemned.

Generation after generation after generation watched household members and neighbors falsely accused as witches and burned at the stake in a deliberate Holocaust of a land-grab. My conclusion? Many of us are suffering a plague of cultural post-traumatic stress disorder from the brutal decimation of our ancestors' Nature-based Spirituality. The unholy, globalized marriage of State and Corporate entities, which so blithely accounts for inordinate destruction and suffering today, wasn't extant in medieval Europe. Well, the State was, only at that time it partnered with another institutionalized player who also lusted for land and power-over any competition, including the large peasant populations.

Who was this unlikely despot? The Roman Catholic Church. How did they accomplish these nefarious ends? Originally by building chapels, churches and cathedrals over Indigenous sacred sites. By condemning traveling minstrels and actors who might put on a more compelling Death and Resurrection (Initiation) show than did the priests. Traveling players had a prop known as the "Mouth of Hell": very popular. Then came Dictates, Crusades, and the Inquisition. All in the name of Christ, mind you, "Jesus meek and mild."

As you can imagine, even a savvy sense of irony must have provided scant comfort when one was being tortured three times, the most excruciating level known as "the third degree." Think of a woman you love being confined in the Iron *Maiden*, stretched on the rack, and ultimately tied to the village-square stake to be set ablaze, scalded, singed, smoldering and scorched. "Conversion" at its most brutal.

If Church and State could thus murder even the valiant, visionary, devout Joan of Arc (and *then* canonize her as a Saint), who among the people could feel safe? (See *The Messenger*). And even today, the Old-Boy's Club oppression continues: As revealed in the documentary *Deliver Us From Evil*, Cardinal Joseph Ratzinger was long in charge of overseeing American pedophile priests. He moved them about like so many scurrilous pawns rather than calling them to task, thus multiplying the number of their victims.

Now he is Pope Benedict XVI, and while victims try to serve him papers for contributing to the endangerment of children, "President" Bush has granted him full immunity from prosecution. We need to take a clear-eyed Shamanic assessment of those who shape our world if we wish to create stories which restore balance. Don't doubt it for an instant: sexual violation = a soul-shattering loss. Ratzinger was once Prefect of *The Congregation for the Doctrine of the Faith*, formerly known as *The Holy Office*, historically *The Inquisition*. What unholy wedding of Church and State have we now: an endorsed Slaughter of the Innocents?

SHAMANIC ROOTS DESTROYED: *THE BURNING TIMES*

The National Film Board of Canada produced director Donna Read's tri-part *Women and Spirituality* film series, of which *The Burning Times* is segment two. Its comprehensive depiction of this horrific historical epoch is surprisingly bearable, thanks to obvious compassion, hope for a Shamanic revival, skillful weaving of the scholastic with the visceral, and hauntingly plaintive music by Loreena McKennit. Bear it we must if we are to absorb that, just as Euro-Shamanic ancestry was eradicated, it might well be restored.

Film consultant and modern-day Witch, Starhawk, surmises that fear of womens' power was behind this Holocaust, that mass propaganda against them was required: demoting and demonizing the wise women, healers and midwives of the day as heretics. She explains that the word 'witch' did not always invoke the image of a diabolical crone: "The source of the word comes from the Anglo-Saxon 'wic,' which means to bend or shape, to bend or shape consciousness, and thus the events in your life. Essentially it is the remnants in the West of the old Shamanic tradition, that tradition of developing within yourself altered states of consciousness" — sometimes via plant spirits, and sometimes via very simple techniques, such as drumming, dancing, and chanting.

The Church began condemning women on the grounds that midwives eased the pain of childbirth, God's punishment for Eve's transgression — misogyny compounded. Any woman practicing medicine without a license was condemned, and since only men were admitted to medical school, their monopoly of this lucrative and influential career was assured.

Then witch-hunts were expanded and facilitated by the mass printing of a handbook, the *Malleus Maleficarum* (*The Hammer Against Witches*), used by the Inquisitors to interrogate the accused. This uniformity of cross-examination is the reason why diverse women in isolated and far-flung European villages from Normandy to Italy "confessed" (under torture) to *identical* transgressions. This truly bizarre litany of heretical sins included: possessing a strange birthmark, living alone, growing old, gathering with other women at night, having sex with the devil, being red-haired, stopping hailstones, suffering mental illness, cultivating medicinal herbs, providing remedies for 'bewitched' animals, and so on.

This persecution grew into quite an industry: there were fees paid for accusing the "witch," seizing her, escorting her to jail, locking her up, guarding her, providing her meals (if indeed meals were provided), and so forth. Thus the Church and State worked together to insure that countless women's lands, homes and assets were confiscated to pay for their capture, imprisonment, trial, torture, and execution. Although there are many movies mourning the horror of Hitler's Holocaust, there is scant cinematic record of this annihilation of peasants' powers.

The Shamanic roots of so many modern-day peoples were destroyed by this systematic scourging and pillaging. Pagan and Celtic victims of this centuries-long reign of terror have been estimated in the millions, 85% of whom were women. It took a lot of horrific effort to uproot Natives from their pleasure in, and reverence for, the land. (Monsanto struggles for similar control today, meeting similar resistance.) The all-too-common truth of the adage, "History is written by the victors," also points to the silence of those falsely accused, condemned, and eradicated.

And so "witch'" stories are found in folk and fairy tales, their credibility reduced to children's' fare. But children are rarely fooled, being still deeply enmeshed in their Unihipili (id, instinct, Nature Spirit), and thus engaged with Cosmic cycles. As the screen goes temporarily black before panning up from the Underworld, one young school-girl in this film sweetly and wisely proclaims, "I think a Witch is someone who comes out of the ground at Halloween and gives everyone magical powers."

Let's celebrate Euro-pagan roots cinematically. After all, what is there about them to fear, and not revere? Start with a crop circle film (for much better inspiration than *Signals*, see Freddy Silva's *Stairways to Heaven*). And let's face it: there is zilch evidence of witches systematically and hostilely killing off millions of priests for hundreds of years.

PILGRIMAGE AS INITIATION:
THE SACRED SITES OF THE DALAI LAMAS

Look at the true-life arc of development experienced by Steve Dancz, narrator of *The Sacred Sites of the Dalai Lamas*, a Michael Wiese documentary which demonstrates the inestimable advantages of timeless pilgrimage over trendy tourism. For Dancz, an accomplished composer, traveling to Tibet was a long-held dream come true, replete with sonorous chanting, chiming bells, and bass-below-bass horns providing a veritable homecoming. When one of his Mentor-guides indicated a well-preserved, ages-old sea-*spiral* fossil in the same outdoor site where incense *spiraled* upward, earth and sky were wed. And when Dancz played a water-filled singing bowl in the Marketplace, it resonated with shimmering visual and aural fore-shadowing of the Lake itself. Beautiful.

The trials and physical demands of this group pilgrimage to the 16,000-foot-plus Oracle Lake were brutal at times, the sort of purifying ordeals typical of many Initiatory paths to wholeness. Upon accessing the

Lake (after visiting a plethora of holy locales, any *one* worthy of pilgrimage), these altitude-challenged devotees were assaulted by a hailstorm. Fitting, since the *I Ching*'s Hexagram #29 speaks of the orienting, sustaining reliability of frozen waters: when they melt, you are left with the solid mastery *within* despite the formlessness without.

Dancz may have intuited this, as he fared relatively well in the punishing climes, even receiving a vision: "As the winds blew across the lake, it created a shape like an hourglass, but with the sand flowing up rather than down — a reminder for me of the fallacy of time." Timelessness, liminal space, an opening to the Eternal Zero Source.

For me, that image triggers something else of Indigenous value: the notion that prescribed, doctrinaire teachings need not be handed *down* from hierarchical institutions; Revelation can also rise up from Nature, to re-orient and inform. The Loa of Voudon rise up the ceremonial center-post (*poteau mitan*) from the waters; the dance of the Hula "raises and spreads the Light." This Earth-based reverence begins to bring a female balancing element to thousands of years of dominating patriarchal canons.

It is some measure of the Dalai Lamas' balance of yin and yang that they are able to read the depths of a lake, even a yang-located mountain-high one. There is another *I Ching* Hexagram, #31, that includes "the Lake on top of the Mountain," meaning "Reflection," but in this case, because of its heightened, liminal location, *Reflection of the Divine*. There is also a note of relative humility when the summit of a mountain is yin, carved out to contain water, rather than yang, jutting boldly upward into the sky. A site of such receptivity counsels "opening the self to receive great teachings." Indeed the case here.

While this film is composed such that the access to Oracle Lake is in every sense its high point, there is a further sweet denouement. Because Dancz has been our narrator, we've been invited to identify with him, from his early dream of Tibet to his sense of Spiritual home-coming. Thus it is quietly thrilling to glimpse the delighted expression on his face during their descent when they visit the cave and chapel of the great poet, yogi, and *musical composer*, Milarepa. Late in his life, the much-beloved Mystic promised that "anyone who even hears his name, even once, will receive an instant blessing, and will not be reborn in a lesser state for the next seven lifetimes." As a musician himself, of refined sensibilities and sacred inclination, this clearly resonated deeply within Dancz — how gratifying to behold!

VENERABLE RESTORATION: *IN THE LIGHT OF REVERENCE*

Natives speak of the "Rainbow Dragons of Creation" going underground when the colonists arrived on North America's shores. But as Thoreau and the Transcendentalists illustrate, even among the Euro-Americans there has always been an ecologically green snake pulsating alongside the oil-slicked, asphalt grey snake of industrialization. It's just that movies, often the in-bred offspring of multinational Corporate mergers, seldom document this vibrant, popular, green strain. Thus they lack a prophetic dimension, and lag behind much of the populace in our love of, and hope for, this planet.

The superb documentary *In the Light of Reverence*, an exception to this retro negligence and eleven years in the making, is conspicuously hard to find for rental or purchase. Nonetheless this award-winning, PBS "Point of View" series production is a "must-see" for any filmmaker or viewer of genuine eco-spiritual passion.

Director Christopher McLeod hopes it will encourage Americans of all ilk to designate particular land-sites as sacred and treat them accordingly. This may run against the grain of "separation of Church and State," but that's an historically-iffy boundary at best: This film informs us that the U.S. Government actually funded generations of Missionary schools to kidnap and indoctrinate American Indian children. And it was a double-crossing Mormon Bishop who, in his capacity as lawyer, sold the water rights of the Hopi out from under them, draining their sacred springs and aquifers to slurry coal as a power source to southern California.

Yet one of *In the Light of Reverence's* more cordial dimensions is that it doesn't do a 100% Red-White polarization, instead including Euro-Americans (from lawyers to scholars to park rangers) who genuinely support the Natives' cause, indeed, are as one with it as they can be.

Wyoming, Colorado Plateau, California

Three Native American Indian sacred sites are featured as threatened:

— The Lakotas' **"Lodge of the Bear"** or "Mato Tipila," (aka Devil's Tower) by tourism,

— The **Hopi Lands**, or Hopitutskwa , by mining, and

— The Wintus' **Mount Shasta** holy spring, by naïve hippies and a ski resort.

What's most astonishing is the lack of cultural curiosity on the part of so many of the non-Natives interviewed. Why aren't they interested in learning from peoples steeped in Earth-based wisdom (e.g. Vine Deloria Jr. here) what petroglyphs represent, what a dream circle means, what their Creation myths are, why a mountain requires an annual phase of solitude?

Director McLeod suggests it is a well-repressed guilt over the violent misappropriation of these lands which aborts humane dialogue. Such avoidance enters the realm of contempt when a bulldozing miner says hey, "They lost the wars," with a decidedly "Get over it" tone of voice. Mayor Bush of the town nearest Devil's Tower complains about the Indians festooning nearby trees with "offensive" prayer bundles, claiming superior regard for the site because "We don't hang out our dirty laundry." And a woman supposedly sympathetic to the Wintu's desire to stop ski resort development on Mt. Shasta implores the Natives to also factor in the ten years of planning she's done. As if a mere decade of real estate calculation equals ages of tribal reverence for the land.

A VICTORY AMIDST BLINDNESS

Yet this documentary ends with the Wintus' victory over the developers, and this hopeful note provides promise that an invisible wave of momentum is gathering strength. A wave of spiritually based, ecologically aware, non-Native Americans who revere this land are joining forces with Indigenous peoples' determination to halt further desecration. Grief and growth are two sides of the same coin, and in claiming that coin as valuable currency, we can move from shameful past to revitalized future.

Each of us in conquered Indigenous lands can work to release any excessive grip the mutant Marketplace may have upon us, and allow ourselves to sink down into the Earth which inspires and sustains us. The Rainbow Spirits can resurrect. Spirits of Native Ancestors who were "disappeared" from the country in stages, via war, via residential school indoctrination, via a plague of smallpox laden "gift" blankets, could be welcomed back via prayer, "grandfather winds," fertilizing rains. They could help those paralyzed from the heart down find engagement with a truly stunning continent, Turtle Island.

ANIMALS AS KINDRED

Our Native-based Ancestors lived alongside animals with a daily intimacy that extended far beyond hunting. (What is our equivalent today — interacting with cars and computers?) Unlike our impersonal, modern-day food-processing methods, preparing for a hunt was as conscientious and sacred as preparing for war. And returning from a hunt often involved the same de-toxing, purifying rituals as those following battle. For the same reasons — so the Spirits of the Dead would be placated and not wreak havoc with the Village.

Animals which modern man would just as soon eradicate were held in esteem. For example, tribal members in South Africa would mix rat fur into their hair before engaging in fights, so that they might be as swift and wily as these rodents in escaping their prey. Imagine honoring rats, giving the wee rodents their due, vs. famously proclaiming, "You're the dirty rat that killed my brother!"

Totemic Animals (the intra-species equivalent of guardian angels), with their incalculably diverse skills, are engaged as guides on Spirit voyages to other worlds. I have worked Shamanically with victims of abuse, whose souls have fled to "the Cave of Lost Children" or, in instances of more de-monic practices, been stolen to darker "Circles of Hell." Retrieval of their lost soul elements has been spontaneously aided and abetted by totemic Animal Spirits whose vision, speed, and cunning capacity for camouflage made rescue possible.

Not everyone wants to undertake such Voyaging, but the prospect of honoring it does provide great cinematic potential. And if we are to perceive the world Shamanically, we must engage with Animals from the depths to the heights. Just as some landscapes seem mundane while others exude Spirit, so too our personal experiences of Animals will vary from the profane to the sacred. And it must be noted that Shamans give as much regard to messages from actual animals as totemic guides, since they perceive all three worlds as sufficed with Spirit.

On a lighter note, it has been said that Sean Connery was chosen to play James Bond because en route to his audition he was seen "striding across the parking lot like a panther." Imagine casting agents drumming for their clients' totem animals!

INTRA~PSYCHIC = INTER~SPECIES HARMONY

It is a paradoxical matter, best illustrated by the Hawaiian template, which sees us as a vertical axis connecting Divine, Human and Nature Spirits. We can think of our Lower self, Unihipili, in this case as a "voiceless" animal which requires our expression, direction and care.

Both the Hawaiian Kahuna who "Return to the Source," and the Australian Aboriginals of "The Dreamtime," have this essential belief in common — that streams of their departed Ancestors' essence can re-incarnate as plants and/or animals to provide their descendants protection, sustenance, and companionship.

Thus that which requires our care — plants and animals — can also be providing care for us here in Middle World, their interventions varying from the inspirational to the tender. Imagine how your regard toward a Lizard or a Calla Lily might change if you believed it animated in part by the Spirit of a beloved departed Ancestor? And when your heart is tugged by the ribboned Aurora Borealis or a wave curling back into the sea, consider the possibility that your Unihipili shares in energetically sustaining this dimension of Creation. Welcome home to the Indigenous world.

REVELATION & SALVATION FROM THE BRINY DEEP

In *Hidden Journey: A Spiritual Awakening*, Andrew Harvey, a self-proclaimed "depressive, over-educated, atheistic Jew" described his encounter with a Hawaiian family's Aumakua. A Native family he'd been living with for months invited him to come play with the Mother of the Family, who turned out to be a Whale: "Then I remembered that I can't swim." "Don't worry," the father said, "just cling to the rock that I show you. The Whale will do the rest."

"When I did so, the most astonishing single thing of my life happened. About five hundred yards away the biggest black whale I have ever seen calmly arose from the waters. That single moment overturned everything I had ever thought of as reality. I was terrified. But then I felt it, I felt the Whale feeling my terror and sending toward me these great, warm, healing waves of energy, pure energy. How can I explain this? I knew, with certainty, that the Whale had felt my terror, knew I could not swim, and was sending me through the sunlit water, wave after wave of what I can only call love, silent, strong, immense.

"She came to within two feet of me, rolled over and let me run my hand along her belly, as if I were her own child, nuzzling against her. Then calmly, she withdrew. I felt as she moved so silently away that she was only moving away in time, in 'biography.' In the dimension where we had at last met, and which she had opened to me, there was no time, no parting, no coming and going. There we would be together always."

INDIGENOUS TOTEMIC ORIGINS: *SPIRITS OF THE JAGUAR*

While it is rare to find films which depict Indigenous apprehension of Animals as Sacred, *Spirits of the Jaguar* is one such beauty. In actuality a layered and complex educational work on Meso-American and Caribbean Indian history, it weaves the image of the Jaguar's importance from embodied beast to acknowledged Spirit, pouncing languidly from gorgeous Myths of Origin to Initiatory paths of migration across the waters.

As Westerners might acknowledge an Archangel or Saint, so do these Native Indians acknowledge this supple cat as an everlasting source of inspiration, courage, and protection: creature as Totem. Demonstrating the capacity of Native Shamans to access the Spirit World *behind* the physical, these sacred animals help maintain the balance of creative and destructive powers. Similarly Caribbean people counter the Hurricane's divine "Spirit of Mayhem" with ceremonial dance. (Even today, Kahuna in Hawaii gather their skills to quell the damage of threatening typhoons and tidal waves).

In *Spirits of the Jaguar*, we learn the need for the Uhane, the Spirit who Speaks, to provide a living bridge between the Natural and Divine Worlds: "The Gods of the Maya created the World. The creatures that inhabited it squeaked, chattered and howled, but could not speak. For that the Gods required people, people who would worship and respect them."

The beasts too were respected for their unique qualities, some worthy to be Temple Guardians for Upper, Lower and Middle Worlds, with Jaguar proclaimed the revered companion Spirit of the Kings. When the Aztecs required that a God enter the roaring Cosmic Flames of the Sun to bring a new dawn, many hesitated, but Jaguar willingly participated in this sacrifice, gaining its dark spots and becoming one of the most revered of Animals. Thanks to this phenomenal feline, "The Fifth World had been created."

CLOSER THAN YOU THINK: *ANIMALS ARE BEAUTIFUL PEOPLE*

At first I found the theme of this playful documentary, with its frivolity set to stirring orchestration, to be somewhat presumptuous: the claim that exotic denizens of Africa's oldest, driest, white-sand-lunar yet seasonally lush, 50,000-square-foot Namib desert region are somehow "just like us." We're talking baboons, anteaters, scorpions, wildebeests, zebras, pelicans, monkeys, tortoises, badgers, snakes, oryx, hyenas, giraffes, kingfishers, meerkats, ostrich. *Just like us.* You know, in a cutesy, Disneyesque, roll-down-the-dune-drunk sorta way.

Perhaps the only *Homo sapiens* who could lay *true* claim to such kinship with these exotic beasts are the Kalahari Bushmen, shown here in a hunting-teaching circle with the youth of their tribe. While these amazing mimics flawlessly enact the jutting, swooning gesticulations of various species, a voice-over proclaims, "They feel a great affinity with all the animals who are both their neighbors and their food."

And yet the truth of the matter is, the line between what we deem "human" and what we deem "less-than" is actually quite blurred. Much more is similar along the continuum from unicell slime to *Homo sapiens* than is often imagined. When Anthropologist Jeremy Narby asked Ashaninca Shaman Juan Flores Salazar what he thought the difference was between humans and other species, his response echoed Huna lore: "Bueno. I can say the difference is that human beings have voices with which to speak, whereas animals have their knowledge but do not have the property of speaking, or rather the strength to speak in a way that humans can understand."

And Donald Kennedy, editor-in-chief of *Science* journal, notes " As more and more is learned about the behavior of animals, it becomes more difficult to get closure on a set of properties that are uniquely and especially human. The zone of what we think of as uniquely human is gradually shrinking, thus reducing our sense of being all that special."

I prefer to see that "they" are decidedly *more* special, awe-inspiring and admirable than ordinarily assessed by scientists. And not just in obvious ways such as acknowledging that flight is an enviable skill, a hawk's vision far exceeds ours, or horses decidedly outpower us. What about the dragonfly's multi-faceted vision that makes ours unutterably dim by comparison? Or this case in point: that butterflies haves eyes on their genitals; imagine the advantages! And floating from the erotic to the scared, does not our depiction of Angels imply tribute to our winged kin?

EQUINE AWE & UNIHIPILI GRATITUDE

Everything in Indigenous life is based on yin and yang. But humans have often mistakenly projected only male qualities into powerful creatures (e.g. rhinos) and female qualities onto more delicate ones (e.g. ladybugs). So I want to take time out to pay tribute to the awe-inspiring racehorse with the scampish name featured in the 2007 movie, *Ruffian*.

Even the descriptive "thoroughbred filly" didn't do justice to this almost divine, Platonically ideal, splendid creature. She brings to mind this Novalis theory which echoes the Aumakua spectrum, "*If God can become man, he can also become element, stone, plant, animal. Perhaps there is a continual Redemption in nature.*"

Forcing this horse into an extreme "Battle of the Sexes" with Foolish Pleasure proved that too much yang pressure to be # I can prove fatal to the more inclusive, yin side of the equation. In a larger playing field, horses can pace themselves; pitted one-on-one, the relentless exertion demanded is clearly excessive. The mythic hoof-prints of a Pegasus should evoke springs of water, not the blood which flowed when this Champion's leg shattered under undue pressure. "I vote to outlaw such 'sport.' "

Ruffian had already differentiated herself as likely the fastest horse ever to live. Yet that wasn't enough to satisfy chauvinism and financial greed, so she was needlessly exploited by the mutant Marketplace, unto death. The ensuing human grief was echoed by Nature churning thunderheads over the Belmont Racetrack that tragic day. To watch this film is to experience heart-break at a deep level of participation in Life, as well as to see rare public resolve to esteem female excellence. Ruffian was in a class of her own and resolutely true to herself, the goal of any true Initiate.

We have much to thank our Nature Spirits/Unihipili for, including containment of emotion and memory. They ground us in Creation, leading us into life with appetite (mouth and belly), courage (heart), desire (loins), awareness (eyes), discernment (teeth) and spirit (lungs). Eventually, inevitably, all those beloved and loving organs of our Nature Spirit will literally die for us, drawing us into the Earth and greater participation in the orbits of the planets, Moon, stars, and Milky Way Galaxy ~ realm of our Loa and Aumakua's splendor ~ the Soul's deep Home-coming.

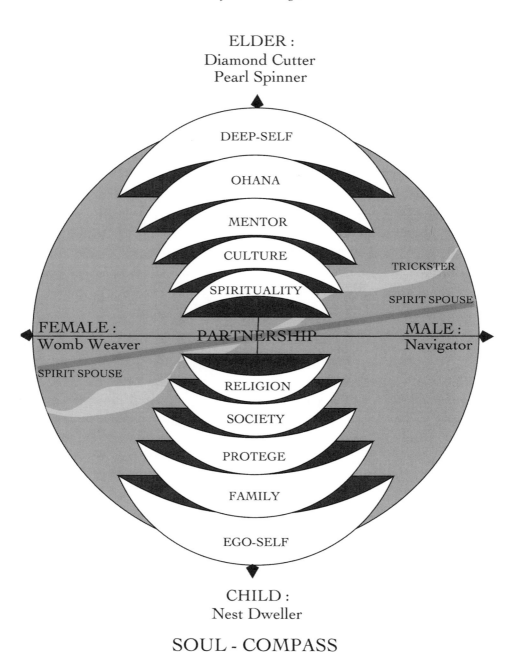

ELDER :
Diamond Cutter
Pearl Spinner

DEEP-SELF

OHANA

MENTOR

CULTURE

SPIRITUALITY

TRICKSTER

SPIRIT SPOUSE

FEMALE :
Womb Weaver

PARTNERSHIP

MALE :
Navigator

SPIRIT SPOUSE

RELIGION

SOCIETY

PROTEGE

FAMILY

EGO-SELF

CHILD :
Nest Dweller

SOUL - COMPASS

FIRST INTERLUDE

THE SOUL COMPASS & DOMAIN BASINS OF INITIATION

This Soul Compass is a template designed to transform life from a series of dogmatic dictates or chaotic occurrences (which act *upon* and define us) into a rich, sacred Self-defining sojourn which we gladly undertake. By "gladly" I don't mean to imply that our destinies become all pleasurable and facile, although some may appear that way: imagine being born into the Bach, Austen, Corr, Wyeth, or Neville Brothers' family, and having your creative gifts encoded and celebrated from the start!

The key here is that life becomes *meaningful*, purpose clearer, our unique talents revealed. This usually requires some lonely epiphanies. But even if it is a matter of becoming like the mythic Sisyphus, rolling the stone uphill again and again, we can take satisfaction in fighting the good fight vs. conforming to deadly programming. Initiation is the means that deepens our process from passive to engaged, flailing to empowered, confused to comprehending, alienated to aligned. Aligned to Zero: the containing and inspiring Source.

We begin as newborns in the South and work our way up through Family, Society, Mentoring, Partnership and Spiritual Sovereignty. All this en route to becoming Elders, which in turn is a launching point for Ancestry and Divine life, as Aumakua or Loa.

SOUTH~NORTH: FLEDGLING BEGINNINGS, WISE ENDINGS

We all begin as Children, Nest-Dwellers, fledglings, mysteriously finding ourselves here with what existential philosophers call "a sense of thrown-ness." Although each of us is endowed with a Soul Compass, we're allowed to embark upon life's journey half-baked, initially projecting elements of this internal guidance system onto parents, grandparents, etc. We sense that we've hatched from the masculine Navigator's Eastern Solar beam fertilizing the darkling feminine Womb-Weaver's egg of the West.

And so we discover ourselves plopped down into our first Domain Basin in the South. Little acorns that we are, our youthful cardinal point is always in alignment with the northern one of Eldership. That mature realm of Diamond-cutting and Pearl-spinning provides our ultimate capacity for accomplishment this life: Everlastingness. What we taste as Wisdom in youth is actually that *knowing* which has been cooked, seasoned and cultivated in comforting Domain Basins as yet vaster than our ken.

In the African Yoruba tradition, parents watch closely to see which drumbeats their children respond to, as this indicates which God or Goddess (Orisha) they belong to, and signifies their spiritual alignment from the start. (Destiny is always revealing itself via what allures you and, conversely, what you suffer.) They are proud that their child's unique characteristics can provide revelations, shatterings, that contribute to the evolving enrichment of the Universe. An American Indian 'naming ceremony' includes splashing the child's head with cold water, blessing its capacity to grow into the bracing Winter of Eldership. While Christianity pointedly celebrates one Divine Child, other peoples respect this Sacred dimension in all children.

Our first experience of environment is that of being a Soul in a body, a body in Nature, Family, etc. I remember in the first grade, when our teacher asked that we write down our addresses: I very assiduously started with my Street, then the City, the State, Country, Seven Seas, Planet Earth of the Solar System "Family," and Milky Way Galaxy. I then felt myself going into a fugue state of Cosmic vertigo as I tried to describe what I sensed spreading out beyond that in the Heavens. Many children come to life thus, some actually "trailing clouds of glory," others at least intuiting our multi-dimensionality of Nature, Humanity and Divinity.

ALL OUR RELATIONS

Moving up our Soul Compass' axis mundi, we become infused by an awakening to our gender identity, rich subject matter for tribal Initiation which usually coincides with this bio-spiritual coming-of-age. The poet Rilke spoke for those who go unschooled about such grounding in sexuality, lamenting:

"Why, I ask you, when people want to help us, who are so often help-less, why do they leave us in the lurch just *there*, at the root of all experience? Anyone who would stand by us there could rest satisfied that we should ask nothing further from them. For the help imparted to us there would grow of itself with our life, becoming together with it greater and stronger. And we would never fail. Why are we not set in the midst of what is most mysteriously ours?" (quoted in *Rilke on Love and Other Difficulties*, by John J. L. Mood).

From an Indigenous perspective, our multi-faceted engagement in Nature gives shape to our unique erotic dispositions. The Fon people of West Africa believe we each come into life engaged with a pod, or web of elements, plants and animals that share in the same life-span or cycle: we rise, fall, and are reborn together, never alone. How comforting!

Imagine that part of your life's work was sussing that out, recognizing your singular web of other-than-human kinship. Maybe then you'd understand why you "fell in love with" a stallion, or perhaps a dolphin (like the woman I read about who *married* one). Why the dew rising from a lake's surface in the morning so tugs at your heart. Why you're galvanized by the presence of a Norfolk pine tree. You're all related! I once heard two documentary film-makers resolutely proclaim *with ardour* that they carried Caribou hearts in their breasts, and the Caribou carried theirs. As we age, our erotic orientation should expand from focused one-on-one sexual engagement to celebration of *all* we love. In the movie *Vitus*, the youth asks his long-bereaved grandfather if he longs for his late wife, only to receive this wonderful reply:

"Up to now I've only written (love letters) to Annemarie, but now I'm getting more generous. I'm also writing to the beautiful woman who sat opposite me on the train, and to the glistening lake, to the lovely figure skater on TV, and to the cool shade under the pear tree."

Such native self-awareness not only grounds you in your particular sexual graces and powers, but enhances them. I've read Aboriginal love poems that work the spirit of standing clouds, splayed palms, groaning thunder and racing rivulets into seductive, pleasurable composition. And there are numerous, most beguiling Hula chants which obviously drove the Calvinist Missionaries apoplectic. If your culture includes a Goddess known for her Flying Vagina (*Kohe lele*), there's certainly latitude for some fabulous verse!

It would make for lovely pillow talk to enquire after your lover's Nature Spirit, what in Creation they're attuned to, and share your allurements in return. A sweet, fun exercise along these lines can be found on the website for *The Golden Compass*: a playful questionnaire to determine one's daemon, or totem animal.

STAR~DICE OF THE HEAVENS

It is also important for Deep Cinematic films to include, either directly or subliminally, some sort of reference to the Cosmos, the living, roiling stars and celestial spheres, the all-encompassing domain of our Aumakua and Loa, from which the elegant, complex galaxies hatched and in which Earthly Creation participates. Watch just such a starry reference sealing the romantic pact in *The Last of the Mohicans*. In explanation to Cora (Madeleine Stowe) of where he believed his deceased parents and recently murdered friends' Spirits to be, Daniel Day-Lewis' character explains:

Hawkeye: *My father's people say... at the birth of the Sun and of his brother, the Moon, their Mother died... so the Sun gave to the Earth her body, from which was to spring all life. And he drew forth from her breast the stars, which he threw into the night sky to remind him of her Soul.*

(Cora is most pensive in response to this, which Hawkeye misreads as disappointment.)

Cora: *On the contrary. It is more deeply stirring to my blood than any imagining could possibly have been.*

From the circulation of blood to that of the swirling Cosmos, Love's covenant is claimed. It is this type of relationship, the Hawaiians teach, where the Higher Selves are ignited and mingled, that draws couples beyond the playing fields of sexual and romantic experimentation into the potential for visionary and enduring Love.

This larger, embedded, Cosmic engagement can be cinematically referenced by some form of fortune telling: attention to omens, animals, signs, cards, weather, or the toss of stones, bones, gems, or sea-shells — anything which allows for that paradoxical mix of chance and destined participation in the Big Picture. Some tribal peoples teach that the ritualistic shaking of rattles is a reminder of the stars (Ancestral Spirits) dancing throughout the Heavens, watching over us. And if we concur with the Huna and Haitian teachings of these vaster regions being the dwelling place of our Higher Selves, we can actually rattle and hum our deeper consciousness awake!

Claim your share of the heavens. Comedian/actor Billy Connolly (*Mrs. Brown*) certainly encouraged his children to do so when he complained that even the likes of Galileo didn't "connect the dots" properly when naming constellations: "There are as many shapes up there as there are people, so we could each have our own view of the sky. Then it would belong to us" (from *Billy*, by Pamela Stephenson). He wants rock stars up there, characters from fairy tales, relatives. Aha, naturally he wants to include Ancestors, Loa.

The best way to keep children star-robed is to give them free rein in Nature, something that's less and less common in a world of malls and techno-addiction. As they grow, and begin navigating the shaping Domain Basins of school, society, church, politics, etc., they will be far less likely to be blown off course if grounded in Nature's Laws. Rilke intuited this necessity. Among the Australian Aboriginals, Initiatory growth is a measure of participation in Nature as Law-men and Law-women. They believe that Souls work their way skyward after Death, only to return to life as shooting stars (see *Ten Canoes*). And in Hawaii, the stones of the *Heiau* (outdoor Nature Temples) are aligned with heavenly bodies. 'Rock Stars' indeed!

TIPPING AND TIPSY DOMAIN BASINS

Once we're adult, an emboldening shift takes place (and without ritualized Initiation this "once" is actually several times) by which we move from outer to inner authority structures, from a cage to a spine, from the Southern to the Northern Hemisphere of the Soul Compass.

Only an ego-self strong enough to helm the ship, and occasionally sacrifice its excess, can move from rigid constraints to more organic, graceful, limber experimentation. Such shifts, when we experience them, are no less world-shaking than Copernicus' discovery that the Sun (larger Self) and not the World (ego) is the center of the Solar System. We may shift from religion to Spirituality, fixed society to creative Culture, nuclear family to broader Ohana, relying upon mentors to Mentoring others, ego self to Deep Self. After cleansing (*kala*) our formative Basins of any negative imprints, we can then invert them into magnanimous cornucopia. When we realize that our past woundings await healing which *we* can provide, a refreshing future unfolds.

One sign of such growth is moving from a harsh good-bad polarization to a more dappled integration of Shadow: food of the Trickster! In this, the Shape-shifter's landscape, we may fall prey to the *unhealthy* temptation for ego inflation, or engage the *healthy* option of integrating heretofore repressed elements.

MIDNIGHT IN THE GARDEN OF EDEN

For each one of us, the demarcations of what was good and bad, kosher and taboo, acceptable and shameful, all played out differently in the landscape of our childhoods. Awards and punishments drove the lessons home, re-enforced by educational and religious mores, until most of us dutifully found ourselves striving to live the Light and suppress the Shadow.

But eventually fissures lace out in the icy moral surface, with the repressed elements seeking a claim on our Souls. Desire, temptation, fantasies of fulfillment via forbidden fruit, rebellion, all weave into the Trickster's bluesy howl 'round Midnight. Sometimes whole generations do the Shadow dance to a revolutionary end: look at how the drug experimentation, anti-war protests and free love of the sixties contrasted with the alcohol-consuming, blindly patriotic, straight-laced fifties. Any new composition of what's light, what's dark, and which of each is valued, does nothing less than reconfigure new worlds.

How much the integration of the dark side enriches our lives, and when we tip the scales too far (or too little) is all a matter of how centered we are in our Upper and Lower Selves, and our yin and yang capabilities. Anchored with that core ballast, that intuition for Wholeness, we'd likely only push the membrane of the acceptable to include *some* spicy, daring, or passionate elements, just enough to enhance our authenticity. A bonus for doing this inner work: Shadow integration often entails humor, as humor of any sophistication involves Shadow. (See *Pushing Tin* for delightfully sparring Shadow brothers.)

Without that Upper-to-Lower plumb-line holding us true, we might do the Dr. Jeckyll/Mr. Hyde flip from what's vital over into what's downright deadly. The other way we can fail this dappled dance of integration is via *resistance* to all things dark, projecting sins onto another while proclaiming ourselves virtuous, innocent, without flaw. Either immersion or resistance is to our decided detriment, because "the Shadow knows" and will keep rocking the boat until we get it.

Often Trickster, shameless in his appetites, has a paw in renewing the World, and so sets things spinning with a twist. Such open-endedness, with fabulously frayed threads of imperfection from the outset, is the assurance that Creation is evolving and we a necessary part of it. Like when Navajo rug-makers leave a segment untied to allow Great Spirit's entry.

From darkness emerges light, and vice versa, and on and on. As the poet e. e. cummings noted, "you cannot have without winter, spring." Even science acknowledges that if matter and anti-matter were equal, everything would cancel out. This glistening, dappled run is fun to swim once you catch its rhythm. Rather than rush to "good/bad" judgment over the next occurrence in your life, take on the open-ended Huna attitude of "Maybe/maybe not," and watch things play out. To gain this perspective is to playfully integrate the Trickster's dimension of the Soul Compass without getting stung by him — too badly!

BLESSED WOUNDING

Haitian Voudon practitioners believe that our Soul which enters the (mutant) Marketplace is most imperiled. It certainly has become tricky territory, often today's largest impediment to engaging Indigenous Soul. "Heathen" Scientists used to provide the biggest problems, but nowadays Quantum Physics has turned them all into Mystics of faith, needing to "believe" in sub-atomic forces which elude their gaze. They *get* the particles and flow of inherent life forces, as Shamans have for centuries.

Too many Corporate moguls of the Market still operate as if Spirit is abstract, and matter (from "mater," Mother Earth, females) spiritless. Manufacturers torque the image of Spirit in matter to seduce us. Think of the countless ads which have gorgeous women hawking goods, as if buying *that* product will include *her* in the bargain. Ultimately it's fortunate that the Nature-Spirit Goddess is *not* for sale. But this also means that disillusionment with false marketing is inevitable, and thus we're primed for another round of deceptive bait-and-switch: feeling "less-than" and needing "more" to salve our wounds. The Fall-Redemption model tries to gain sway over increasing Self-reliance.

I love it that (Saint) Thomas More (see *A Man for All Seasons*), in his book *Utopia*, had children playing with precious gems such as rubies and sapphires, like so many marbles, sea-shells, or wooden blocks, so that they would never lust for them. If gems were not *hyped* as exclusive commodities, no one would ever *die* for a *Blood Diamond*. My idea of decent advertising is something as simple as "Fresh Fish at the End of the Dock on Wednesday." I find ads which create and inflate a false need into a status symbol, in order to shame people into purchase, to be quite vile. We need to restore the Marketplace to its best, Natural/Human potential. Imagine your values as gems — personal emeralds, diamonds, dusky Tahitian pearls — musically cascading softly along the core of your bones as you stride through the Marketplace like the Loa/Aumakua you're becoming. Do you glow from within?

One way we experience wounding is when the gems we're attempting to carry into life go unpolished, "uncooked" and unseen. Uninitiated. Or we may suffer trying to retrieve the "Lost Coin" (self-value) from its exile in the Underworld. There are examples worldwide of burgeoning Shamans enduring psychic dismemberment at the hands of demons (Underworld), and then being "re-membered" by more angelic entities (Upper World). In surviving this ordeal, the Initiates henceforth have the skills to be *Wounded Healers* (home again, home again to Middle World). Attend carefully here: what makes their story so compelling is the Rebirth piece. Anyone can saw a body in half, how many can mend it? Shamans can: blessed woundedness (unraveling) and re-weaving are among their essential skills.

One suffers to become a Shaman, "suffering" coming from "su-frerre," to get beneath and carry. "Lift up your bed (unconsciousness) and walk." It should be a (simple?) matter of descending into the Underworld in order to wrestle with demons and retrieve lost gold. But the mutant Marketplace has raised so much Hell into Middle World that we need goggles (the Shamanic "Strong Eye") to see through the sulfuric fumes. Too many poor Souls struggle just trying to claim a legitimate sense of home here. That's so wrong. Only by learning the lay of the land (artists, that includes budgeting and marketing skills!), and insisting upon bringing no less than our deepest values to bear, can we restore Middle World to Nature and humanity — a *creative, inspired* Marketplace! A site of home and hearth-fire, not Hell-fire.

"NEXT"

The "Burden Basket" is found in various Indigenous cultures, with differing uses: for gathering crops, as part of a girl's Initiation to womanhood, etc. One concept is its use to symbolically carry the burdens of the day. (The first time I saw one, I was thrilled at how small it was!) If you were then to enter a household it would be proper etiquette to hang your basket outside, so as not to bring your troubles to another's table. To exhibit such dependence implies you can't access your own solution from the inner Spiritual realm. If you *do* confide your problems to another you are then obliged, at the very least, to *attempt* any solution they offer. And this is because Self-reliance is of such high value.

As we spiral up the Soul Compass, we gain broader perspective so that we may eventually compensate for past deprivations, shed injurious impressions, restore fled Soul elements. We get to know (Uhane) when old memories and emotional programming (beleaguring the Unihipili) are thwarting us. So, like an adult with a benighted child, we lovingly cleanse these impediments by lifting them up to our parental Aumakua for dissolution, reminding Unihipili of its Divine heritage (*The Prince and the Pauper*). Our prayers sent aloft, we await in faith for the waters of blessing and inspiration to rain down. Mmmmm...

This heartfelt work never ends. Well, yes and no. Even with the worst of circumstances we only endure a finite amount of childhood woundings. Once we realize that our adult wounds usually feel overwhelming because they are amplified by the inner child's helplessness, we can enact cleansings, healings, "shrink the heads" of the perps, and grow into an Adult emotional body. Since we heal childhood wounds by tapping into our Higher nature, we can grow ourselves from child-identified to juicy, playful adult-identified, finally living ever more from our Spirit Greatness.

At this point, our empathy with others, and our awareness of our holographic interconnectedness, allows us to extend our healing, cleansing skills. "Next." Like a competent shoemaker at his work-table, "Next," we know the damaged goods are gonna keep on coming. Kahuna welcome these opportunities to restore alignment to the Source, one inner cleansing at a time. Instead of doubt we begin to festoon the collective Heavens with diamonds of confidence. Instead of pointless gritty suffering, we contribute to the Underworld a sea-bed of lustrous pearls. Diamond-cutting and Pearl-spinning align Nature and Cosmos with such scintillation that henceforth everyone can avail themselves of the healing vibrations, like so many strings on a Celtic harp. Indeed, the more the merrier.

COSMIC MENTORING

The East-West latitude of the Soul Compass is met halfway up the Child-Elder axis. It is here that a sense of personal Adulthood is prodded into play as we take a measure of our parents' influence upon us and Soulfully cast about for a mate of our own (inner and/or outer). Native American Indians have rituals which warn against too much Sunlight (masculine energy) drying up the growing corn (children). Mythic tales also depict how cold the hearth becomes and how bereft the family, if the maternal element (sometimes described in African tales as "honey") is absent. Of course the opposite themes are also found: missing fathers and smothering mothers do us no favors. Such stories reinforce the Universal understanding that parents should demonstrate both relational skills, of objectivity and of intimacy.

The qualities we seek to develop in hatching identity and entering partnership are no less than Cosmic in origin, even while they're as close as our heartbeat. The Dagara tribe allows that parents' contribution to their children can end with the biological, after which mentors provide instruction. And here I gladly draw upon a favorite graduate school mentor of mine, Cosmologist Brian Swimme, who can be viewed in his DVD compilation, *Canticle to the Cosmos*. For this Interlude I recommend Part 4: *The Fundamental Order of the Universe*.

This provides a *Cosmological* ethic, not one based on any single culture or religion. The order is comprised of *Differentiation*, *Subjectivity*, and *Communion*. In terms of the Soul Compass, I site the bold sense of Differentiation — *naming who we uniquely are*, in the East. Subjectivity — *the capacity to sound out infinitely compassionate interiority*, I see in the West. And Communion as a task of the all-embracing Diamond-Cutter and Pearl-Spinner partners (inner and outer wedding) at true North. The contained Nest-Dwellers in the South can initially just bob and float in these nurturing Initiatory Basins.

EVOLVING MALE NAVIGATIONAL SKILLS

The power of the East is air, illumination, inspiration, navigating, thrusting forth, masculine. So many books and films written by men have been devoted to this Heroic journey that we needn't recapitulate it here. But from a Shamanic, inclusive, harmonizing perspective, the all-too-common use of this model proves inadequate: that of growing a male ego into a personally victorious state of fulfillment, period. It usually celebrates *one* dramatic chapter in *one* man's life, with women, children and elders marginalized at best.

I'm not complaining about films where someone comes into their own, comes of age, *differentiates*, as this is the stuff of Initiation. But we know all too well the macho version of a "hero" who carves, shoots, bombs or chisels out his identity at the expense of others, thus violating the female principles of relatedness, intimacy and inclusivity.

In a plot with such macho men, genuine women are in absentia: dead, silenced, co-opted, divorced, or missing altogether. Just look at the semi-comatose spouse (*whomever*) of the bombastic, hypocritical, Military man (Chris Cooper) in *American Beauty*. Or look to the film *Robin and Marion*, where we have the telling example of an aging Robin Hood (Sean Connery) ruining his chances for a loving retirement with Maid Marion (Audrey Hepburn). His stubborn refusal to drop his Warrior persona, the very weight of it, his armor and weaponry, leads to his ultimate destruction.

Yet there are Indigenous alternatives, much more engaging: think of the Native American Warriors' concept of "counting coup" which avers that riding up to your enemy to assert your presence, waving your staff and trilling, is more courageous and impactful than brutally killing them. To proclaim that *your ideology* does not require *another's blood* is an enormously preferential advancement over "Shock and Awe." Australian Aboriginals are so disposed toward tribal harmony that violence between men is largely limited to inflicting corporeal punishment for transgressions of The Law. Thus the concept of competitive sport was wildly disturbing when introduced to them, and, like many Indigenous peoples, they'd continue playing such games until both sides "won."

We could also film stories of modern-day players taking time out for the equivalent of Vision Quests, Walkabouts, or Pilgrimages which prove profoundly revelatory. Someone motivated by a divinely-ordained sense of purpose in Life is unlikely to be swept up in the worst machinations of the Marketplace.

Increasingly, men today are evolving beyond the tired old paradigms, are creating work which allows them more time at home, more time with spouse and family, as well as more pleasurable engagement in Nature. A return to tribal values. Such men are daring to Navigate their vessels into

Westerly waters, off-loading the hair shirts of beasts-of-burden, integrating subjective qualities, becoming "yin-sane"!

At the same time, more and more movies are being made which show men relating to other men, primarily or period: Apollo and Narcissus in love. Women are currently getting less and less screen time. I see this as a need for men to bless one another precisely in their male identities, something they've rarely received from their fathers, and one reason some may resent or fear females. And I see this as a challenge for women to do whatever work required to get our authentic life experiences onto the screen. As soulful, spirited, original women, and not mere fantasies.

WOMANLY WOMB~WEAVING POWERS

When women are encouraged to move into the world as harsh and destructively as the worst of men, without the opportunity to sound out their unique natures, I perceive them as Yangsters (the male corollary being Yinners). Not that women shouldn't be vital and impactful or men vulnerable and receptive; please do. This is a more subtle matter. You alone know when you've crossed the line into false male or female identification, and thus self-betrayal. One example might be the American Olympic figure skater Tonya Harding, hiring thugs to cripple her top rival. That heinous deed certainly tarnished any womanly graces her performance purported to embody.

Soon after that incident occurred I was returning to the States from New Zealand and had a stop-over in Tahiti. There I encountered gorgeous Native women preparing for a dance competition by helping one another dress and adorn themselves, copping each others' moves, and giving helpful suggestions. No private coaches in isolated gyms. When I spoke with a goddess of a dancer about how ashamed I felt about the American way, she responded wisely, "We just have a different concept of competition in the islands. Com-petition for us is petitioning the gods together." Ahhhh...

The power of the feminine West is as splendidly darkening as a Tahitian pearl in a shell, involving interiority, seduction, enchantment, containment, dreaming, elimination. If men are served up too few examples of viable Indigenous manhood in cinema, women are truly at a loss. The few times I see a woman in film who seems real to me, I come out of my usual viewer's trance and sit bolt upright, with all the avidity of one encountering an endangered species thought to be extinct, that might actually be saved.

There is a Native Meso-American teaching which says that women belong to the Earth and the Moon, men to the Sky and the Stars, including of course the Sun. Men are able to introduce women to their realm of brilliance, expansion and objectivity, but women are strongly cautioned not to fly sky-ward and star-ward with a man who hasn't demonstrated true respect for her Earth and Moon, in other words for the bodily, cyclic, nocturnal, and emotional/oceanic realms.

A woman's womb is a microcosm of the Cosmic Void from which the inspiring light of the Sun and stars stream to Earth. The fecundating, inspirational, airy male energy of the East, and the child-like, all-consuming, fiery enthusiasm of the South, are given a measure of value in the watery mini-Void Womb of the West. There the female *knowing* decides what deserves to be nurtured into the final, enduring, earthy maturity of true North (e.g. become a Chief) and what should be eliminated: Whoosh!

Elimination, *Menstruation*, the "M" word, "the Curse," symbolizes the ability to say "No" (through blood-red lipstick) to any growth and supposed "progress" which falls far, far short by female, relational standards. While a man would go on a Vision Quest once in his lifetime, our Ancestresses the world over withdrew some four hundred times to return to the Source, their bodies partaking in remembrance of the fluid formlessness before form. And when they came back to the community, they were welcomed with care and reverence, their Moon-time dreams avidly attended to, as they might well prove prophetic.

"She who bleeds and does not die." Today scientists are developing means to eliminate menstrual flow altogether. May as well blow up the Moon, destroy the tidal rhythms. This is a power which was once celebrated and treated with awe as Sacred, and which modern Western life has cancelled out in favor of a female model which is always receptive, sexually willing, and maternally nurturing. As a young Irish tourist once said to me, "It's a grand fookin' scheme for someone, but not for me."

On the cover of this book is a Mermaiden, a fantastic symbol for a beguiling Archetype found world-wide. In Haiti, she is the Loa *Sirene*, whom

Voudon serviteurs call upon for seductive powers and wealth. In Hawaii is found *Nahenahe* whom Connie Rios, author of *Ka Hana Pono*, describes as a Polynesian woman in the fullness of life, possessing the strength and compassion to swim around our endangered canoes and help us get back on a righteous course. Such lovely Tricksters are sometimes required to seduce men into the depths of the feminine West, until men come to learn that the Death they encounter there is a necessary one for them in order to be stripped down and Reborn, restored to their Soulful trajectory.

Anyone wishing to appreciate Shamanic skills must learn Western Compass-point elimination in order to dislodge and dissolve any obstacles and make way for the new. The solar sun-rising Male must face his mortality in the West. We are all destined to die and truly foolish not to prepare well for that fantastic passage of Transformation. To avoid this awareness is to cultivate a childish resistance to it, which makes the inevitable feel like annihilation, rather than birth into our Divine nature.

In every death of identity we can evaporate the dross of life and become more centered in that which endures. Death and Rebirth. It's paradoxical: an intimate enfolding of deep values which then spread out into greater engagement with all three dimensions of world and self. Come on board for that challenge, mates! Or rather, "Walk the plank and c'mon in, the shark-infested water's just great!" In Old Hawaii, the Shark was the totem animal of the West, and women had to swim among them calmly to earn their Initiatory rank. Yeow, Mama — Nahenahe, don't fail me now!

A~VOID~DANCE & ENGAGEMENT

South Africa was the site of seclusionary lunar enclaves known as "the Huts of the Maidens with no Hearts," the opposite of females when conciliatory and nurturing. And in the Pacific Northwest, the menstrual hut was at enough distance from the Kwakiutl tribal domestic dwellings to be known as "the place where women stay when they disappear." Even their gaze at this time of elimination was thought to be potentially lethal, and dining utensils were secured (e.g. sipping through swans' bones) so their touch wouldn't render the food poisonous. Serious juju.

If women no longer ritualize their monthly cycles, those profound energies are submerged into unconsciousness. Some woman's tendency to default to the Womb, the Cosmic Void, the dark female Source, makes it easy for them to a -"Void" pro-active engagement in this culture's yang-oriented life, and for others to void them out.

Too many women are still being asked to discount their true experiences, even by men who claim to know better. How many (yawn) movies have you seen where the man is impelled to noble action because his woman has died? The movie male-as-widower is largely an idealized fantasy, his mourning a sentimental measure of *love* which requires no give-and-take, no serve-and-response, no rock-tumbling friction with a flesh-and-blood woman. Back in the nurturing Void, she too is idealized, and able to womb-shape her man into a heroic chapter she no longer *humanly* shares. Silent too — how convenient!

You need only contrast the artifice of, say, Mel Gibson's character in *Lethal Weapon* to the authentically anguished widowers in documentaries *Strange Culture* and *Trudell* to see what a cheap shot the former affords.

Women's challenge is to sound out the watery, enchanting, lunar, emotional, soulful layers of Western, sunset-streaming, opal-flashing subjectivity. To distill their evolving earthly and lunar comprehension of Death and Rebirth into a frequency of shrewd and compassionate sovereignty. She must also claim the East of the Compass, moving equally back and forth from the sea-cave to the Marketplace with the powerful, star-spangled dark ballast of her womb intact.

LIVING THE COMPASS

So let's launch out and examine this spiraling Compass as an inner/outer measure of the Soul's life from pre-womb to post-tomb, as illustrated by films.

To distinguish male from female, we can imagine men, via their thrusting phallic natures, coming to earth and moon *from* stars and sky, "the Word made Flesh." And women, via their contained, womb-based capacities, announcing the inner knowing of earth and moon *to* the stars and sky: "the Flesh given Voice."

The best of plots will have the protagonist undergoing an Initiatory round of Death and Rebirth between maturing identities. The death may be sudden and startling, or a more gradual morbidity, wherein the current Domain Basin becomes less and less vitalizing, more cramping, boring, or even toxic. Or a Death and Rebirth may be prompted by prophetic vision, when one tosses their heart (Will) over the fence so that the horse (Nature spirit/Ancestry) may follow.

Look for or create these elements: when Actors are conceived as potentially Shape-shifting Shamans, their consciousness cannot remain blithely on the surface. "Suffering" (carrying) a vaster, Upper World, Prophetic consciousness, they penetrate the Ancestral realm of what preceded them, that which is not merely manifest but compacted with repressed elements, both lead and gold. In that Underworld they encounter demonic and/or divine spirits, and resurrect with a truer knowing, a sense of meaningfulness that informs Middle World and renders the Underworld no longer so threatening. (Think of the Pacific Northwest Native fable in which a band of captive children were able to explode a Witch into a cluster of mosquitoes, thus reducing an overwhelming threat to a pesky, but easily conquered one.)

Once you sound out this tri-level model, your plots can sizzle with challenge, since one person's Ancestry and Prophesy can so eclipse another's as to thrust them into liminal space. Thus we see the Colonialist and Corporate lust to destroy the Indigenous "Other's" culture whenever encountered: there goes the neighborhood!

And always, always watch for the Uhane, the power of the human Voice to define reality. This registers as leadership in a plot, sometimes *falsely* (think of Hitler's rants twisting the impulse for patriotism to vile ends, or his inversion of a timelessly generative symbol into the regressive, enervating swastika). And sometimes *truly*: let the movie's desired, revered and winning "star" be one who listens and speaks for both Unihipili Nature and Aumakua Cosmos.

Brian Swimme tells us that the Fundamental *Dream* of the Universe begins with each living entity presenting itself in its singular nature, *differentiating* its unique contribution to life, a task which is profoundly commissioned from both within and without. Thus we see that Initiation is ordained from a Cosmic longing for the authenticity of everything in Creation!

You don't have to journey to the outer reaches of our Galaxy to locate deep prompting and support for your life's fulfillment; it pulsates from the heart of the Cosmos into yours. Into *yours*, which you'll eventually learn actually *is* the heart of the Cosmos. No less than the beauty of an orchid or the splendor of a sea storm, the sultriness of a panther or the grace of a gazelle has been invested in your unique and necessary nature. Planted there from your beginning and renewed each moment, each breath, each heartbeat.

Finally, everyone is implored to sound out their sacred *subjective* depths, their compassion, emotional truth, hope and inner knowing, resulting in a gorgeous, compassionate *communion* at all levels of Creation: Heaven-on-Earth indeed!

PART III

CHILDREN AS NEST~DWELLERS

"Each child lives deep inside his or her own psychic house, or soul castle, and the child deserves the right of sovereignty inside that house, without invasion."

— Robert Bly

EMERGING FROM THE VOID

From Tibet to Timbuktu, Tasmania to Tahiti, Indigenous cultures have great spiritual regard for the development of children in their mothers' wombs. Many even attend to the parents' dreams *prior* to conception for indications that the time is ripe to ripen. It only makes sense, if we are to study the Soul's experience in evolutionary terms — Nature to Human to Divine — to give weight to *past* lives as well as concern for *future* ones.

In the light of Reincarnation we must value the Unborn as one who has already lived, perhaps many, many lifetimes. Australian Aborigines make the distinction between human and spirit children, and designate certain water-holes as dwelling sites where Souls cluster, looking for opportunities to be reborn — such as the chance to dive into a potential father walking by (see *Ten Canoes*).

In the Dagara Tribe of Africa, there is tolerance for children who change their minds once conceived, and detach from the mother's womb; they interpret miscarriage as a choice, not an accident. Tibetans have distinct rituals for all the different phases of pregnancy. Hawaiians believe you can determine a fetus' nature by its mother's appetite: hunger for shark-meat signifies boldness, for a gentler fish like mahi-mahi, a more docile offspring.

Hawaiians also see the Unborn as emerging from *Po*, the velvety dark Land of the Dead, where the *Ali'i* (Royalty) sup on butterflies (metamorphosis) and honey. As the Soul approaches Earth through the Heavens, it chooses the lights by which it intends to illumine Life. This is a reference to what some Native American Indians call 'Night Medicine,' and Westerners, 'Astrology' — a convenient way for screenwriters to illustrate the contours of Upper World, if only in their preparatory character sketches. Casting directors could also factor this in. Want a somber, brooding, responsible leading man? Ralph Fiennes and Denzel Washington, both Capricorns, surely fit the bill. Desire luminous compassion in a female lead? Pisceans Juliet Binoche and Rachel Weisz can always deliver, shimmeringly.

Even in the West, where Science has dominated in a cold, empirical manner, many women still dream their child before conceiving, and are informed by the fetus of such essentials as its desired name. Indeed, this is probably where the concept of Cherubs arose: sweet winged babes hovering around the parents, seeking incarnation.

Like menstruation, which cycles from order to bloody chaos to re-ordering, the phenomenon of pregnancy is rife with Initiatory potential. Our Ancestresses faced a high mortality risk every time they bore a child. They were dancing close to an Ultimate edge from which they may or may not return with a new identity, that of Mother, approaching the Land of the Dead which might actually claim them, or from which they might claim a Soul for its rebirth.

The teaching of this next film is that we hold a dream in our hearts prior to birth. This strong sense of *prior intent* haunts us throughout life. We are always looking for *causes* of effects, or rummaging around in the half-forgotten dramas of childhood for explanations of conditioning to deliver to therapeutic sessions. What seed grew *this* harvest? Initiation could take you farther back, between lives, to recall your true purpose this incarnation. As you chose it.

PRE~NATAL COMMUNICATION: *BETWEEN HEAVEN AND EARTH*

Truly, Carmen Maura is to be cherished for her facility in roles requiring that she swim through Upper and Lower realms without appearing woo-woo in Middle World. You may well have seen her playing the no-nonsense "ghost" of Penelope Cruz' mother in 2006's *Volver*. But you probably missed her in Marion Hansel's 1992 European "fable for the future," *Between Heaven and Earth*. Do make the effort to find it if you want to experience the rare enchantment of a modern story centering on Mother-Child pre-natal communication.

Maria (C. M.) is a sensual and sophisticated Parisian newscaster, a career journalist for whom the world's conflicts (e.g. violent political dem-onstrations) are pure catnip. One night after sharing dynamic airtime on a hot, breaking story with a suave, out-of-town celebrity journalist, she finds herself trapped in her apartment elevator with him. Their sizzling on-camera chemistry takes a more intimate turn, and quicker than you can say "Action!" Maria is pregnant, and her married one-night stand gone back to his legit family.

Affluent and independent, Maria decides to keep her lover blissfully clueless, and his identity a secret from her friends and colleagues. In a nice bit of sub-plotting, we see her ongoing interactions with a young neighbor, a latchkey-less kid who enjoys time in Maria's apartment while awaiting his parents' homecoming. Her warm rapport with the boy foreshadows her capabilities as a single mother.

But even this cosmopolitan feminist is rattled when her in utero baby begins speaking to her, claiming to be in Nowhereland (similar to the Hawaiians "Po"), "*where we know everything: Forgetfulness comes with birth.*" Also echoing the Dagara tribe's tolerant beliefs, it informs her, "*Nothing obliges us to live. We decide if we want to come earlier, later, or not at all.*"

Any plans Maria may have to distract herself from this odd phenomena by burying herself in work are dashed by a new assignment — investigation of a slew of overdue pregnancies resulting in stillbirths when the doctors try to induce labor.

She meets another mother-to-be in their obstetrician's waiting room, the young woman clearly driven to the edge of insanity by her fetus' anguish: she hears her child screaming in the night that he doesn't want to come to

Earth. Maria's unborn echoes this reluctance, proclaiming the world too violent, corrupt and ecologically devastated to appeal to any of the Cherubs in Nowhereland, that they are planning to stop coming altogether if the adults don't clean up their act. While this prenatal mutiny was originally thought to be a local dilemma blamed on the tides, statistics on stillbirths begin sounding a world-wide alarm.

EAST~WEST IMBALANCE, NORTH~SOUTH SAVVY

We've already noted that the Unborn's Father is out of the picture, resulting in an emptiness in the East which sets up an imbalance in the Soul Compass. Such an occurrence can weigh matters towards the West, drawing a soul back toward the original Void of Deep Mystery. Or it can amplify a child's yearning for its father, casting its consciousness out into the transcendent realm of Great Spirit. Either way, the connection still lives, in every cell.

Without a husband's spousal support and protection to allow Maria the womanly largesse of brooding over her ambivalent babe, she becomes devastated at the prospect of loss. Some assurance is provided by her young neighbor's surmise that if only *one* more baby can be persuaded to come to life, the rest may follow. Balancing his Southern point intuition with Elderly, Diamond-cutting savvy is a seasoned Chaos Theory Scientist who agrees with Maria's fetus that we are threatening the fragile threshold of life itself by interfering with Nature. If more women would listen to their unborn children, he avers, Chaos could reorganize itself just fine, on a more elegant plane.

The passionate showdown between Eros and Thantanos comes at another threshold, the seashore, to which the overdue Maria has fled after her doctor tried to force her into the delivery room. As with Carmen Maura's role in *Volver*, while the circumstances are supernatural, she manages to make the exchange most human. Stakes are high and emotions raw. No extraordinary promises are made from either side, nor assurances that life as it is will undergo some fabulously swift renovation. Yet Maria's passionate love for her child, and insistence that his life is valuable and desired in part because the world *is* troubled, are enough to persuade him to be born. But only after an angel gently hushes his hyper-awareness of Nowhereland, inducing the great forgetting that sets us all innocently on our life paths.

TREACHEROUS REALMS: DAMNATION OR RESCUE

There's a rather severe Tibetan Buddhist warning: "Children aren't safe from anything in this world, not even from Death." Sadly true. Add to that the Buddhist belief in Karma and we can mistakenly slip into magically blaming the victim. However, I think most of us share an innate longing that children be safe, be cherished, be recognized as unique and necessary. To subdue or override that protective longing in the face of a child's pain is to scorch an essential dimension of human-heartedness. To dismiss a child's suffering as their Karma, without first empathizing with their distress and trying our utmost to prevent it, is to fall prey to a moral relativism that borders on cynicism.

Yes, it may be in a child's fate that it suffer, but might it not equally be its Destiny to be rescued, and someone else's choice to be just as courageous as the perp is exploitative? Tropisms are at play: one character may well turn toward destruction, another towards life — with the audience avidly invested in knowing who's Uhane, whose human will and voice, will determine the outcome.

As a quarter of the Soul Compass, and the first chapter of every life, Childhood/Nest-dwelling is foundational to all that flourishes or falters thereafter. In many African tribes it is considered the utmost in rudeness to greet neighbors without asking after every member of their family. Deep Cinema encourages more inclusion of children in our cinematic storytelling, with soulful regard to their multi-dimensional natures.

In this chapter I am recommending a troubling litany of films which show that children can face treachery in every imaginable Domain Basin, some being damned and others escaping any enduring curse. We'll observe which options stand available for them, or how harrowing it is for them to face possible destruction solo, *without* human orbits of support surrounding them.

My thrust here is to encourage films which restore a more tribal consciousness to the relationships between adults and youth. In Hawaii, many non-blood-relatives are referred to as "Aunty" and "Uncle," with the subsequent sense of intimacy and security being truly palpable. What if children felt they could turn to *all* adults as family, and adults perceived *all* children as in their care? Even factoring in the need for discretion, just imagine the comforting sense provided by that World Tribe.

FAMILY: *THE WAR ZONE*

Tim Roth is always an intriguing actor, but even his best performances gave me no preparation for the sterling skills illustrated in this, his directorial debut — *The War Zone*, with cast and crew matching his high standards at every turn. In my therapeutic workshops on *Film as Biography* and *Film as Initiation*, this one has proven most skillfully evocative of suppressed emotional memories for numerous victims of familial abuse. Steel yourself: daring the dark as none other, Roth has chosen to tell a tale that is no less than excruciating to behold.

The metronomic syncopation of "apparent vs. true" is shown from the very opening scene, with adolescent son, Tom (Freddie Cunliffe) shown gliding a bike along a languorous coastal road to his Devon family home. What initially looks to be an enviable locale soon proves to be vulnerable and even creepy in its considerable isolation. Initially too, the family seems sweetly bonded, as they rally to speed the very pregnant Mom (the ever pitch-perfect Tilda Swinton) en route to the hospital after her water breaks. It's night, the unlit road rural, and when the Dad (Ray Winstone) is distracted by the back-seat antics of Tom and daughter Jessie (Lara Belmont), he hits a bump and careens off the road, violently flipping his precious cargo.

Amazingly, baby daughter Alice is actually born wailing in that crushed, dark, and steaming wreck. As they crawl out, bloody but unbowed, there has seldom been a more shocking picture of a family in extreme distress meeting it with extreme resilience. Which quality will prevail? You have to wonder.

TOM'S TRI~PART SELF

The rest of the plot focuses on young Tom's discovery of the father's incestuous relationship with teenaged Jessie. The awkward, acne-pocked, sullen virgin lad confronts his sister with a jumbled mix of righteous indignation, accusation, and sexual envy. Preoccupation with his own congested, unresolved erotic issues (Nature Self) compromises his brotherly capacity to draw on transcendent principle (Divine Self) in order to speak out (Human Self) and protect his sister. Her main concern is that their mother not be told.

Only after stealthily following the perverted father-daughter couple out to an abandoned cliffside war bunker where Jessie is sodomized, does Tom realize how profoundly and helplessly she is suffering. And since his older sister has always proven the more confident, capable sibling, Tom's determination to disclose the dark deed crumbles in the face of her anguish and vulnerability.

Things will have to get worse for Tom to rally, and incredibly, they do. Watch for a small but pivotal scene with the Mom busy in the background and Tom lounging while Dad walks about with the newborn infant on his shoulder, cooing sweet nothings in her ear. Red alert! If you replay and listen closely, you can just barely hear him whisper "I can't wait."

Apparently he doesn't. Soon afterwards, the newborn Alice has to be rushed to the hospital running a temperature and mysteriously bleeding from her wee bottom. This transgression against his infant sister (pure Unihi-pili: Nature Spirit) gives Tom the courage to verbally (Uhane: Spirit who speaks) confront his Dad, enduring violent denial in return. It grows the lad. Meanwhile, with the mother away in hospital, Jessie huddles trembling at the kitchen table as lone witness.

CLUELESS MOTHER, TRANSGRESSING DAD

The War Zone is a stormy, tragic story of what happens when children are isolated, betrayed, and left to their own devices to make things right, a responsibility far too great for them to bear.

Young Lara Belmont's acting is incredible throughout. Her character has no Elders to turn to for rescue. The mother is failing her Western point covenant with the quality of intimacy by remaining naïve in the face of the husband's violation. The husband, of course, is failing his masculine, Eastern point covenant to model requisite distances, transcendence, boundaries.

When the mother berates her daughter for having stayed out all night on the beach with a new boyfriend (a very young Colin Farrell), the look in Jessie's eyes — of daring, hauteur and contempt — is a wonder to behold. And in this trembling, climactic showdown scene with the father, she manages to convey a layered, poison parfait of being wound too tight to bear (desperately trying to contain her outrage) all the while humming comfortingly to herself between ravaged sniffles. When she finally ignites her Uhane, giving voice to her savaged flesh, it's a raw, red-eyed, overdue issuance from too-long a private Hell. Not to be missed, if you can bear it.

AND SO IT GOES

We could go on into ever-expanding Domain Basins which fail to shelter children:

Work: *The Devil's Miner* has fatherless children forced into treacherous labour in Bolivian silver mines. *Blood Diamond* shows the horror of child soldiers blindly supporting a marketplace which never benefits them.

Celebrity: And who wears the blood diamonds in the magazine ads? As Angelina Jolie's biographical turn as *Gia* tells it, anorexic, addicted young models. In this case one emotionally abandoned by her star-struck friends and criminally-heartless mother. Whose tainted blood spilled for whose haute couture benefit?

Church: Does the Church protect children? Endure *The Boys of St. Vincent*, a reenactment of true-life sexual abuse on the part of priests running a fortress-like orphanage in Newfoundland. Only in Part II do women come on the scene, one a radio newscaster (Uhane), another a marriage partner of a former priest. They're willing to go toe-to-toe with these once isolated, insulated, and entitled pedophiles, and the truth comes out.

Therapy: Look at the child's nightmare that is *The Sixth Sense*. A boy with extraordinary psychic ability, barely launched into life, is allowed no measure of carefree innocence. Instead he is assaulted by hungry Ghosts, veritable Zombies, walking Dead who believe themselves still alive. This film makes the plane of life-force so hostile to the lad that the color red, the color of blood, life, love, passion, vitality, the womb, and the root chakra is here used to represent all that is sinister and threatening. Even the boy's one source of possible rescue, his Therapist, is among the discombobulated deceased who require the youth's Shamanic Psychopomp skills to help them accept their demise and finally cross over.

Spirituality: While many Indigenous peoples express anxiety at learning that their child may be Shamanic, fearing these extraordinary qualities might alienate them from the ordinary pleasures of family life, at least they have Medicine Men and Women to acknowledge such powers and shape them. Instead we have movies showing the very good dying far too young, as in *Pay it Forward* and *Powder*. What message does this give young people who may have a highly tuned sixth sense and are fascinated by the realm of Spirit? — Sacrificial lambs.

End Times: The uniquely innovative director Michael Haneke echoes the sentiment of Leonardo Di Caprio's *Blood Diamond* character who implored, "When was the last time the world wasn't falling apart, huh?" But Haneke was frustrated that it only seems to be the Apocalyptic End of the World for folks *other* than those of the First World. So he set *Time of the Wolf* in modern-day Europe, where a young boy gives up on the adults and determines to sacrifice himself to save humanity.

We can do better by them.

Let's celebrate at least one example in which the Domain Basin of early loving containment sustained an Indian girl throughout kidnapping and attempted indoctrination. May it be a lesson for us all, that we too can be restored to Indigenous Soul, providing ourselves and our youth protection and purpose.

SCHOOL: *WHERE THE SPIRIT LIVES*

Canada 1937: Right out of the gate, *Where the Spirit Lives* dares to begin with a young Canadian Indian girl discovering her first menstrual cycle and being ceremonially initiated into Womanhood. The joy on her face is radiant as she probably imagines a future lover, courtship, marriage, children, and deeper participation in village life. In attendance is a younger tribal member, Ashtecome (Michelle St. John) who clearly longs for her welcoming day to come.

Before that can happen, Ashtecome, her little brother Pita, and a handful of other Indian youth are seduced into a biplane and flown off to a wretched boarding school where the all-too-usual atrocities take place: brutal de-licing, haircuts, imposed names (Ashtecome is now "Amelia"), physical punishment for "talking Indian" or even mentioning the past, "conversion" to a harsh brand of Christianity, sexual exploitation, lies, adoption, etc.

A new teacher on staff, Kathleen, is idealistic enough to respect "Amelia's" past, but is of little use when the girl announces her first Moon-time, pleading for the white woman's ritual: "Well, there is no ritual, dear. That sort of thing is part of your old ways. You're a Christian now. Go see the Nurse." Could be funny — "Huh? Christian women don't moon-flow?" — if it wasn't so pathetic. But remembering the tribal ceremony, Amelia enlists another Indian resident to paint her forehead, first with a swath of blood-red and then an arc of moons, saying:

"You are my friend, and now we are sisters.
The Moon is our Grandmother.
She brings Life to the Earth in the dew of the Night,
As you will bring Life to the Earth.
You are Amelia,
And now you will be Ashtecome again.
Even when we become Stars in the Sky,
In your daughters and in their daughters,
Where you have given life,
You will live forever."

A strangely beautiful variation on Initiation: Death to an *imposed* identity and rebirth of her Native one. Tri-Part self: Cosmos, Earth, and Human: Ancestry, Prophesy, and Verbal Spirit all coming together in passionate resonance. Through this traditional rite, as well as in a sweet-grass ceremony and a burial ritual, Ashtecome shows that the seeded Domain Basin of her past has ripened enough to uproot any European-based indoctrination the school attempts to impose. Like the Australian Aboriginal girls in *Rabbit-Proof Fence*, she determines to steal away with her kin and make her way home. And we're left with little doubt that she can. Splendid!

ENCHANTMENT:
ETERNAL CHILDREN VS. ENDURING TALES

Tragically, some children never grow up. A classic, *The Little Prince*, gives us the reason for this arrested growth: he lives on his own planet which doesn't engage in the normal cycles of day to night, or the ongoing passage of months, years, decades. In the Hawaiian language the word for *nurturance* is the same as that for *cycles*. Without these nurturing, Initiatory cycles he's stuck, and unfortunately seems fine with unending youth. Funny he isn't an American creation.

The French author of this tale, Antoine de Saint-Exupéry, was a considerable Puer Aeternus (eternal boy) himself, and died in a plane accident in midlife.

If the Puer avoids growth by flying too high and not touching down onto all that Earth's cycles imply, then a Puella (eternal girl) avoids Lunar nurturance. Our image-driven society has tragically spawned a modern-day plague of eating disorders, and a record-high suicide rate for obese and anorexic girls. The industries that standardize and commodify beauty are truly cannibalistic, asking us in turn to commodify ourselves or else be judged as fallen short.

Not only are grown women held to impossibly youthful standards, but little girls are prematurely sexualized by bizarre products: Bratz Brand manufactures a padded "bralette" for the pre-pubescent crowd, and Mattel launches a make-up kit aimed at six- to nine-year-olds. What next — cod-pieces for little Junior? Botox for babies? Just take a look at the serious plasticized contestants, culled from real-life players, in the final scenes of *Little Miss Sunshine* for a repugnant hit of just how grotesque this all has become.

I ask myself why American films are so relentlessly puerile, so gleefully charging apace in the dogged foot-race from *Dumb & Dumber* to Dumbest. Why do they have so little orientation toward true North of the Soul Compass, the cultivation of a rewarding sense of maturity? I chalk it up to avoidance.

Not merely avoidance of aging and mortality, but avoidance of the true Eldership of this culture, its Shamanic profile, the life of and on the land that is North America. Since the descendants of the oldest dwellers, those who revere and replenish the sacredness of spiritual hills and watering holes, have an ancestral history of displacement and genocide, non-Native filmmakers can't comfortably turn to them for stories on how to age honorably. To do so would be to enter a round of grief and growth, and face a reckoning that's long overdue.

ARRESTED GROWTH: *LOVERS OF THE ARCTIC CIRCLE*

Often, arrested youth have no Elders to model life's full trajectory, so they never get hooked by their Higher Selves, and don't age past midlife. In *Lovers of the Arctic Circle* two doomed childhood sweethearts, Otto and Ana, cling to one another in compensation for parental Domain Basins which have been destroyed by death and divorce. As teens, they even become sexually active together, but are still clearly reaching through one another for the love of the lost parent. Ana suspects that her late father's Spirit possesses Otto. Sadly, the superficiality of his commitment to her is displayed when he attempts suicide after his mother's sudden demise, then implores Ana to mother him.

The fact that their names are palindromes, spelled the same way forward and backwards, echoes their stultifying one-step-forward, one-step-back dance through their short lives.

The plot book-ends with Otto, now a pilot, flying to the Arctic Circle on the day the vermilion Sun is shown rolling across the horizon but not setting: the Land of the Midnight Sun. (Again, the curse of *The Little Prince*.) There awaits Ana, living in a cabin which, wonderfully, has the latitude of the Arctic Circle curved across its wooden floor. Otto's voice-over: "It's good that lives have several cycles. But mine, my life, has only gone around once." And so he crashes. With Ana dying soon after.

This inability to get with the spiraling rhythm of the Time-Space Continuum is tragic indeed, in that here are two entranced youth who will never grow old enough to shine in the Midnight (Northern point, Eldership) of their own Soul Compasses.

WONDROUS ELDERS

Every human is born with a promising Soul Compass, but initially we only experience ourselves as dependent Nest-Dwellers projecting our capacity for

Partnership onto our Parents, that of Tricksterism onto "Enemies," that of Eldership onto Grandparents, etc. Only as we grow can we withdraw and transform those projections in order to individuate and live more authentically.

Among African tribes it is understood that parents are needed biologically for reproduction, with Mentors and Elders then on hand for the deeper initiatory and spiritual teachings after birth. Without such culturally endorsed objectivity, the growing pains of the parents often tangle with the growth spurts of their children, leaving everyone trashed in a shallow quagmire (*The Squid and the Whale*).

Even if obviously flawed, Elders by their very presence energetically sustain an Archetypal Domain Basin onto which the Child will project an umbrella of potential and protection. And if the Elders don't exploit or excessively disillusion the Child, it has a decent chance. But much more kinship is possible (see *Vitus*) with one Soul arriving from the Source and the other soon returning.

Having a Wise-enough Elder on hand is like having your heart hooked by your Higher Self, Grand Tete, in Voudon: a larger Domain Basin of acknowledgement and potential is kindled, activated, electrified. Without them, the wee Irish lass of Roan Inish here would still be doing a sorrowful pub crawl trying to get her grieving Father to love her, instead of coaxing her seal pup of a brother back on land.

WATER SPIRITS: *THE SECRET OF ROAN INISH*

John Sayles, this time with a "brother from another species," displays childhood Shamanism at its mythic, totemic best. The Selkies celebrated here are of an ilk found world-wide: mermaids, sirens, the half-human, half sea-creatures of irresistible seduction.

No matter what your philosophy on evolution, you have to admit that, during one epoch, our ancestors were necessarily pretty wild creatures living amongst some pretty wild animals, all of whom shared in predator-prey exchange. This exchange was so intimate that when we managed to domesticate species (tame horses from the wild, wolves to dogs), we also tamed and domesticated ourselves. But that sense of kinship endures, with folklore averring that for some the shape-shifting tipping point may not be that far afield, as with werewolves, for example, or, on Roan Inish ("Island of the Seals"), with Selkies.

Slight, fetching, blonde Fiona Coneely (Jeni Courtney) is a thoughtful, "listening" child, with a lot to listen for, having lost the voice of her mother to death, her wee brother's to the sea, and now her father's to work, grief and "the drink." Fortunately, this Nest-Dweller has an option: two loving Elders, grandparents on the West Coast of Ireland, glad to take her in. Off shore from their mainland dwelling is an island, Roan Inish, home to a cluster of empty, decaying, thatched white cottages, once the family's ancestral compound.

FROM TOMBSTONE TO BLARNEY STONE

If the girl's life before this move was far too silent, sorrowful and lonely, her grandfolks more than make up for it with their loving good spirits and considerable gift of gab. It's from the old man that Fiona learns of her brother Jamie's fate that day the Coneely family was forcibly evacuated from Roan Inish during World War II.

While the adults were busy loading their household possessions aboard ships, Jamie was resting in his wooden cradle on the lip of the shore, the cradle being some artisan's exquisite nest of carved shells and seaweed. Then the sky darkened ominously and a commotion of gulls conspired with a band of seals to draw Jamie too swiftly out to choppy sea, beyond his family's desperate grasp. The old folks are resigned to the infant's fate: "The Sea had taken poor wee Jamie. It was angry at us for leaving Roan Inish."

But rather than accepting as absolute that "the Sea gives and the Sea takes away," Fiona resolves that it can also give back. She can secretly work with her teenage cousin Eamon to refurbish the island cottages to their former domestic beauty, convince the family to move back there, and thus release Jamie from the Seals' enchantment.

Another more menacing "dark cousin," Tedhg (John Lynch), while violently going about the bloody business of cleaning fish, tells the ever nonplussed Fiona that their family pedigree includes the seals themselves, Selkies. A Coneely Ancestor found one of these quaisi-mermaidens in beautiful human form (Susan Lynch), having slipped from its black, shiny skin. This pelt he stole from the rocks and hid in the attic. Years and several children later, her seal-skin is found and she is drawn irrevocably back to her watery home. Thus Fiona is assured by Tedhg that Jamie's not lost at all, but "just with another branch of the family."

THRESHOLDS AND THRESHOLDS

Having arrived so recently from the other side, a child has passed the threshold from "Po" to Earth, from the Spirit land to the plain of incarnation. In the best of all possible worlds, their very first, organic stage of mourning, if at all, would only come with the bittersweet, organic passage from childhood to adolescence. So it feels unnatural for a wee one of Fiona's age to have already grappled with death. Her poignant loss is brought home when she awakens from a dream visitation with her deceased mother, and plaintively calls out to her.

Another meaning of "threshold" is "threshing grounds," that place where the ordinary necessary work of the world gets done to sustain us. Being so young, and already tipsy with Spirits, Fiona clearly benefits from the hard, grounding toil of white-washing and thatching the cottages to their former familial warmth. At first she finds hints of life on Roan Inish, wee footprints in the sand, ashes in the hearth, an enchanting child-sized dining display of shells and crabs. And then she begins seeing Jamie himself, a skittish, naked, tousled-haired "dark" Coneely, so wary of human encounters that he always speeds away in his trusty cradle, much to Fiona's dismay.

ONE DARK AND STORMY NIGHT

One of the great, rare benefits of *The Secret of Roan Inish* is that, while the male characters in it are indispensable, it is ultimately a young girl's story, with a womanly resolution. The wee girl needs a Wise Old Woman to blaze the path from Nest-Dwelling to Diamond-Cutting and Pearl-Spinning, to provide assurance that living a full, long life with Soul intact is indeed possible. So when the Grandmother, hanging laundry, tells Fiona of her parents' splendid courtship, you can see the child glowing from the love that created her, and dreaming her own romantic potential, as girls always do.

So the East-West of the Soul Compass is provided from the mature Womb-Weaver. And it is from this same source that Fiona desperately needs her visions of Jamie validated.

Yes, cousin Eamon is wonderfully helpful, and tweedy, pipe-smoking Grand Da' the greatest, but it's the Grandmother who wears the shawl in this family. And when she whips it around her head and begins packing for a wild nocturnal passage to the island, we know she's been convinced against all logic and Catholic doctrine that her grandson Jamie is still alive and can be restored to her ample and loving bosom. So too the harmony between humans and Nature — restored. And somewhere in the smoky warmth of the island cottage's peat-moss fire can be sensed the ghostly spirit of Fiona and Jamie's mother, suffused with relief at this loving reunion.

With this tale comes a beginner's lesson on the surprising sweetness Death can sometimes provide, and how intimately it becomes woven into our lives. Those of us who have lost family members, friends, role models and mentors to the mysterious depths know that part of the human heart is a cherished necropolis, a city of the dead. And surprisingly, that catacomb can become as sweet as a honeycomb due to the exchange of love ever flowing across these liminal thresholds. And that is one of the key Secrets of Roan Inish.

STEALING FIRE FROM THE ELDER: *WHALE RIDER*

Because the modern world is dominated by the mutant Marketplace, and Indigenous peoples have by and large been literally run off, or ground into, that crooked playing field, they have to resort to embodying legend in order to "talk story" which manifests their cherished mythic powers. Such can be found in the many mythic re-enactments of *Dreamkeeper*. And such is the case with *Whale Rider*. But these profound tales microcosmically display what usurped Natives have suffered through Corporate Colonialization: to move from the depths of Whale Rider to the shallows of, say, *Thirteen*, is to get painful, psycho-spiritual bends in your very Soul.

'Survival,' a British-based organization which works to preserve Indigenous cultures, points out 100 tribes worldwide who adamantly *don't* want interaction with the modern world, as all they see coming their way is cultural disrespect, deadly disease, forced labor, sexual exploitation, and dire destruction of their environment: land, water and animals. New Zealand has already been strongly invaded by Colonial interests. Otherwise we'd still know it as *Aotearoa: Land of the Long White Cloud*. Still, this film is nothing less than a slice of what life can be like as ever more Indigenous practices are revived by the Ngati Konohi tribe of New Zealand's east coast. It valiantly heals a hole in the Ethnosphere.

In many tribes, the bond between Grandparents and Grandchildren is considered the strongest, because the child has just emerged from the Source and the Grandparent is returning to it. Sometimes the Elder and Child will call one another Brother or Sister, or an Elder will even call a Child Grandfather or Grandmother, sensing them to be that reincarnated Spirit. And such is the long unacknowledged yet indomitable kinship in this Maori story.

A vital Huna teaching is that when one is caught in one's Unihipili/Nature Spirit in a wounded, childlike way, one must be reminded of one's Aumakua/Divine Nature in order to be healed. And while *Whale Rider* is based in the Maori tradition of the Land of the Long White Cloud, awareness of such Divine inheritance is key to the adolescent girl's confidence and development. Respect for animals as Ancestral also resonates throughout, thanks in part to a gorgeous musical score by Lisa Gerrard (of *Dead Can Dance*) which echoes the undeniably authoritative, booming depth charges of Whalesong.

BOOKENDS

This movie book-ends with two hospital scenes: the first at the birth of Paikea, an anguishing ordeal which claims the lives of both her mother and twin brother. At that time the infant's Grandfather (Rawiri Paratene) could barely acknowledge her, so invested was he in having her brother grow into his inherited role as Tribal Chief. The final hospital scene shows the same Grandfather keeping humble watch at what he prays won't be the deathbed of the now adolescent Paikea (Keisha Castle-Hughes). What happens in the decade or so between these scenes is an arc of development that pulls everyone's Soul a thousand fathoms deep.

While this story is about the Maori peoples' Sacred origin and their need to stay aligned with that Source, it is not set in some fabulously re-imagined epoch, but in the present. Unlike *Once Were Warriors*, there is no harsh contrast shown with European culture, other than the obvious facts that most of the youth are apathetic about their tribal traditions. Not so young "Pai" who is as passionate about claiming her chiefly lineage as her sexist, patriarchal Grandfather is about preventing her. Although the girl's Father (the always wonderful Cliff Curtis) abandoned her in grief on her day of birth, his last defiant gift was to name her after the Maori's originating Ancestor. Paikea was the Whale Rider who led his people across the Sea from *Hawaiiki*, whose name of honor had henceforth been bestowed only upon first-born sons in the chiefly lineage.

As cold and resistant as is Pai's Grandfather Koro, so is her Grandmother Flowers (Vicky Haughton) warm, turning every one of her husband's "Stop" signs into a temporary and enriching "Detour" for the girl. In league with her is Pai's Uncle Rawiri, who was once a champion of the Maori stick combat known as *Taiaha*, and is now become something of a debauched beached whale. Having been scorched by Koro's contempt for his status as second-born son, he's glad to help Pai defy the old man by teaching her that Warrior skill. Soon she is besting even the best of the tribe's first-born sons who are being trained by Koro in the old ways to compete for the esteemed role of Chief.

SUPER NATURE = SUPERNATURAL

The superb, natural, Aotearoa coastal locale of *Whale Rider* is so lush and primordial that the film can go easy on the supernatural elements, such as Pai's connection with her late Mother, and her kinship with the Whales. These soulful notes are deftly sketched and subtly amplified by the ongoing chanting, watchful sacred statuary of the *Marae* (Meeting House), and Pai's retreats to her father's half-carved *waka* (community ship). Ultimately they weave a layered resonance that make the mythic climax credible:

Drawn by Pai's prayers, several Whales have become stranded on the shore, including a venerable, barnacle-encrusted one whom they recognize as the original Paikea rode to these islands. Sensing that it is so heartbroken over the Maori's cultural devolution that it is willing to die, the tribe strives futilely, with ropes, tractor and personal brawn, to turn the Whale around and return it to the depths. They know that all the rest will follow its lead. If only…

When they have given up, Pai, who's been exiled from the community efforts by Koro, approaches the Whale solo and makes intimate contact, pressing her nose to it in Maori greeting, and climbing aboard the Ancient One. She kicks it with her bare feet, the way a rider would prompt a horse. And so she guides it back to a watery realm where the Souls of the Ancestors are assured that once again their people have a leader willing to die for them if need be.

She doesn't die, and even gains her Koro's long-withheld respect when, sitting alongside her hospital bed, he implores: "*Wise leader, forgive me. I am just a fledgling new to flight.*" Soul to Soul connection. Life in the word. Paikea's eyes open briefly, somberly acknowledging him, and then return to healing rest. Imagine: a young teenager who hungered enough to stay invincible in the fight for her Destiny, even if it meant stealing fire from an intractable Elder. Earlier, her tearful father had proclaimed, "Koro is just… he's just looking for something that doesn't exist anymore." And Pai had countered, "A new leader? They exist."

What a mantra that could be: "A new leader? They exist." Let that become a prayerful chant for girls coming of age, and the sacred Moontime age around "Thirteen" will be restored to its Initiatory dimensions.

PART IV
PATHWAY THROUGH PARENTS

"On the rough wet grass of the back yard my mother and father have spread quilts. They talk quietly, of nothing in particular. As I am little, I am taken in and put to bed... as one familiar and well-beloved in that home. But they will not, oh will not, can not, not now, not ever, will not ever tell me who I am."

— James Agee

FAMILY AS DEADLY DYNASTY / DESTINY

One decided benefit of Initiation is that it separates youth from their biological parents and connects them to Mentors and Nature-Spirit as a higher/deeper resonance of male-female nurturance. Re-engagement with family comes after the ritualized acknowledgement that the Initiate has a new identity, often accompanied by a new name.

Without that clear demarcation, families can engulf their offspring far too long, dictating their social, sexual, political, and vocational choices. Sometimes Nest-Dwellers are born into toxic, devouring or benighted Domain Basins and never make it out alive, physically or spiritually.

GANGSTER DADDY, IDEALISTIC DAUGHTER: *MANDERLAY*

At *Whale Rider's* joyous end, there's a scene in which the handsomely carved, triumphantly festooned *waka* (community ship) has been completed and is being rowed out to Sea. Pai sits in a middle row alongside her Grandfather, wearing the Whale's tooth Sacred, Totemic pendant and leading the chants, as is befitting a newly recognized Chief. And while this is clearly a traditional ritual, the fact that Pai earned her status in such an original, radical manner *and* as a female, promises that she'll be ushering in new leadership. The spiritual wisdom and human kindness modeled by her Grandmother Flowers contribute in no small measure to this assurance. A Brave New World, and a loving one too: Navigating and Womb-weaving integrated.

There's no such hope for the idealistic, would-be leader Grace (Bryce Dallas Howard) of *Manderlay*, the second (following *Dogville*) in Dane Lars Von Trier's trilogy on the dark, thuggish side of America. Grace's father (Willem Dafoe), a widower, opens the story by averring that there isn't a woman alive who doesn't fantasize about serving in harems or being pursued by torch-bearing Natives: "However much they go on about Civilization and Democracy, sexy it ain't." The spunky Grace's only recourse in times like these is to remind her boorish father that he wouldn't behave that way if her mother were still alive. But she isn't, and so the worst of this man is left to bloom like viral overgrowth in his all-male company of thieves.

I don't know if having watched *Dogville* makes the no-frills stage-like set of *Manderlay* (think *Our Town*) more palpable or if it's just better rendered, but it works. The year is 1933, and Grace, her Don of a Daddy, and his gang of henchmen happen upon an isolated Southern Plantation where masters and slaves still abide some 70 years post-Abolition. When Grace determines to move in (accompanied by a cadre of Daddy's best goons of course) and liberate the ol' homestead, he's patronizing at best, warning that her good-hearted efforts may well prove as tragic as when, as a child, she liberated her yellow canary Tweety, only to find it frozen in the snow beneath her window the next morning.

CYNICISM CONFIRMED?

To say that Daddy is proven right is to judge by appearances alone, and not to give his savvy daughter any credit for being a dogged, devoted quick study. But it's the books that fail rather than the student who falls short. Unlike Pai of *Whale Rider*, Grace is uninitiated, with no sense of Destiny and the imaginative rein it allows, and so can only play by pre-fabricated, man-made rules. Her father predicted that Grace's year-long experiment of turning a slave plantation into a successful, democratic agrarian co-operative would go bust.

But her efforts could only be compared to the Tweety bird debacle if young Grace had taken to shooting her pet canaries. Yeah, it gets that dark.

Women, children, men, animals, and the Manderlay land itself all suffer under the well-meaning Missy's rule, because she's ruling via a male model: the Word made Flesh vs. the Flesh given voice. Without discovering just who these African-descendant people actually are, what they know and dream, believe and condemn, desire and fear, she merely attempts to impose a white-washed version of Freedom and Democracy upon them. (Sound familiar?) Von Trier is conveying that, while idealism is something indulged in the children of America, the ruling Elite (and the only truly free) are power-mongering gangsters. And they will *never* unravel their self-serving, tightly-knit system of haves and have-nots, exploiting and exploited, masters and slaves.

Since the original plan for American freedom and democracy was a *Declaration of Independence* and *Bill of Rights* for a handful of white men, not women, not Natives, and certainly not the Founding Fathers' slaves, we can see the *Manderlay* plantation atrocities as yet another toxic boil erupting on this hypocritical body politic.

If an Initiated Womb-Weaving Woman were given Grace's opportunity to shape freedom, her "Bill of Rights" would include safety, security and nurturance extending to Ancestors, humans, animals and the environment, as well as all Spirits entailed. That would be Indigenous and Shamanic "democracy." (The time for this has surely come again, and shouldn't be all that hard to re-integrate as we launch an Ecological Age: after all, humanity lived under Tribal values much, much longer than we have in warring "civilization" or finally, this brief and highly destructive Industrial Age).

But the daughter of the Mafiosa-style Don can't pull off such visionary exploit. Instead we see Grace escaping the now-restored slave plantation and high-tailing it back into her crooked Father's world of brutally gained entitlement.

The movie ends with a searing montage of photographs depicting the fate of "freed" American Blacks, rendered in true-life colours that seem garish after *Manderlay*'s monochromatic design. David Bowie, who's married to an African woman, can be heard singing "Young American" while the screen flashes onto KKK lynchings, Civil Rights opposition, Martin Luther King Jr. in his casket, rank poverty for the segregated, and a Black janitor buffing the despondent face on Abraham Lincoln's statue in Washington D.C. The latter is a precursor, no doubt, of the final segment of Von Trier's trilogy, working title *Washingtonia*.

OVERDUE DEFIANCE: *PANIC*

With a dead mother and a criminal father, *Manderlay's* Grace was caught in a toxic cauldron with no means of escaping its slimy slopes. In *Panic*, it is a grown son, Alex (William H. Macey) who can't get beyond the invisible fencing that is the dominating domain of his corrupt father (Donald Sutherland). Such an overwrought dependency has all but crippled this middle-aged man, collapsing him into passivity, a stance that is wonderfully conveyed in the opening shots: Alex leaning against the bluish glass wall of a high-rise building, Alex smoking, Alex riding an escalator to the office of his shrink (played wonderfully well by John Ritter). The very first words out of this reluctant client's mouth tell all: "Do you ever get the feeling you're dead?"

But even before this, on the DVD version of *Panic*, the *pater-familias* gets the first word. We are shown a blurry shot of Alex with his Father's voice corrupting the very essence of Initiation: "*Every man has a Destiny, Alex. Life is not random. The trick is discovering your Destiny.... Once you know that, everything else comes easy, everything flows.*"

We later learn that this instruction was given Alex as a boy when not-so-dear old Dad was inducting him into the Family business, a vocation he's revealed to no one before this visit to the Psychologist. After saying his employment is operating a particularly tacky-sounding mail-order business out of the home, Alex blandly confesses that he also works for his father.

Dr. Parks: *Doing what?*

Alex: *I kill people.* (Drum roll, please).

SINS OF THE GRANDFATHER

The repressed desperation of *Panic* is wonderfully rendered, with the debilitating effect of the father on his grown son shown in their every encounter.

Take the luncheon scene when Alex arrives at the restaurant only to learn that his father has already ordered for him: Chicken a la King. Could anything with a Regent's name possibly be any closer to soppy baby pabulum? It implies that Alex must swallow whatever Dad dictates, and not engage the discriminating powers of biting, chewing and, heaven forbid, spitting out.

Alex's nasty-piece-of-work of an ice-queen Mother is every bit as possessive, ever probing into her son's sex life and looking smug to learn it's pretty non-existent. But his wife Martha (Tracy Ullman) and six-year-old son Sammy (David Dorfman) comprise a beloved family worth fighting for, which Alex finally manages to do when he learns that Grandpa has begun indoctrinating Sammy into *his* violent "Destiny." That, and the truly horrifying disclosure that Alex's next hit should be Dr. Parks, is enough to finally get the lead out of Junior's pants. At great cost.

Yes, the mortally oppressed son, in his role as loving father, finally takes a bid for defiance, and in doing so manages to pressure at least one facet of the dark lump of coal that is his Soul into Diamondhood. The final scene shows the truly adorable (vs. sappy) Sammy in Dr. Park's office, pondering some serious existential bedtime discussions he'd had with Alex:

Sammy: *I used to think there was no such thing as Infinity, I used to think that everything began and ended. I don't think that anymore.*
Dr. Parks: *What do you think now?*
Sammy: *Now I think that nothing really ends.*

OUTGROWING PARENTS: SHEDDING THE GHOSTS

Indigenous teachings, with their bodily engaged, from-the-ground-up respect for the interdependence of Creation, are always asking that we audit our energy flow. Imagine: you awaken in the morning with all the powers of your Soul Compass flowing heartward to sustain and inspire you. But within moments 20%, 40% or even more of your juices are drained off toward ghostly, vampirish emotional snares that serve no value. A parent's curse, a mentor's judgment, a lover's rejection, can all re-loop devastatingly, even if they are long-gone from our present-day lives. The Unihipili is displacing Uhane's clarity and must be healed to make way for Aumakua's inspiration.

The Toltecs recommend what they call a "Recapitulation," which is a broad-based, decade-by-decade review of all the relationships we've ever had throughout life, to disengage from those that are negative or even neutral. The Hawaiians warn that our emotional bodies can become as rancid and odiferous as our physical bodies if they go uncleansed, and teach the dissolution of *aka* cord connections (sticky psychic threads) from outgrown associations. This can be done individually, as works best when a relationship has been long-term and intimate. Or you can employ a swifter process, allowing severance of all debilitating connections in one fell swoop. The quickie version: scissor your fingers and snip, snip, snip, all around your aura wherever you feel a drain. Refreshing!

Sometimes this severance involves family. Because our parents comprise our first human nest-dwelling Domain Basin, we begin with maximum innocence and minimum savvy as to their influence upon us. Like a fish in water, a fetus in amniotic fluid starts out clueless that there could be options to the Mom/Dad Realm.

This next example is much more hopeful than the last in that it looks at a grown child becoming aware of, and growing past, the negative imprints his parents made upon him. Successfully cutting those cords, this offspring is free to reclaim enormous inflows of vibrant energy, now made available to shape partnership more in the image of his Divine Aumakua than his merely mortal Mom and Dad. He can claim the East-West latitude of his Soul Compass free of debilitating negativity from parental ghosts.

COVERT COMPETITION: *MOTHER*

This next film addresses what must be done when a dream of fulfilling partnership has been planted in a wedding basket woven by the parents instead of the true partner, who would instead ignite awareness of the Divine Marriage of Aumakua. Like the best of comedians, Albert Brooks is able to take a serious topic, Mother-Son travails, and resolve it with enough droll wit to make the psychotropic medicine go down deliciously. In terms of Initiatory passages, this one delivers even more than it promises.

PART V

CLASSIC INITIATION

"There was a ship — on a calm sea — itself becalmed. From the ship a long line descended down to an oyster shell on the bottom of the ocean: 'Waiting for the Pearl.' It was clear that the oyster was not yet ready to be opened — it was still in the process of forming. . . that pearl which in many cultures symbolizes the Self — the pearl of greatest price."
—Edith Sullwold, *The Ritual-Maker Within at Adolescence*

MENTORS FALSE AND TRUE

While there is a quietly impassioned movement afoot to re-invent coming-of-age rituals for non-tribal peoples, this vital restoration is still sparse and hasn't rippled out to the mass culture or the big screen. Even then, the worthy and doable cinematic challenge will be to keep the sacred elements *Sacred* while still conveying the transformative boon they afford youth seeking to blossom into adults.

You can look at many, many films as men-mentoring-boys sagas — whether in educational, corporate, military or even criminal settings — but these are too often a matter of homogenization, enforcing a common com-munitas at the expense of each youth's unique Destiny. Women mentoring girls onscreen is almost non-existent. You can only watch *The Miracle Worker* so many times, and that biography (of the young blind and deaf Helen Keller and teacher Annie Sullivan), unless viewed symbolically, is unique to its subject.

Indigenous cultures find at the basis of life the distinction between male and female powers, and the necessity for both. An Australian Aboriginal gesture, easy to adopt and most telling, is to indicate the number "2" by raising the index fingers of both hands, right and left, male and female. Amongst the New Zealand Maoris, there are the mingled waters of tapu (male) and noa (female) energies, without which harmony cannot be achieved. But the invading European missionaries had the audacity to bless the former and condemn the latter, as if a bird could fly on one wing. Modern Western men still secure most positions of authority and so often end up mentoring young women, an oddly suspect stance by many Indigenous standards.

Trouble occurs when a young woman comes up against a devouring Mentor who engages her not solely for her benefit, but largely for his sexual gratification, career advancement, and overall libidinous rejuvenation. Instead of being allowed to first cultivate their identities and only later approach intimate partnership with their Souls intact, young women find themselves pressured to barter away their intimate sexual gifts en route to self-possession, thus undermining both. On so many levels, blossoming women often feel helpless in the face of this kind of fraudulence, flattery, and manipulation.

It happens to young men too, who, via their pro-active yang enculturation, may have a better chance to resist or escape such exploitation. I'm forever grateful to one director, the camp John Waters, for bringing us the character *Pecker* (Edward Furlong). This teenaged Baltimore portrait photographer gains fame and fortune after being discovered by a New York City art dealer (Lili Taylor). When she decides it'd be a buzz for them to get it on, Pecker bobs and weaves, squirms and fidgets, and finally states flat out "You *shouldn't* have sex with people you're suppose to be helping."

Perfect. You *shouldn't* have sex with people you're suppose to be helping. Put that in Latin over the social room thresholds of every school, church, and place of employ. Tres succinct.

Pecker, however is the exception. So I have chosen for a "False Mentor" example male-female perversion of that purportedly helpful tutelage, and for a "True Mentor" example, positive male-male guidance. Because this is largely how it still stands today, not that the half of it should perjure: young women deserve better options in life than merely surviving damaging indoctrination.

PREEMPTIVE KING, REDUNDANT QUEENS: *GUINEVERE*

The Pacific Heights Sloane family is one of those schizoid clans whose glowingly prosperous exterior masks their dismal, emotionally-twisted hearts. This is sketched out swiftly in an opening scene charged with all the Archetypal energy weddings invoke. Younger daughter Harper (Sarah Polley) is commandeered by her irate Mother (Jean Smart) to go upstairs and break up the overlong "Greek Tragedy" of a farewell between the Bride and the Father reluctant to give her away. It is some measure of how "at sea" modern women are mythically that the Mother refers to this as "Oedipal crap," when the correct reference for Father-Daughter enmeshment is the "Electra Complex." Talk about tragedy.

The gangly, unpolished Harper is next in line in a family of attorneys to be heading off to Harvard Law School in the Fall, although she deeply resents her presumed place on the family production line. With the razor-sharp sonar of a predatory shark in bohemian clothing, wedding photographer Connie Fitzpatrick (Stephen Rea with an Irish-Afro) picks up on the girl's potential for rebellion and begins circling her seductively. Coming from a clan where the hottest vibe is between father and elder daughter, Harper is ripe for romance with a man decades her senior. In a twinkling, she's kissing off the big "H" and moving into Connie's book-lined studio-loft as his latest "Guinevere."

It's all promising and chaste at first, with the artist priming the protégé for more by comparing their relationship to that of seasoned photographer Alfred Stieglitz and the much younger painter, Georgia O'Keefe. He claims Harper's only condition for staying there is "to create something — photograph, paint, write, or dance" to which she demurs, "Oh, you're mistaking me for someone with potential." But he insists that he truly sees the swan within the awkward duckling. It's all seduction of course, focused on their potential sex life rather than her potential creativity, which gets pushed onto a back burner that never heats up.

HONEYMOON SOURS

When Mom catches onto Harper and Connie's living arrangement, she confronts the pair in a truly pointed manner rarely seen in film. Asking the protesting Connie what he has against women his own age, she herself supplies this theory in answer: "I know exactly what she has that I haven't got. *Awe.* I mean no real woman, no woman of experience would stand in front of you with awe in her eyes and say, 'Wow! Look at that bohemian wedding photographer with holes in his jeans. Gosh, isn't he *something?*'" After this disdainful slice and dice castration, she leans toward Harper's ear and hisses, "I know what you're doing and it makes me sick."

Such a sizzling confrontation certainly has its impact, but falls far, far short of true efficacy because Mom is *always* so bitchy, always *so* bitter over her husband's obsession with daughter #1, that she sees this second May-October pairing as that redux. When she haughtily insists that Connie refer to her as "Mrs. Sloane," it's pathetic to note how heavily she leans on wifely status, when she's the first to call out her marriage for the miserable sham it is.

Trouble really does set in, however, when "Guinevere" realizes that Connie is neither an august King nor a noble Knight, but something of an aging lecher who's "Lanced-a-lot" of nubile naifs before her. She's only the latest in a long line of loft-educated virgins, snared into what a graduate calls "The Cornelius Fitzpatrick School for Young Ladies." Billie (the ever sexy, and here something more, Gina Gershon) really provides the Initiatory guidance here, warning Harper of Connie's usual lines and ploys: sketching out his forthcoming curriculum of asking for a five-year commitment, and then lecturing her on being a ruling class enemy so she'll feel guilty enough to supply the rent money.

It's not that Harper doesn't gain much of wonderful value by moving beyond her family's WASPish orbit (evening meals dominated by legal tort discussions) into a far more vibrant realm of artists, writers, and musicians. But she only signed on for that life due to Connie's promise to teach her to become a creative player herself. The falsehood of this stance hits home when his sad combo of physical and economic decrepitude requires that they hock her camera before she's taken even a single photo.

FANTASY FAREWELL

One of the key elements of Initiation is closure, not just closure of a chapter in one's life, but closure of the suffering one underwent as an Initiate. This comes about most naturally in a larger solution of a tribal container that recognizes the former protégé's pain, hard work, and new identity. This is why I believe so many sad, genuinely anguished American victims seek out public television as a forum for their disclosure, in order to have the Domain Basin of celebrity, however tinny, brief, and impersonal, validate what they've gone through so they can move on.

Director Audrey Wells works this need for social containment and recognition into the final chapter of the plot, which takes place four years after Connie and Harper break up. His pending death from alcoholism prompts the latest naïve Guinevere to gather together as many of his past "pupils" as she can find, to provide help for herself and a send-off for Connie. We learn that some have moved on to success, with Harper now a photographer herself, complete with an agent and pending shows. It is here that Billie, a thriving painter, once again hints at Harper's next potential Initiatory step by mentioning that she can't cater to Connie because she has to get home to her partner.

So Harper is alone with Connie at the last, with the Mentor once again leaning heavily on the Protégé, asking that she guide his Atheist soul over the threshold to Death. And while this is hardly the rich matter of Aboriginal Women ritualizing a man's demise, it has some paltry echoes, which is all a po' uninitiated white girl can provide. She guides him along "the Connie Special," an imagined corridor with side chambers from which his past concubines bid him farewell. And, at the very end is found a comely, blonde 19-year-old, lifting his hocked camera to lovingly blind him with a flash of Eternal light.

Whether Heaven, Hell, or prolonged Purgatory awaits this poor benighted soul with too few diamonds as his legacy, we can only surmise. Harper moves on intact, little thanks to Connie's paltry excuse for Initiation.

HERITAGE RESTORED: *THUNDERHEART*

While there are many, many Man-Boy Mentor-Protégé tales that address the coming-of-age process in a more classic, teacher-student, age-appropriate manner, I've chosen Michael Apted's *Thunderheart* for one very important reason. It illustrates that, regardless of years lived or accomplishments gained, a beckoning to Initiation can, if needed, interrupt our conscious game plans at any point with urgent entreaty for deeper authenticity.

Creation never goes stagnant to rest at a pinnacle of apparent perfection, nor does it collapse into what for us seems a nadir point of despair. Creation goes on creating, with amazingly unpredictable generativity, allowing for phases of testing, triumph, celebration, decline, death, discovery, and rebirth into further Evolution. It will rock our boats, time and again, which is why Navigating skills such as forbearance (patience for life's cycles) are so important. And if there's a Spiritual guide on hand to give the turmoil meaning, we are blessed indeed.

Such is the case for *Thunderheart*'s sharp, young Raymond Levoi (part-Cherokee actor Val Kilmer) who had surmounted his troubled family background to become an FBI Agent smack in the urbane heart of the game, Washington, D.C. Trickster sounds the story's first note, with the Bureau having unearthed the very dimension of Ray's past he wishes kept hidden: that his heritage on his father's side includes Lakota Sioux blood. Worse yet, Ray is being assigned to investigate a murder in the Badlands of South Dakota precisely *because of* that heritage, and the word's been sent out in advance to the FBI (Full Blooded Indians) on the Rez.

The reluctant Ray's only allurement to the assignment is the opportunity to work with legendary veteran agent Frank "Cooch" Coutelle (Sam Shepard) in apprehending the crime's prime suspect, Jimmy Looks Twice (John Trudell; see *Trudell: Independent Lens*). Jimmy is a shrewd, slippery shape-shifting opponent who's proven too savvy to be nabbed. We don't know this initially, but he's also (with a heartfelt nod to real-life framed prisoner, Leonard Peltier) actually innocent.

TOTAL SOUL COMPASS

Perhaps due to its American Indian subject matter, *Thunderheart* sounds out all dimensions of the Soul Compass which, after all, was inspired by many a Medicine Wheel. It has the Trickster element in on-the-lam Jimmy, an *apparent* Mentor in the corrupt Cooch, a truer Eastern Ego ideal in Rez Sheriff Walter Crow Horse (Graham Greene), a Womb-Weaver in schoolteacher/activist Maggie Eagle Bear (Sheila Tousey), Nest-Dwellers in her students as well as Ray's flashbacks to his childhood, and a true Diamond-Cutting Elder in Medicine Man Grandpa Sam Reaches (Chief Ted Thin Elk).

While Ray is shaken from the get-go when Walter immediately sees through his ruse as an Indian Agent of any active heritage, it's Grandpa who really rattles him to his bones by Shamanically recalling Ray's anguished childhood, overshadowed by his father's alcoholism. Ray is also reminded of a past life of participating in the Ghost Dance leading up to the Wounded Knee Massacre of 1890. When Walter learns that this very White-identified Indian was at "the Knee," his envy is quite comically conveyed.

In fact it's the ongoing competition between these two, in matters professional and personal, that supplies *Thunderheart* its much-needed levity. When Walter outshines the urban agent in tracking finesse, Ray can only respond with a terse "Fuck you," to which Walter sassily retorts, "You'd love to." We get it. He would, not literally, but yeah, he'd "love to" get closer to Walter's Native wit, savvy, wisdom, everything Ray could have been but squelched. He'd *love* to.

HOMECOMING?

And he just might make it home, a Prodigal Son reminded of his Diamond-cutting potential. Grandpa's skillful mentoring is sometimes delivered pointedly and sometimes on the sly. He's not depicted in a ceremonial, awe-inspiring, sanctimonious manner, but as an impoverished old man who lives in a shack and enjoys watching *Mr. Magoo* on TV. And this makes the acuity of his visions all the more impactful, as he repeatedly slam-dunks Ray smack into the wounded core of his life, and lovingly contains him there to cook a truer identity: Initiation.

Coming from the materialistic sophistication of the modern nation's capital to the raw poverty of an older nation's spiritual center, Ray is stripped not only of his pretentious possessions — chic watch & sunglasses — but also of any willingness to help Cooch perpetuate a cover-up about what's really going on in these tense, violence-saturated Badlands of South Dakota.

By defying this false Mentor out of loyalty to a true Elder and to his deeper roots, Ray sets himself a conundrum. The story ends in suspension, with his heart drum-beating at the center of a literal cross-road (the Loa Legba's territory) facing his Destiny's most radical Soul Compass choice: *to be or not to be* authentic, and how best? All told, *Thunderheart* displays the vital, multi-leveled anguish of this modern, reluctant Initiate, lovingly tempered and beautifully rendered. Bravo!

PART VI

SHADOW-BOXING
& DANCING

....

"Coyote traps Badger in his own inflation, in order to get him out of the way so that Coyote may seduce his wife. But there is a spiritual dimension with which Coyote has not reckoned."

— Madhi, Foster & Little, *Betwixt & Between*

The Shadow is created by Light (approval) shining on one's chosen Persona (mask), casting repressed, conflicting characteristics into the dark. It's often generated when our surrounding Domain Basins compel us to repress dimensions of ourselves. Which is why the Shamanic voyage to the Underworld proves so compelling: there may be gold in them thar caverns, or at least some fertile shyte.

Here we shall look at two examples: one of dark, truncated projection by which Shadow integration is rejected, and one demonstrating warm, glowing acknowledgement of one's golden Shadow.

DARK TRICKSTERS:
THE LURE OF DANGEROUS ATTRACTORS

Le Mot *Unjuste: Capote*

Right up front we are given plenty of input as to the preferred self-image of author Truman Capote (Philip Seymour Hoffman) in this rendering of his life-chapter devoted to writing *In Cold Blood*. His personal virtue of jealous choice: honesty. So we know his fatal flaw, the Trickster tripping him up, will be any steadfast denial around *dishonesty*. The irony is his name: "Truman," True-man. But don't stop there: "Capote" means "cloak," a "long hooded cloak." So we have here a man whose truth is hidden. And that truth has to do with ambition, woundedness, and a bottomless hunger for recognition.

In the film's opening scene we see Capote chatting up a circle of high-society friends, complaining that author Jimmy (James) Baldwin is far too controversial in his writing while he, Truman, is merely *honest*. Both men are gay, only Baldwin is intense and Black, providing a convenient shadow to Capote's blond, fey self. And when his childhood friend, author Nelle Harper Lee (Catherine Keener), accompanies Truman to Kansas to investigate a gruesome murder, they have this exchange:

Nelle: This make you miss Alabama?
Truman: Not even a little bit.
Nelle: You lie.
Truman: I don't lie.

But he does, and oh how he does, in ways large and small but mostly around feigning compassion for others' woundedness in order to get at the juicy bits of the case. He's shrewd, he's foxy, evasive, inventive, manipulative, and every other winsome "cloak" of dishonesty one can don. He finds the perfect scapegoat in Perry Smith (Clifton Collins Jr.) to transport his darker elements onto the center stage of fame and fortune. Smith, along with an accomplice, attempted to rob an isolated Kansas farmhouse, and ended up shotgun-blasting all four of its innocent family members from here to eternity.

Like Truman, Perry can protest his innocence in the face of all evidence to the contrary.

At the time of the murders, Capote is already a social fixture in international celebrity circles. As he bounces back and forth between the high-life of the Big Apple, tony hotel suites, a villa in Spain, and visiting this inmate in a sere Midwestern penitentiary cell, it reminded me of these lines of Hermes, a mythic Trickster: "Better always to live in the company of other deathless ones — rich, glamorous, enjoying heaps of grain — than forever to sit by ourselves in a gloomy cavern."

No, that's Perry's job. Although by the time he gets done seducing the sensational details of the killings out of him, Capote's "deathless, glamorous" disposition has started the process of zombification.

SHADOW BROTHER/SHADOW KILLER

Nelle Harper Lee is not only Capote's life-long friend, she's also his conscience in a world of glitterati who apparently prefer witty back-stabbing and upscale indulgence to lives of moral rectitude. Another of their conversations, about Perry, is most telling:

Truman: He wants so badly to be taken seriously, to be held in some esteem.
Nelle: Do you?
Truman: Do I what?
Nelle: Do you hold him in esteem, Truman?
Truman (pause): Well, he's a gold-mine.

Well, buried under a shyte-pile, the dark side of the equation. Years later, Capote confesses to Nelle, "It's as if Perry and I grew up in the same house, and one day he stood up and went out the back door, and I went out the front." Shadows, one golden, one a lump of coal. Capote purports to want to restore Perry to the light of humanity, assuring him, "If I leave here without understanding you, the world will see you as a monster. Always. I don't want that."

Oh, but he does: *In Cold Blood*, after all, isn't a simpatico title. Truman thinks he can amp up his own *front door*, red carpet treatment by pandering to his trendy circle's elitist fears of the likes of Perry, even if it means pushing him out the prison's *back door* to the warehouse gallows. Capote out-cons the convict by playing on his most vulnerable note — a wretched childhood, saying they share a past of abandonment and grief. He even feeds Perry baby food to coax him out of a hunger strike — can't have him dying before full disclosure. At the same time he marinates his prey in faux pity, Capote distances himself more and more from his own early life suffering which fuels his current ambition.

Most notable is the world premiere of the movie based on Harper Lee's book, *To Kill a Mockingbird*. Capote drinks himself into a stupor of self-pity ("They're torturing me!") rather than celebrate this cinematic version of his childhood as Nelle's best friend, protected by decency personified, Atticus Finch, and fleeing the *innocent monster* that is Boo Radley.

By the time Truman is reduced to consuming a soppy mixture of baby food and whiskey, we know his efforts to quell his wretched inner child have become desperate. At the same time, his sham attempts to truly save Perry have grown tissue thin, with Capote revealed to be every bit the stone-hearted killer (albeit passive-aggressively) as he paints his duplicitous, wounded Shadow-catcher to be. Only Perry murdered four people for a measly forty dollars, while Capote's investment in these killers' deaths paid off much more handsomely with this runaway bestseller. *In Cold Blood* indeed.

A HOLY GARBAGE COLLECTOR

Naturally, Indigenous peoples arranged ways to deal with societal transgressions long before modern courts and jails, with exile being the most extreme consequence, not the first resort. There is a movement afoot today to bring back these methods, called Restorative Justice, which deal relationally with guilt, accountability, and atonement. And in Hawaii, the method of resolving family discord, *Ho'opono pono*, is being used to good effect in prisons.

Hawaiian Haleakala Hew Len PhD's tale is certainly worthy of cinematic record. Profiled in Thomas Freke's *Shamanic Wisdomkeepers*, he illustrates the Kahuna belief that we are "all in the same stew together." Ergo, if we consciously work on ourselves, we automatically effect the whole pearly net of interconnectedness. In relating this story, he very humbly refers to himself not as a Kahuna, but "a garbage collector":

"No one wanted the job I did with the criminally insane. They were averaging about one psychologist a month. But I got asked. We had about 25-30 people. Half of them would be in shackles at the ankles and the wrists because they were dangerous. They could either kick you or slam you. Everyone would walk with their back toward the wall so that they wouldn't get struck. They had no family visits. No one could leave the building.

"A year and a half later there was none of that. There were people going out on bus rides. Nobody in shackles. The level of medication dropped. What did I do? I worked on myself. I took 100% responsibility. It's an inside job. If you want to be successful, it's always an inside job. Work on yourself."

One method this wondrous Kahuna provides us to do such cleansing work is "The Indigo Bowl:"

"It is best performed twice a week before retiring at night. Imagine placing all of your problems — to do with yourself, your family, friends, ancestors, cars, pets, animate or inanimate things — into an indigo bowl which is suspended over the center of the crater of the Haleakala volcano in Hawaii. Allow whatever you have placed in the bowl to turn from indigo to icy blue, and finally to white. Then Divinity will finish the treatment and the situation will change."

Too bad Capote hadn't been initiated by the likes of this Shamanic healer. Then he too may have moved his considerable consciousness into the shared snarled and knotted *pilikia* (troubles) of Perry's Unihipili and lifted them both up to the miraculous Light of the Poʻe Aumakua (collective Higher Selves) for *kala* (cleansing) and renewal. And who knows? Maybe Capote's avid audience was tired of tinsel, and at a deeper level sought a more compassionate and deeply-engaged resolution to dealing with our criminal faction than condemning them to isolation and death.

The Aborigines say that the Big Dreams are hunting us, stalking one who is able to hear and give voice (Uhane) to Creation's much-needed stories. After being brave enough to come out of the closet in a conventional age, perhaps Capote was stalked by the Domain Basin of the Dreamtime to tell the deeper story of the incarcerated: that their captivity as scapegoats deprives us of understanding their motivations, and thus discovering means to transform the very society which may have contributed to their criminal excesses. But maybe, being sexually marginalized, Truman was eager to make another look worse than he (carry his Shadow). Or perhaps he was too spent by the risks he had already undertaken to go the distance here.

Sadly, by so strongly resisting his Shadow of vulnerability and dishonesty, he actually became it: deception led to destruction and increasing isolation: from Hermes' dens of the "rich and glamorous" to the "gloomy cavern." *In Cold Blood* was the last book Truman Capote finished, despite its enormous success, and he proceeded to drink himself to an early death at the age of 59. A sobering thought as to the consequences of repression and projection.

LIGHT TRICKSTERS: CLAIMING YOUR GOLD

The Queen & the Virgin: *I, the Worst of All*

Sometimes what we've repressed and disowned is not what we judge demonic but that which we revere as golden, qualities which actually would give us great joy if only we deemed ourselves worthy of cultivating them. In the case of Maria Bemberg's historical work *I, the Worst of All*, it is a particularly pitiless, patriarchal society which judges two exceptional women harshly for their golden aspirations. It is some measure of how little encouragement our psyches need to actually bloom that these two kept one another afloat for some measure of time, cultivating passions which the powers-that-be would prefer to condemn. Only the dual calamities of the Plague and the Inquisition could ultimately divide and depress their amazingly complementary Spirits.

It is 17th-century Mexico. When the new Viceroy (Hector Alterio) and his wife (Dominique Sanda) arrive from Europe, one of the first people they ardently wish to meet is Sister Juana Ines de la Cruz (Assumpta Serna), celebrated in Spain as the Tenth Muse. Juana has all the earmarks of an omni-genius, equally splendid as a playwright, poet, scholar, herbalist, astronomer, musician, and even accountant. While the two regents clearly delight in an in-convent staging of Sister Juana's latest witty and surprisingly ribald theatrical production, another audience member is decidedly *not* amused.

Rising to power at the same time as the new Viceroy is a new Arch-bishop (Lautaro Muruo), and in this instance, God's and Caesar's tracks are clearly parallel. While Sister Juana bathes in the temporal rulers' applause, praise and affection, this purported man of God denounces the nunnery as a bordello, and decides to work the back rooms. The current Abbess, who dotes on their beautiful, brilliant in-house artist, is coming to the end of her term. Knowing this full well, the Archbishop bribes two malleable sisters to manipulate the upcoming election, throwing it toward a stricter nun more aligned with his conservative mode. But he cautions that they must do so "with discretion. Secrecy is the source of the Church's ascendancy." Aha!

SOUL SISTERS

Vicerene Maria, bemoaning the lack of cultured women in the world, takes to visiting Juana as often as possible, and soon their bond deepens. Both were curious and solitary children for whom learning was an adventure. It is gradually revealed that Juana is equally enthralled with Indigenous as "Civilized" teachings, and has the largest library in the Americas, including dangerous books no one would dare read in Spain for fear of bringing down the wrath of the Inquisition. Her vocation, it seems, was not so much a call *towards* God as an *avoidance of* marriage and children, which would not have allowed her the solitude she needed for study and creativity.

Maria, on the other hand, clearly a polished denizen of the world, loves her wonderful husband dearly, and is pregnant. When talk turns to children, Juana delightedly indicates the treasures of her splendid study: "My telescope, my sundial, my obsidian mirror in which I see the past and glimpse the future, my automaton, my astrolabe, my lyre, my magnets, my quills, my writing... *my children!*"

While the differences are obvious, Maria's loving heart teases out the similarities: "You wear a veil, I wear a crown. You are locked up in the convent. Do you imagine I can escape the palace? You abide by the rule, and I by protocol. At 20 you entered the convent. At the same age I was married off. I wonder which of our worlds is the most stifling?"

To which Juana responds with the first of many poems composed for this true and beloved friend:

"There is no prison for the Soul,
Nor shackles for it to be hindered by,
The only bonds that restrain it
Are those the Soul itself creates."

THEIR GROUNDING: CULTIVATED, AND SUNDERED

The new, stringent Abbess fulfills the Archbishop's agenda, and soon is doing her best to rein Sister Juana in. It is here that Maria pulls rank, successfully, and Juana blossoms under the patronage and protection supplied by the Crown. A gathering of male scholars who come to meet with her regularly, and debate through the bars of the convent's visiting cell, worry about her intellectual exuberance. When she speaks of "an infinite longing for knowledge, a limitless daring!" one responds "And perhaps a certain attraction for the abyss?" Aha — the Void, here named as a threat she recognizes all too well, and from which she will not shrink: "Why not? Knowledge is always a transgression, all the more so for a woman."

Intellectual innovation is a golden ring a woman dare not grasp without dire consequences. It is the golden Shadow of the culturally-endorsed qualities of predictability and drab servitude, especially expected of a nun. Nonetheless this exceptional Sister is savvy enough to reserve her most feminist teachings for her young pupils' last day of school:

"I would like you to always remember that God did not give you perception and curiosity in vain, that none of that is the private hunting ground of men. Neither is the freedom to explore the secrets of the Universe a privilege of man alone."

Clearly the Virgin and the Queen have consolidated a loving exchange that emboldens and secures them both in larger Domains than either could have ventured alone. For Juana, love, eroticism, the body and worldly politics carry the Shadow of her religious, contemplative and celibate life. For Maria, corseted by state sanctions, Juana opens up the inner realms of spirit, intellectual daring, and creative beauty. Fluid loving potential dances through them both. Maria gifts Juana with a resplendent headdress of sacred Quetzal plumes, honoring the native Queen in *her*. And Juana gifts Maria with passionate poetry, carving out her inner, virginal Sovereignty.

When the Inquisition worms its venomous way across the sea, the Archbishop gets the upper hand and the Viceroy and his family are sent back to Spain. Severed from one another and otherwise anguished, each woman is tempted toward a vortex of sorrow. But we know that what could have proven treacherous for each is now sustained by uniquely Golden underpinnings.

The worldly Vicerene, upon the loss of her husband, has an inner virgin Queen to fall back upon, thanks to Juana. And Juana, deprived of her library and her scholarly artifacts, commanded to denounce even "her ideas," is reduced to scrubbing the floor during the Plague. But the Viceroy and Vicerene have seen to it that her collected volumes of poetry were published, so this Tenth Muse is preserved in the very world she renounced. Thanks to the golden penumbra of love between two Archetypal women.

Second Interlude
A LARGER OVERVIEW

There is this cave
In the air behind my body
That nobody is going to touch:
A cloister, a silence / closing around a blossom of fire.
When I stand upright in the wind
My bones turn to dark emeralds.

— James Wright, *"The Jewel"*

By the time we're contemplating Marriage, outer and/or inner, we are at the Heart of the Soul Compass, and crucial elements come into play. Do we have a *sense* of our ego self's connection to both our Nature Spirit and Divine Self? If not, we're still unripe for partnership, vulnerable for an unhealthy co-dependence. Can we dance with the Trickster into ongoing integration of our Shadow that is neither too much nor too sparse? If not, we may engage in an idealized partnership unaware of the dark side of Love's Shadow until it becomes unconquerably destructive. Are we struggling through some swampy morass of past conditioning, or flying into a fantasized future?

The Heart of the Compass is the place of Sovereignty, and once we claim this, we live from it, with the energies of the four Cardinal Points flowing toward us as needed, seeking harmony: all cylinders firing more skillfully. We should be at a stage of development where we've begun to cleanse and reformulate lower Domain Basins to heal any Nest-dwelling wounds and provide nurturance for others "unto seven generations," as the Native American Indians say. And we should have begun to sense our mortality, a sure nudge toward personal fulfillment, which makes the enduring skills of Eldership more desirable.

We are not living in a vacuum when Love beckons us, we are weaving and navigating various nesting, quasi-permeable Domain Basins. I take this Interlude to interrupt a sense of mere ongoing progression, which can prove too shallow. I want time-out to ask where potential East-West mates (inner or outer) stand in relation to their South-North axis. Do they comprehend the blessings and the wounds of each other's Childhood? Are their Destinies, their aspirations, compatible? Are they willing to cultivate one another's sense of Sovereignty?

Our Unihipili, the Nature spirit who "never sleeps," is engaged in sustaining our physical and emotional life. The Uhane is occasionally flooded by emotion from below, but is largely logical and more objective. Being receptive to the Aumakua's Divine wedding of yin and yang (for which our earthly marriages are both preparation and echo) provides inspiration to create a new future.

Let's take it straight up, documentary-style, going backwards, and forward on the time-line of life. One biographical film will restore us to our Cosmic Ancestry which sustains us, followed by a feature which engagingly teaches how ancient wisdom and modern science are finally making thrilling bedfellows after too-long an estrangement. And then we'll see highlights from a documentary on a number of visionaries determined to create a better future, one passionate dream at a time.

At this marrying point of the Soul Compass we need to Womb-Weave enough of a nurturing Domain Basin to allow our Navigator the adventure and largesse to fulfill unique dreams. Let Thomas Berry remind you of your deep past, and TED (Technology Entertainment Design) invite you to expand the envelope of imagination for your most exhilarating future. *Mindwalk* between these extremes, allowing them to funnel a bracing (but manageable) gale, freshening your Soul Compass' parameters.

RECLAIMING CREATION: *THOMAS BERRY, THE GREAT STORY*

Father Thomas Berry may be formally known as an Historian, Ecologist and Theologian, but to those of us fortunate enough to have studied with him, he is known fondly as a "Geologian." His strongest teaching here is that the Universe is an ongoing story, the Great Story, and we humans are "stark, raving mad" to have lost our place in it. Because we have an I-It vs. an I-Thou relationship with our Planet, we are in the process of destroying no less than the last *65 million years of life development*. Take a moment, or better yet, 65, to let that begin to sink in. (And some thought we'd only the melting polar ice caps to worry about).

This truly wise Elder also has a broad and deep comprehension of world cultures, and notes that most peoples have their values rooted in some kind of Cosmology. This informs them how things came to be from the Origin, where humans fit in, and how best to proceed. He is most passionate about our need to be restored to a sense of the sacred in Creation, of which it cannot be apart, restored to a sense of reverence, a Cosmic liturgy of the seasons and the larger heavenly cycles. Nature as Sacred and Revelatory, certainly not mechanistic. And we humans as no less than the self-reflective capacity of it all.

Born in 1914 in North Carolina, Thomas Berry oriented himself early on toward the wilderness and away from commercial enterprise. Like Sister Juana of 17th-century Mexico, he understood his nature well enough to know that he needed time to study and reflect, time which he determined could best be found either in jail or the monastery. Studies in History, Paleontology, and World Religions gave him broad contexts from which to view life, as well as appreciation for the development of consciousness in all species.

OUR TASK AT HAND

Berry sounds a key element of Initiation when he notes that each period of History has a great work to be identified and accomplished. And the nobility of the people of each epoch has everything to do with their discernment of, and fidelity to, that work. He names our current task as that of stopping Ecological devastation and bringing about renewal. He also resonates with the Huna template when he notes that our big problem is exploitation of the non-human as inferior, when *everything* was created to manifest a face of the Divine.

This devastation of the environment continues because everything in America has become subservient to what Berry calls the financial, industrial, commercial Corporate Regime. He cautions that we must be cognizant of exactly which World Order, destructive or sustainable, we're contributing to. And claims that chemical pollution of waterways, extinction of species, and disappearance of the mysterious view of the night sky due to "light pollution," constitute a lamentable "soul loss."

We need to return to Nature, the wild, to remember where the real powers dwell, psychic and physical, cosmic and foreboding: "Put somebody in the wild, they become reverent real quick." And because we are profoundly grounded in and comprised of the world's elements, any destruction of them will be wrenching: "The deepest tragedy of losing the splendor of the outer world is that we will always have an inner demand for it. We are genetically encoded to live in a world of immense beauty."

Berry plaintively shares that he "thinks constantly of the children," not just human, but plant and animal: "It takes a Universe to fulfill a child." To prove that necessity he points out that no matter where you find yourself in the Cosmic story, the Universe is expanding, receding away from you. And if you run the camera backward it will scroll back to the originating point of the Universe, "and that will be you." What a blessing of an Elder we have in him!

LOCATION, LOCATION, LOCATION: *MINDWALK*

The underlying holographic *inter-connectedness* of Creation is the keynote of *Mindwalk*. It manages to make most engaging a Manifesto of modern physics, no less, by situating it in a conversation between a politician (Sam Waterstone), a physicist (Liv Ullman), and a poet (John Heard) while they stroll around the majestic, Medieval, monastic environs of Mont Saint Michel.

Directed by Bernt Amadeus Capra, *Mindwalk* was co-written by his brother, theoretical physicist Fritjof Capra (*The Tao of Physics*) based on his book, *The Turning Point*. We can see that the artistic brother is enacted by the poet Tom and the scientist by Sonia, thus leaving the politician, Jack, out of this creative familial loop. But, as the Devil's Advocate, he speaks for those people unaware of these subtle scientific perceptions. Altogether these three characters supply a prismatic reinforcement of a paradigm both new and timeless, showing how it's been illustrated by the teachings of many, from Shiva to Blake to Nostradamus to Jefferson to Neruda.

Of course enemies always spring up to oppose free thinking, but often the biggest enemy is mental lethargy, in this case regarding mechanistic vs. holistic perspectives of the world. And it is here that *Mindwalk* succeeds most effectively on a subliminal level, due to its locale. Both the scientist and the poet are disenchanted former Americans who have chosen *flight* to France over Jack's willingness to *fight* things out right in the belly of the beast, the political/lobbyist arena. The tidal mists, parapets, terraces, graveyard, charnel house and all-around Medieval structure of this gorgeous, cathedral-dominated, rocky islet set it solidly in another era. And the discussion invites us into a cutting-edge awareness of spiritual/scientific truth, the Laws of the Cosmos. Indigenous Domain.

IN~"SPIRED" DEBATE

As these three thoughtful companions walk through a chamber containing the inner workings of a huge clock, discourse turns to the dated teachings of Rene Descartes and Isaac Newton. Amidst the pendulums, wheels and pulleys of the 17th century, they contrast today's quartz crystals, quantum physics and microchips. Sonia, with her creamy Norwegian accent, is impassioned about our need to rectify centuries of patriarchal damage via much more female/relational Systems Theory thinking. This endorses preventative medicine and sustainable ecology and economics, as well as the American Indians' resolve to measure a tribal (now global) decision in terms of its value "unto seven generations."

The politician, used to courteous debate, doesn't hold back in questioning and challenging the scientist. But she manages to convince him that, as Huna teaching has long purported, we are inescapably alive only due to a web of relations. We are energetically disposed not toward being "finite things," but toward an ongoing exchange of photons and electrons, toward *probabilities* of interconnectedness. This sustains everything from the dance of sub-atomic particles to the Music of the Spheres.

By the time poet, politician, and physicist stroll the evening shore, the highest tide of the year is about to roll in. It is apt that they have a view of Mont Saint Michel's handsome spire as Sonia teaches that life forms are "self-organizing, self-maintaining, self-renewing, and self-*transcending*." Thus while we may be *dependent* upon our environment's immediate Domain Basins, we are not *determined* by them. The basis of evolution is not adaptation, but creativity, surpassing that which is already manifest.

At the end of the day, not even a proton is what it was at the outset.

This tidal, peripatetic stroll made me think of a writing by Galileo, *Dialogues on the Ebb and Flow of the Sea*, a title which the Inquisition wouldn't allow. So his *Dialogues on World Systems* debated Ptolemaic vs. Copernican thought: is the Earth the center of the Universe or does the Earth orbit the Sun? The answer is evident today. And by the end of *Mindwalk*, the truth, poetry and political application of Systems Theory thinking makes anything else seem as archaic as this Medieval isle, with none of its timeless beauty.

GOOD LIVELIHOOD: *THE FUTURE WE WILL CREATE*

And what kind of blessing do you hope to convey? We don't need to scrap every element of the Industrial Age to contribute to global harmony. Wonderful films like *The Next Industrial Revolution* show that manufacturing can leave a soft footprint on the Earth, or even a healing one. *Go Further* iterates everyday dietary choices to benefit self, Earth, and animals. And 2007's *The Future We Will Create* shares highlights from one of the electrifying annual TED (Technology Entertainment Design) conferences in Monterey, California, where a thousand visionaries connect with one another to cast sparks far and wide.

Al Gore is in attendance at this one, successfully cruisin' and smoozin' for his anti-global warming campaign. And while it's a TED instruction that nobody discuss politics, it does slip out, as in this exchange between Gore and motivational coach Tony Robbins. Robbins asks the audience what people usually say was *lacking* whenever they fail to reach an important goal. While most shout out the usual: they didn't have *time*, they didn't have *money*, or technology, or contacts, Gore called out "the Supreme Court!" to riotous response. This doesn't stop Robbins from making his point: that such *resources* are never the defining factor, it's *resourcefulness* that makes or breaks the game, including emotional motivation, which he notes that Gore certainly has in spades of late.

Everyone attending TED did, including MIT Professor Amy Smith who, on a rostrum of presenters with high-tech, state-of-the-art inventions, passed around a handful of modest corncobs burnt down to charcoal. These will provide Haitians and others safe cooking fuel and good income as well as halt the horrendous depletion of forests: recently 30 million trees per year. But mainly such natural briquettes will help eliminate the number one worldwide cause of death for children five and under: respiratory failure due to inhalation of wood-burning, indoor, cooking smoke.

AWARDS AND WISHES

The majority in attendance at TED are white and male, indicating cultural imbalances which must be brought into harmony. It's understood that our Aumakua are flooding into play whenever we receive creative impulses, impulses toward creating a better future. We're all composed to activate this dimension of Deep Self, and Goddess knows women's dreams and those of Indigenous peoples of both genders, could provide inestimable value to the world. The majority of "TEDsters" are also wealthy, with that last characteristic coming in most handy when three annual awards are passed out, and each winner allowed to voice a wish which the TEDsters will then strive to fulfill. Wouldn't you love an auditorium full of gazillionaires backing your dream? Pretty thrilling!

Filmmakers among you will be glad to note that one of the winners was documentarian Jehane Noujaim, whose wish is "to bring the globe together for one day a year through the power of film." Her project, Pangea, asks people from around the world to create and submit "short powerful films that deal with universal themes such as food, home, water, laughter, sorrow, hope, landscape, despair and joy." TEDsters came forth with offers of advice, website creation (*www.pangeaday.org*) , monetary donations, as well as advertising and marketing support.

If Bono's success in getting his wish granted the year before is any indication of the TED's efficacy, Jehane Noujaim is well on her way. Bono wished for a social movement of one million American activists supporting his causes in Africa. ONE.org was created along with funding, marketing, and media access allowing fans to sign on at U2 concerts. This has doubled the outcome he'd desired, to *two* million.

One of the more indelible segments of *The Future We Will Create* is a nocturnal drum-fest on the beach of Monterey, where Physicists and Nobel Laureates let down their hair and boogie. A drum-beat (rather than a shot) heard 'round the world is something to laud and cherish indeed. To all TEDsters worldwide, Bravo! Only please, can't you begin to honour the feminine by getting together monthly? Besides, we need all the vision we can drum up to bring this End Culture to a Rebirth!

PART VII

INNER & OUTER WEDDING

"The Tanka people of South China have a range of ghosts (including) Young Ghosts, who die before coming of age. Even though they have died, when they do reach the age of adulthood, their parents perform a marriage ceremony for these young ghosts."

— Sukie Miller, PhD, *After Death*

HUMAN SPOUSES, SPIRIT SPOUSES

From a Shamanic perspective, human spouses are not just two people traversing Middle World, but are human/divine/natural beings, multi-dimensional combinations of frequencies lower, middle and upper, past, present and future. It's such an immeasurable stroke of genius that Hawaiians have us evolving toward a sacred marriage, represented by Aumakua, as that goal gives the thrust toward harmonizing our marriages a boost. It also encourages our inner evolution toward being "the perfect Soul," a wedding of our unique yin and yang proclivities.

Imagine wedding vows that pledge going the distance together in all directions: "for better or for worse, richer or poorer, upbringing and dreams, home and society, Ancestry and Loa, Unihipili and Aumakua." In Dagara African tradition, a naming stone is selected by the Soul in utero. At the time of marriage it is immersed in a water-filled container and joined on an altar along with the spouse's stone. After Death, these become the partner's headstones at their gravesite. They're planning to be in it for the long run. As is the betrothed Southwestern Native American Indian who descends into a kiva to weave a garment that will be used as the naming cloth of his newborns, as well as his spouse's shroud.

Since Indigenous marriages are believed to be formed by Spirit, all that occurs within a marriage should first be perceived from a Spiritual perspective. Even the troubles. If you can hold to the concept that your marriage is comprised of a mutually-rewarding vibrational affinity, then discord means this patterning is out of harmony and needs restoration. If you hold that a marriage is best between two partners each fulfilling their Destiny, then partnership is enhanced when each spouse is deeply invested in seeing that endeavor achieved by both.

One of the key Hawaiian instructions is how to stay upright in your canoe as you navigate through life. Upon wedding, there are now *two* in a canoe, learning all the requisite sensibilities to dip and row harmoniously in a mutually-rewarding direction. You probably *know* how tricky that can be!

In most Indigenous cultures, marriage is hardly a personal matter between two people. Rather it is an opportunity for all in ceremonial attendance to renew their vows, as well as pledge to help the fledgling couple when the going gets rough. It is also a blending of Ancestral clans into a new, dynamic configuration. I once met a sculptress from the Wampanoag Nation of Cape Cod who explained that as her Father's clan was known for its wealth of historical knowledge and her Mother's for its psychic powers, so she and her siblings were entrusted to combine these talents to "see" into their next historical era.

In Africa too, the individual's commitment of alignment to their Grand Tete or Higher Self expands via marriage to commitment to a Shared Spirit singular to partnership's potential. Thus Indigenous wedding vows have everything to do with claiming a new foundation from which to comprehend and/or heal your past as you pledge devotion to your future Destiny. If we don't take such vows, our bonds can shred in any number of directions, as we'll see in this upcoming South African drama. Here a couple with a comfortable past lacked a compatible Destiny, and so could not go the distance into the future together.

IMPENDING SACRIFICE: *A DRY WHITE SEASON*

A Dry White Season is a wonderfully-wrought adaptation of Andre Brink's novel directed by the Martinique-born, Paris-educated, Black and female Euzhan Palcy. One of its most deft strokes is depicting the central White character, Ben du Toit (Donald Sutherland) as a prep school history school-master. That alone says all that need be said about his upper-middle-class orientation: elitist, insular, and oriented toward those former times which created Apartheid — allowing a small minority of Whites to brutally rule a vast majority of Blacks. Even the name Ben ("been") subliminally consolidates a sense of the past.

There's irony in the casting of this teacher's racist wife, since superb "British" actress Janet Suzman is really South African born, as well as niece to an aunt who was a liberal politician there. Another satisfying note: it so often seems that films about Native people have to focus on White stars to obtain production funding, *but* if you really tune in you'll discern that this one gives the most enduring, Diamond-Cutting nod to Stanley (Zakes Modae), a cab-driver/activist from SOWETO. He's the liaison between worlds and the originating catalyst for change, as indicated by the gorgeous *black and blue* butterfly painted on the hood of his *white* cab. Telling. And he's the one who finally takes out the worst villain of the tale. Also telling, as that is a coup traditionally reserved for the Hero.

THE GARDENER'S SON

There is much to laud about this production, not least of which being that it lured Marlon Brando out of a decade of retirement to indelibly play an obese, grumbling, sardonic, progressive barrister. Again we note the dif-ference between amoral, arbitrary White laws and Nature-based Native Law: whenever this solicitor wins a case, the State just changes the laws surrounding the issue to deem his victory flaccid.

But I'm focusing here on Ben's relationship to his feminine, relational Soul and how its expansion shatters the familial Domain Basin. At the outset, this schoolteacher is depicted as a contented family man, with wife, daughter, son, grandson, and extended relatives gathering at his attractive estate. The missus, as noted, is thoroughly biased toward her "own people" and contemptuous toward the Blacks. The daughter too, with her white-blonde hair and icily chiseled, delicate features, thinks everything should be hunky-dory now that the servants are sequestered away onto reservations, such as SOWETO (SOuth WEst TOwnship), even if those deplorably impoverished locales aren't even noted on official maps.

The du Toit family's delusional satisfaction gets spun tipsily off center the day Ben's Black gardener Gordon (Winston Ntshona) comes looking for legal help after his innocent young son Jonathan (Bekhithemga Mpofu) has been caned by officials for protesting his inferior education. Ben demurs, saying there's nothing to be done to help. And, after all, the lad must have done *something* to provoke the punishment. Things escalate atrociously when Jonathan is arrested during another, grander-scaled SOWETO uprising, interrogated, tortured, *killed*, and buried at an undisclosed location. Again Ben protests he cannot help, so the destitute Gordon tries taking matters into his own hands, only to meet the same fate of incarceration, interrogation, torture and death.

"KAFFIR LOVER"

When the official cover-up preposterously claims the clearly bludgeoned and burned Gordon to have been a suicide, this finally stirs Ben into sticking his neck out for the bereaved mother and widow, Emily (Thoko Ntshingo) by hiring Atty McKensie (Brando). At the same time this Historian is risking his bourgeois well-being by publicly supporting a very different sort of woman than his wife, he meets Melanie (Susan Sarandon), a liberal reporter. These two females, each in their own way, ravage and reconstitute Ben's *anima* — his inner feminine capacity for compassion and relationship.

Emily opens up the feeling realm via the Blacks' suffering, shredding a pathway to the benighted regions of Ben's heretofore naïve heart. Her personal daring invites him to *make history* rather than merely help *preserve* an entitled chapter for the Whites. Melanie is shown to be the brilliant offspring of an equally savvy professor and pianist, so her Spirit offers a contrast to Ben's narrow-minded, double-crossing informant of a daughter. This progressive reporter travels to Zambia to get evidence that

Gordon and son were indeed killed. (The journey is telling in that the north is thought to be the direction the African feminine Spirit fled or formerly dwelt, e.g. the 10th-century BCE Queen of Sheba).

While Ben du Toit is increasingly expanded internally, he is outwardly isolated from White colleagues, friends and family, destined for a courageous and sacrificial role which only his young son admires. Ultimately doomed in the temporal realm and blessed in the Eternal, he is led there by iconoclastic women of daring and great contrast to those from his once-complacent world.

SPIRIT SPOUSES

There is another dimension to relationship often found in Indigenous cultures, which is that of Spirit Spouses. This is sometimes a matter of genuine psychic encounter, with visitations from a spectre interrupting the more mundane weave of one's life. In Voudon, such a phantom partner may be so jealous of its married human mate's attention that it demands a separate sleeping area be made for them alone. In other instances its essence can be contained in beautiful statuary or a powerful mask kept in a private, darkened chamber. Some African traditions simply assume that each one of us married a Spirit Spouse before human birth, who now lovingly watches over and gifts us with blessings.

You can imagine this in the case of Ben du Toit in *A Dry White Season*: had he not met Emily and Melanie, his dreams may well have been illumined by shattering insights from the deep Cosmos, a Spirit Spouse reminding him of his intended Destiny.

So, such heavenly Mates can range from indicators of the most scintil-latingly profound, visionary communications with the Universe, to idealized reminders of the beauty, grace, generosity, and virility of the opposite sex. Such is our need for Archetypal reminders of all that male and female energies comprise, that entire cultural institutions have sprung up to satiate it, from vestal virgins to temple prostitutes, warriors to priests. The trick is how to tap into this realm without allowing your humanity to be subsumed by it.

MORE & LESS THAN HUMAN: *MEMOIRS OF A GEISHA*

There is sooo much to be found here about this "business" of a Geisha-in-training and full flower that is alluring: the commitment to a disciplined art, the intimacy found in a mentor-protégé bond, a heritage of dress, ornamentation, dance, astrology, calligraphy, music, and all-around exquisite elegance. But it's also freighted with much that is repellent: forced servitude due to rank poverty, cruel competition between women, idealization equaling dehumanization, and the need for the Geisha to marginalize the true passions of her heart. Bottom line: study Hula instead.

It's easy to get intoxicated by the lush rendering of this tale, but again, always keep your antennae attuned to whose human voice prevails and whose is stilled. If one is not allowed their Human Spirit, they are either reduced to their Nature Spirit or elevated to their Divine. A Geisha's humanity dissolves into both extremes, resulting in a woman who is such a physical work of art as to appear other-worldly. Even the voice-over at the beginning of this tale is an apology for speaking: "A story like mine should never be told. For my world is as forbidden as it is fragile. Without its Mysteries, it cannot survive."

The problem is, these are not true Mysteries, for if they were, they wouldn't be fragile; they could be tapped into via prayer and petition, for true power. What we have instead with these Geisha are women voiding themselves out to create space onto which any man can project his fantasies.

"EYES THE COLOUR OF RAIN"

This is the story of young Chiyo (Suzuka Ohgo) who was brought from a seaside fishing village and sold into servitude at a Geisha house when her mother was dying. But that same mother left Chiyo with the blessing of understanding her true nature: "like water, which can carve its way even through stone, and when trapped can make a new path." Trapped by poverty and falling in love after a brief encounter with The Chairman (Ken Watanabe), this mere girl determines that becoming a Geisha is her ticket to fame, fortune, and fulfillment of romantic desire.

She should have been paying more attention. Her first instruction at the Geisha house was, "You must not speak; I will answer for you." When a worker dares entertain a man she desires, she is rebuked by the equivalent of a Madam, "You are never to see him again! What do you think — a Geisha is free to love? Never!"

Apprenticed to the elegant and kindly Mameha (Michelle Yeoh), Chiyo's original maternal blessing is reinforced by this Mentor's recognition of her true Nature: "I see water in you. Water is powerful: it can wash away earth, put out fire and even destroy iron. You have not yet drawn on these strengths, have you?" But Chiyo's training only brings her tantalizingly close to The Chairman, even while she is instructed to focus on another man as potential patron.

INITIATION INTO A PRACTICED EXTINCTION

At the completion of her training, Chiyo casts off her childhood identity and becomes Sayuri (Ziya Zhang). But all her resplendent skills and public acclaim cannot grant her one wish: "I want a life that is mine!" To this heart-felt exclamation she is told, "We do not become Geisha to pursue our own Destinies. We become Geisha because we have no choice." Truly a death in life, an exquisite Zombification.

And that's the rub. Even when Sayuri wins the long-desired patronage of The Chairman, she has already eradicated so much of her will as to have become a beautiful spectre and nothing more: "It is not for a Geisha to want. It is not for a Geisha to feel. Geisha is artist of the floating world. The rest is secret, the rest is shadow." And that shadow bleeds into the Void not for revivification, but in order to allow men their idealized projections of the feminine. "To a man Geisha can only be half a wife. We are the wives of Nightfall."

Tragic. More tragic still that this is said with such resignation rather than an upwelling of grief and outrage which is the right of any obliterated Soul.

DOWN TO ZERO: *BLISS*

Joy is felt when the human and Spirit partners unite. One way that modern, non-Indigenous folk can cultivate the spiritual dimensions of sexual reciprocity *with our human mates* is via another source of cultural enrichment, Tantric Sex, as endorsed in *Bliss*. There are also rare elements here of an Elder initiating youth into the mysteries of Love. But like any cultural pump that hasn't been primed forever, this story has spurts and dry patches as well as flow. Still, while explicitly "romantic" movies usually bounce from the too-safe pre-fab to the tastelessly pornographic, we've got to be grateful that director Lance Young (!?) strove here to unite our three Soul selves: the physical, human and higher Spirit elements of marriage.

Joseph (Craig Sheffer) is en route to his wedding when he confesses to his best man that he's concerned for his fiancée's emotional well-being. Giving a litany of her neurotic behaviors, he builds to a dark crescendo of "She's always locking the bathroom door, and gets suicidal from time to time," concluding with fervor, "God, I love her!" Clearly this guy has issues too. Soon this couple are in marriage counseling, where Joseph learns for the first time that Maria (Sheryl Lee) has been faking her orgasms. He's crushed.

To make matters worse, this newly-wounded newlywed works on a construction site across from an apartment building where sex therapist Baltazar Vincenza (Terence Stamp) meets with a steady flow of clearly satisfied clientele. And one day he sees Maria walking up those very steps! With the aid of a telescope, Joseph decides the man is sadistic and abusive and confronts him on the matter. The Doctor explains that he's merely playing it as it lays, that Maria has to act out certain fantasies so they'll lose their grip on her: "When she stops asking for abuse, her need for it will be gone."

CHANGING OF THE GUARD

There's a reason it was often Indigenous *women* who initiated tribal youth of *both* sexes into love-making. And as many would find a male Sex Therapist with a large female client base somewhat suspect, if not downright unseemly, *Bliss* does its best to make Baltazar as refined as possible. His apartment is elegantly appointed with an Old World charm, he dresses with Zen-like impeccability, tinkers ably with his antique auto, and in his spare time plays violin in a Symphony Orchestra. Of course. It gets to be too much, and you wish he'd just once allow himself a satisfied chuckle, if not a lascivious wink, given his vocation. At any rate, the most intimate physical exchange we see between him and Maria is a chaste waltz. Whew!

Joseph wants to come to Balthazar, to learn "all he knows," so that he can become the source of his wife's healing. And he'll do so only under the condition that Balthazar terminates therapy with Maria. And so a dance of insight, transference and counter-transference begins, with Joseph discovering his own depressed inner feminine isn't far different from Maria. And Baltazar realizing that he, like Joseph, works hard to help women while getting too little personal satisfaction in return. Everybody's evolving.

There is some echo of Huna wisdom here when the Doctor notes "the mind cannot change the mind, that real change is not a mental process": the Uhane must impress the Unihipili in order to make contact with the Aumakua. And so he gives Joseph a series of homework assignments which largely involve genital abstinence but emotional contact with Maria, and daily masturbatory play with himself. Tentative at first, Joseph finally has a break-through, resulting in one of *Bliss'* funnier scenes: his strutting down the street announcing to perfect strangers, "I love myself. I love myself three times a day!"

Loving Maria is another matter altogether, with this film preferring perfectly lit and choreographed love scenes to psychological reality. It glosses over the long-term hard work involved with anyone suffering from her diagnosis: Borderline Personality Disorder (BPD), brought on by her father's early sexual abuse.

BPD means there's no Uhane (ego) yet hatched to deal with the Unihipili (id) and Aumakua (super-consciousness). Certainly the plot moves too swiftly in growing Maria from girlish petulance to womanly regard. But it does make appealing the opportunity that Tantric love offers: an ecstasy that can heal from the Heavenly heights right down to the Unconscious sub-stratas. Scintillating unity of all three dimensions: *Bliss* indeed.

ADULTERY AS LIMINAL BATH VS. LIMINOID RIPTIDE

Many Indigenous traditions allow for multiple spouses, while at the same time noting that the Spiritual bond is so intimate that adultery can prove deadly. Once aka-cords are connected and fleshed out, a couple is never truly separate, which is why some partners bemoan that they can't "get away with" anything. Neither can they undergo great joy or trauma, even at a distance, without their spouse being aware of it.

Modern Western culture, on the other hand, has a distressingly high divorce rate, many of them occurring in what therapists rate as "low-conflict" marriages. This is what comes of not first sounding out potential mates Spiritually, probably due to the culture's puritanical split between Spirit and Sex, a schism Indigenous peoples rarely suffer.

Also, if we don't make peace with our upbringing and resolve parental complexes, you can see how we might "marry" into more of the same (*Mother*), or with someone who only *appears* to promise compensation for the damage and deprivation of our early years (*Sylvia*). And if we don't make the discernment of our life's purpose a priority, how can we know if our Destiny is compatible with our partner's?

This is not to say that any one chosen partner can perfectly fill out the true contours of a man's Soul, or echo the unique light of a woman's Spirit. That would be boring. But if we begin telling Deep Cinema stories which show that enduring partnership is about conjoined Destinies rather than mere glamour and lust, we'll be getting culture back on the right track. In Indigenous worlds, even lust can be a ticket to potential Spirit, but it's up to you to discern where that ticket might actually take you before jumping on board. If the attraction is scintillating on the surface, but the deeper Souls are incompatible, trouble sooner or later ensues.

Sometimes the marriage is bankrupt and the 'adulterous' option "just the ticket" to provide the requisite re-orientation.

SEXUAL HEALING: *THE SISTERS*

Inspired by a classic, Anton Checkov's *Three Sisters*, this story is both updated and moved from rural Russia to urban America. What would have served for acceptable social constraints in Checkov's day and age are here served up as repression. On the far end of the emotional spectrum, there's blisteringly expressed neurosis. Such mind-blowing extremes demonstrate the wisdom of the Hawaiian teaching: "Don't repress your anger, or express your anger, confess your anger." Dialogue that would have served for witty banter on stage initially sounds a tad arch and literary here. But this is actually something to be thankful for in this *Dumb and Dumber* epoch.

You know these siblings are weighted down with early conditioning by their surname alone: Prior. The eldest's career path followed their late Father's footsteps into Academia, and the family does its socializing in a hallowed faculty lounge which includes a formal portrait of this *paterfamilias*. One sister is a closet lesbian, another a closet addict. And in the middle is the only married kin, who keeps none of her fevered discontent about that bond closeted in the least. It is her circumstances I shall address.

Marcia (Maria Bello), "the beautiful sister," could be Maria from *Bliss*, only with greater sophistication and a more acerbic tongue. Whenever we hear a woman relentlessly using her tongue in a sword-like manner to fend off or destroy relationships rather than cultivate them, she is usually doing so in a desperately male-identified way, as a last resort. ("Life in the Word, Death in the Word.") Such is the case here, and the cause is revealed. When Mrs. Prior died during Marcia's adolescence, this daughter became the substitute wife in every sense of the word: as Southern hostess, protectress of her younger sister, and her father's bed partner.

She finds the whole lamentable chapter "unsavory" now, but it was worse than that. Marcia's lack of boundaries catapulted her into an affair with her college Psych Professor (who *really* should have known better) whom she later married: "Rue the day."

THE PAST RENEWED

On the occasion of the youngest Prior sister's 22nd birthday, family and colleagues have festooned the college faculty lounge with festive decorations, only to be surprised by a visitor: Vincent (Tony Goldwyn), in town on business, had been Dr. Prior's teaching assistant in the past, and had also idealized this family. Miserably married now, with daughters of his own,

Vincent is about to learn from "the beautiful sister" how illusory his earlier impressions had been. He is also immediately drawn to her romantically.

Vincent's candor about his desire is frightening for Marcia, who'd rather publicly degrade her opportunistic husband than cheat on him. Her scathing verbal *orientation* is thus revealed as more of a *fixation*. This under-nourished daughter is stalled in the oral stage because she is both hungry and dares not move on to the anal phase (elimination) for fear of punishment. Also for her, the intimate genital phase is fraught with violation.

Due to incestuous abuse, Marcia is using her starchy spouse as a substitute punching bag, not a true partner, even as he's using her as a trophy wife. Vincent is both familiar enough (father's former teaching assistant) and different enough (emotionally wounded) from the main men in Marcia's life to provide her healing. Yes, he's a bit of a Daddy substitute, but one who loves his own daughters absolutely and honorably. His honesty actually exceeds Marcia's caustic candor. So he graces her inner Spirit with a constellation of *principle*, providing her with the kind of inner foundation a good marriage should supply.

They *do* have an affair, and it's a touching relief to see Marcia able to emerge more lover than shrew. And they do *end* the affair, out of Vincent's loyalty to his daughters who otherwise would be primarily trapped with their toxic, mentally-skewed mother. His farewell to Marcia, "Goodbye my girl," is a variegated, shimmering blessing that shines right down from the Archetypal Masculine realms (father, lover, spirit spouse) to launch her into authenticity, as her possessive and selfish father and husband never had.

This is one example where the so-called "adultery" proved more true than the so-called "marriages" involved. Evolving on to Aumakua, we're inherently primed for true harmony.

LANDSCAPE AS SOUL~SHAPING: *AN AFRICAN DREAM*

If it's obvious that a measure of our sexual allure can be found in our Nature Spirits, then *where* a couple lives and *how* they dwell there is also a measure of their compatibility. Indigenous cultures name as Totemic affiliations not only animals, but plants and even weather systems. Can't you feel that? Having our Soul so beautifully dispersed throughout Creation also provides protection.

In the biopic *An African Dream* we see a "headstrong" turn-of-the-century woman lured by her fiancé from cramped, drizzly England to vast, sunlit South Africa. Despite her groom's catalytic help in getting her there, it is soon evident that it is the land she truly loves. Furthermore an African Native can better ground her there than an insipid Little Lord Fauntleroy of a racist spouse. This film also provides clear viewing of the *pilikia* (troubles) that ensue when we don't operate with consciousness of our tri-part selves. You can just see the woman here speaking (Uhane) from her visionary Aumakua time and again, while her husband's aka cords stream out from the comfort zone of his Unihipili. One has the marriage buggy in Drive, the other in Reverse. It's bound to splinter and collapse.

Katherine (Kitty Aldridge) is one of those spirited women whose beauty is entirely matched by her intelligence. Tall, willowy, and animated, you can tell from the start that she exceeds the constraints of her corseted age. She is also a schoolteacher and an artist amongst aristocratic "Daughters of the Empire," and soon finds herself rebelling against their gossipy teas. This is much to the chagrin of her husband, Reginald (Dominic Jephcott) who is more of a son of the empire than a spouse to his bride. Currently a gentleman farmer, Reggie earned his military stripes fighting against the Blacks, so the Natives' segregation to a Reserve is a validation of efforts he wishes to preserve.

This comfortable colonial imperialism is upset when Katherine meets the son of a deceased Chieftain. Khatana (John Kani) was London-educated and now finds himself suspended between cultures. He is also the Reserve's schoolteacher, and when Katherine volunteers her services to teach alongside him, rumors quickly spread.

A MOST SUBTLE COURTSHIP

While there is no overt sexual infidelity enacted, it is evident to all concerned where Katherine's heart lies, even if she does her best to engage her husband and community with the Natives in general, and Khatana in particular. As the racial divide deepens, and the honeymoon sours between the official newlyweds, *An African Dream* displays the most subtle of courtships between the two actual kindred spirits: *via wardrobe*.

Katherine, upon first visit with Reggie to their handsome marriage bungalow, whips off a blindfold and strides across the floor to throw open curtains and windows. Thereafter she spends as much time as possible outdoors in this beloved Africa, often exploring and painting solo. She meets Khatana upon catching her clothes on thorns in the wild. This can be read as her willing embeddedness in the land, as well as a rending, a tearing open, a loss of virginity. When Katherine blithely relates this encounter to her snooty, appalled, female circle, she is suddenly steered away from them by a friendly host who happens to be an apiarist. Draped in a veiled beekeeper's hat, she appears more bridal and contained than ever she did with the more brotherly Reginald.

Soon afterwards, the assured equilibrium of a dinner party is unhinged by the arrival of the Black schoolmaster, per the "brazen" hostess' invitation. When the enthused Katherine welcomes Khatana at the door, he is elegantly garbed in formal attire, and carrying hand-picked wildflowers. Thus, upon entering the parlor arm-in-arm with Katherine carrying the bouquet, they look for all the world like a pleased couple at their Wedding feast. Sadly parting that night, he kisses her hand, which would be a shocking intimacy by that community's standards. Indeed, a consummation.

And so it goes. After her beloved Black colleague is clearly exiled from White society, Katherine attends an elitist, festive outdoor gathering garbed in the darkest of indigo "blues." And finally, when Khatana is killed and his schoolhouse burnt to the ground, we see his true Spirit's spouse in ebony "widow's weeds," the mourning fashion of the Victorian Age.

Of course the marriage is over between Katherine and Reginald Hastings before it gained a footing. But with the husband planted in the past (Unihipili) and his wife striding into a much more liberal future (Aumakua), they haven't a common ground, even in all of vast Africa, to call (Uhane) their own. She leaves him, a trial separation that becomes permanent. Katherine allows Khatana's heart to resurrect in her Soul, as she starts her own school for the Natives, never to return to this mentally gated community of entitled British ex-pats.

Here too is an example of apparent legal and emotional 'infidelity' which in actuality points to the woman's true nature and Destiny, obviously blessed and guided by the supernal wedding of the Male-Female Divine that is her Higher Self.

INDRA'S NET: STREAMS OF CONNECTION

It's one thing to show geologians and quantum physicists, poets and visionaries with insight into our innate interconnectedness. But what about our daily lives? It helps to consider that we move in pods of people, plants and pets that extend our heart's circulation. I've asked clients of mine to imagine bringing the qualities of love-making into the world. Of course they all imagine "orgasm" would have to stay private. But why, when foreplay, mutual gratification and fond closure can be the aim of every well-meaning exchange? We can "make love" to many aspects of our lives, which only amplifies the frequency of *Aloha* throughout.

A TANGLED WEB: *LANTANA*

For the longest time I was amazed when I sang the praises of *Lantana* to cinephiles, only to hear they'd never seen it. I loved it! My only consolation was that it swept the 2001 Australian Film Institute Awards — the equivalent of the Oscars Down Under — winning Best Picture, Director, Actor, Actress, Supporting Actor and Actress, *and* Screenplay. Then I learned that publicity for this quiet stunner, including screening at a Canadian Film Festival, was interrupted by the horror of 9/11, explaining to some measure its lack of repute. All I can say is, if you haven't seen it, do.

Lantana is a tropical bush that flowers prettily on the outside but is a tangle of knotted branches within. It's a good metaphor for this "Adult Mystery" about the affairs of the hearts, minds, and bodies of three couples, and all the sundry offshoots of their lives. Note that the upper-class couple display a hellish alienation and the lower-class one, a heavenly accord. No less than a polar inversion by the standards of the Marketplace.

This movie also belies the scriptwriting dictate that too many coincidences prove a plot incredible. This story serves up *nothing but* coincidences, from subtle overlap to outright head-butting, bringing Systems Theory home. On the surface alone it reads somewhat like soap opera. But I invite you to sink down and perceive the conflicts and challenges from a level of Spirit seeking Love in human intimacy and knocking on every last door, from adultery to Death, to find it.

It helps to take paper and pen to map out this cast like a genealogy, with Leon (Anthony LaPaglia) at the middle and all others branching out.

Leon is the main character, a middle-aged, middle-class, married (with children) cop, acting out a mid-life crisis via a middling affair that matters more to the woman involved, Jane (Rachael Blake), than it does to the numbed-out automaton he's become. Meanwhile, his beautiful wife, Sonja (Kerry Armstrong), is in therapy with Dr. Valerie Somers (Barbara Hershey) where we learn that Sonja's disappointments with her marriage eerily echo Valerie's insecurities about her husband, John (Geoffrey Rush), a Dean of Law. Only that tony, well-to-do professional couple are also suffering a dark whirlpool of loss threatening to swamp them: the recent murder of their only child, an adolescent daughter. Talk about a depth-charge of a sub-plot: the Underworld itself.

PARANOIA ABOUNDS

Claudia (Leah Purcell) is Leon's partner on the force, a thoroughly decent young woman who suspects his affair and doesn't appreciate any part of it, especially when it involves her covering for him. Single, Claudia has her eyes on a man who frequents the same restaurant as she does, also solo. Leon literally runs into this guy while jogging, only to have him break down weeping in his arms, a vulnerable state which astonishes the more macho cop, and which he resists in himself for the longest time.

Leon's mistress lives next door to the plot's only happy couple, the unemployed Nik (Vince Colosimo) and over-employed Paula (Daniella Farinacci), who have a young family and economic stress. Paula makes no bones about her intolerance for any potential straying on her spouse's part with the flirtatious Jane: "She's lonely, Nik, and you're bored. That's a lethal combination. You fuck with our marriage, I'll cut your balls off and hang 'em on the line between your socks and your jocks, hey?" Duly noted.

Meanwhile Valerie has a gay client who loves playing head games with her, so much so that she begins to suspect him of having an affair with her husband, casting her as the "bottomless well of need" in their triangle. This throws the therapist so off-keel that one evening she verbally accosts Jane's estranged husband at a sidewalk café, who then commiserates with a stranger, Leon, in a bar. And when Valerie fails to return home one night, Jane has reason to believe Nik was involved in her disappearance. She reports her suspicions to the police, who send over Leon and Claudia to interview her, even as the ex also shows up. Quite the tangled root system, and yet it works flawlessly.

Once on Valerie's case, Leon sees his wife's name on the client list, and helps himself to cassette recordings of their sessions. Hearing how lackluster the marriage has become for Sonja, as well as her concern that he's having an affair, Leon initially can't bring himself to listen for the answer to the taped question, "Do you still love him?" Pause....

FRIENDSHIP, SOULSHIP, ROMANCE & SPIRIT

All the social inter-connectedness of *Lantana* is very Indigenous. In most tribal cultures if a person stays isolated for even a day, it would arouse concern. And yet pairing off in isolation is a keynote of Western marriages. And many times this is necessary because, without Initiation to demark adulthood from childhood, many newlyweds need to migrate to get proper distance from their past. But our longing for *communitas* is innate. Think of the *Ohana* (extended family) value of Hawaii. The multi-layered entanglement of players here reveals the sub and supra-conscious energetic network that unites everyone anyway.

Lantana's adulterous activities, indulged or attempted, show the dark side of 'Hollywood standards,' which purport that sexual allure is everything. For the African Dagara tribe intimacy is the delicious icing on a cake that's been carefully mixed, spiced, and baked. To them our Western emphasis on romance seems addictive, illusory and disorientating. Their relational foundation is friendship, or what I like to call Soulship: a clear-eyed knowing of who the other is in terms of their Destiny, strengths and frailties. The common phrase "the honeymoon's over" says it all: we're encouraged to begin marriage in such a *high* state of impassioned fantasy that we're often bound to crash once back in the quotidian routines of life.

If we weren't indoctrinated into believing there's a split between Spirit and Matter, we'd know to take the time to sound out the Spirit of any sexual attraction. Are you drawn to that older partner due to unresolved issues with your mother or father? Fine, and as *Mother* and *Bliss* show, sometimes an inevitable conundrum, but do you *really* want to marry a parent substitute? And then there are potential affairs that seem compelling because they promise the love we never got from a problematic sibling relationship. Again, maybe important for healing, but not the best spousal material. Much better to marry outside the tribe.

Sacred space is required to process the emotional and spiritual complexity of something as rich as wedding, and for Westerners such as Sonja's character in *Lantana*, therapy may be the best container for this. And sometimes it requires Death itself to open people to the liminal depths of renewal. For Valerie and John the death of their daughter proved destructive to their marriage, their momentum toward a shared future subsumed by an unabating whirlpool of grief. But for our man Leon, Valerie's death awakened him from the stagnant trance of his life into a renewed ardour for Sonja. So much so that we can imagine their final waltz onscreen carrying them into a season of true intimacy. "Do you still love him?" Indubitably, and requitedly, she does.

PART VIII

THE SHATTERED PATHWAY

"The greatest source of evil and of things going wrong in people's lives, is the failure to deal with and get over hurt feelings."
                    — Marie Louise von Franz, *The Feminine in Fairy Tales*

FATAL FLAW: RESISTING INITIATION

We never know exactly how our promptings for growth will arrive, ascending from beneath, descending from above, or straight at us: will they come from natural, divine and/or human realms, from the past or inspired by an intended future? Regardless, it's always an invitation into process, and so requires submission to transformation. Depending upon our investment in our current Persona, we may resist a little, a lot, or not at all. For men this often requires self-sacrifice, for women self-declaration.

An important part of Initiatory growth is assuming responsibility for our increasing consciousness as we mature. Take the schoolmaster in *A Dry White Season*. After taking an eye-opening measure of the oppression of Apartheid, he's invited from several White quarters to shut his eyes, ears and mouth (Uhane) on the issue. It is to his great moral credit that he doesn't. In the case of the French film, *Cache*, a similarly comfortable bourgeois man is haunted by the memory of damage he caused in his youth which has personal and political reverberations. Now that he is in a position to atone, the question arises, "What then shall he do?"

HIDE & SEEK: *CACHE*

Watching *Cache* ("Hidden") is like pleasantly strolling with a loved one through Paris, pausing on a bridge to gaze down at the Seine, only to be chilled by a gathering of clouds overhead and a summoning of ghosts from below. No matter how plaintively you wish to restore your winsome weekend idyll, it's just too damn late. *Merde.*

Georges and Anne Laurent (Daniel Auteuil and Juliette Binoche, reigning royalty of French cinema) make you want to believe their culture is alive and well-polished. You've come to love these two charming actors, to want to identify with them, certainly not to doubt or suspect them — clever casting indeed on the part of Austrian director Michael Haneke. Anne works a leisurely schedule at an upscale publishing house, and Georges is the celebrity host of a TV talk show which discusses, again, books. Even their dining room, where they entertain equally erudite friends, is a floor-to-ceiling *bibliotheque*. And they have an adolescent son, Pierrot, a swimming champion, who is every bit as aggravatingly sullen and opaque (cache) as boys that age can be. Their lives are full.

But the complacency of their privileged existence begins to erode when, mysteriously, videotapes begin appearing at the Laurents' door, videotapes showing that they are under surveillance. At first what is filmed is neither personal nor invasive, is, in fact, quite quotidian: hours of comings-and-goings from the front door of their apartment building. But next a tape arrives showing a ride to the countryside shot through the metronomic beat of windshield wipers in light rain. The vehicle turns into the driveway of a picture-perfect stone-built farm estate, stopping abruptly. Then the camera resumes its static, watchful gaze, recording Georges' childhood home where his aging, ailing, mother (Annie Girardot) still resides.

And there's also the unnerving matter of the tapes coming wrapped in juvenile black-and-red drawings: of a small child spewing blood, a chicken (the *coq* being the national bird of France) with a slit throat, etc.

The police aren't willing to initiate investigation until something more sinister occurs, so Georges takes matters into his own hands. A street sign shown in one of the tapes pinpoints a neighborhood where his key suspect lives in a cramped, messy apartment, the antithesis of the Laurents' tastefully appointed abode. Majib (Maurice Benichou) was the son of two Algerian servants employed by Georges' parents in his youth. The immigrant couple were killed, drowned in the Seine along with hundreds of others, while protesting a racist curfew on October 17, 1961. It is one of France's darker post-Colonial chapters, one they've done their best to keep hidden (cache). And while pondering this ghostly Seine, remember the trenchant note that the Laurents' son is a swimming champion. Who dies and who thrives?

After the shamefully tragic loss of his parents, Majib was to be adopted into Georges' family, but what occurred instead leads the adult Georges to determine that Majib is now tormenting him with the tapes. As Alexandra Fuller notes in her African memoir, *Scribbling the Cat*, soldiers don't cause wars, just bear the brunt of them; how much less responsible then are children for the political Domain Basins in which they find themselves growing? But if, as an adult, you can spiral over what shaped your earlier years and make amends for youthful cruelty of grave consequence, shouldn't you?

MORALITY PLAY, ALLEGORY, WHODUNIT

On the Spirit level, atonement requires Soul retrieval for all involved. Anything less is disingenuous and rings a false note to our Higher Self. How do we live with guilt when it pinches our conscience? That is the central challenge of *Cache* as Morality Play.

The lead character played by actor Daniel Auteuil (ironically, b. 1950, Algiers) can be seen as a defensive and arrogant version of France, his wife the distraught populace pleading for transparent disclosure. Majib, the descendant of Algerian immigrants not fully welcomed into the fold, pushed into a one-man terrorist act to wake Georges up. And the two sons (George's and Majib's) the next generation which might continue racial discord, or dispel it. That would be the allegorical version, which works quite well.

Then there's the whodunit version (who sent the damn tapes?) which can prompt wonderfully futile, wine-and-cheese hours of post-screening debate. Here are just some of the theories that can fly:

— *Majib* (Georges' Shadow) sent the tapes, having discovered the celebrity on TV and wanting to blackmail him because of their youth, which certainly included violent betrayal and may have included some homo-erotic elements (listen carefully when Georges edits his show).

— *Majib's grown son*, seeking retribution, after learning of his father's deprivation. The combo-platter theory: he may have seduced the Laurents' son into complicity to haunt Georges. Without adequate maturation on the part of the parent, "the sins of the Father" devolved onto the next generation.

— *Anne* sent the tapes as a last-ditch effort to make the guilty, stultified, inchoate Georges come alive emotionally so she can desire the marriage again. She also may be making Georges' childhood sins an issue to distract from her possible affair with her employer, Pierre. They seem quite intimate, and her son is named Pierrot.

— Then there's *Georges' aging and ailing Mother*, who let herself be manipulated by her son into depriving Majib. She keeps her bedroom lights on all night while, in a later scene, Georges wants his boudoir lights kept off, both for the same reason: evading consciousness. She may have sent the tapes from the perspective of death-bed guilt, hoping for a reconciliation between the two now grown boys.

DEEP ANALYSIS

Spill the wine, pass the brie, and finally let all such desperate theories sink like stones into the haunted Seine. You're shape-shifting at the sandy bottom by now, growing gills and conversing with the ghosts. Because the true question is not "Whodunit?" but the one repeatedly asked by the Linda Hunt character in the romantic political thriller *The Year of Living Dangerously*: "What then shall we do?" If someone's slumbering, guilty conscience is awakened with the classic Freudian thunder of "the return of the repressed," it ultimately matters not a squat how it awakened. It matters what one does about it.

Shamanism and Parapsychology overlap on this issue of "ghosts," saying that communication between the realms of the living and the dead (Psychopomp work) requires just the right mutual frequency (ritual) for the apparition to be actualized and maintained. Georges' consciousness, being assailed from all sides, from his anguished wife, alienated son, dying mother, multi-racial friendships, and historical advances in civil rights, can no longer bear a complacent disregard for his heinous youthful transgressions.

With such pressure on, the "tapes" of his entitled youth replay to haunt him, and they certainly don't jibe with his adult persona as a liberal, literary, erudite television celebrity. That's the theory I subscribe to — that the tapes came from the *watchful eye* of Georges' conscience, the evolving god's-eye-view of his Higher Self which, at midlife, he should certainly feel reeling him in to that watery Voudon throne of eventual reckoning.

Thus, for example, when Georges has an encounter with his employer who has received a "tape," it is really just a matter of Georges having a normal exchange regarding program content, but *imagining* what his boss would make of him if he knew of his destructive, arrogant behavior toward Majib. His Persona is cracking at work. When he and his wife argue over his lack of disclosure, this is just more evidence that their marriage has devolved to a state where a "tape" of emotional dishonesty is being played and replayed. Georges has jammed on his brakes regarding veracity, inner and outer, his East-West harmony shredding due to obdurate secrecy. Finally, his North-South/Child-Elder axis is bracketed by his son's sullen sense of privilege and his aging mother's disingenuous denial.

THE MORAL GAUNTLET

"What then shall we do?" comes from the Bible, when John the Baptist strides in from the clear and dry liminal perspective of the desert and chastises the Pharisees for their selfishness, seeing them as moral vipers. They ask this, *the right question*, and get instruction in compassion, generosity and peacefulness. Whether *Cache*'s Georges Laurent will manage such wisdom and humility, or adhere to an obdurate entitlement, is yours to surmise. It doesn't look good. Initiation resisted results in a muddied psycho-spiritual backwater.

Oh! And don't shut down the film too swiftly. (Most people *don't* wrap up a Haneke film quickly, since he likes to push his characters and viewers to the end of our ropes and then leave those ends frayed.) Watch the credits, and a final scene: it's the static recording camera eye again, watching the Laurents' son and his friends gathered outside their school building, amidst all the bustle of the end of the day.

Cars circle around the school, some repeatedly. Surprisingly, Pierrot is approached by Majib's son for a brief, *apparently cordial* exchange, their words hidden (cache) from us. This scene is a bookend to the film's opening one where a static camera watched the Parisian abode. In theaters, the silhouetted heads and upper torsos of entering patrons shadowed the screen, as in some modern-day Plato's cave. The school scene being videotaped, the boys under possible surveillance from a circling car, and the sense of the theater patrons both watching and being watched from behind, provides concentric, fractal circles of consciousness radiating out — as from a wishing coin cast into the Seine.

Each generation has its individual Watchful Eye, its own challenges and obligations to fulfill or betray via Initiation, or resistance thereto. I like to believe that Eye watches over us not with a cold threat of judgment, but with a Loa/Aumakua's wise forbearance and longing for our utmost accomplishment, for the sake of all three worlds.

ADDICTION: LIMINOID OVERLOAD

Another way we can jam the gears of the Initiatory round is via Addiction. Let's look at how this all-too-common modern detour shreds both the Indigenous and the Initiatory processes.

If you live in a world where you participate respectfully in Nature, knowing the sacredness of it, then there can be no doubt that Nature is a font of Revelation. And as we cleanse our Unihipili of childhood woundedness, there is more circuitry opened to such inspiration. Not only are there divinely wrought impulses, intuition, signs, and omens to be read on an ongoing basis, but there are plant Spirits which invite our consciousness into better appreciation of our participation in the Web of Life.

And once you grasp this innate interconnectedness, it's self-sabotaging to engage in divisive behavior like waging war. Note that Africa's Gabon is a uniquely peaceful country amidst warring tribal lands. This is attributed to the local legend that Pygmies introduced their once violent enemies, the Bantu, to the sacred entheogen *iboga*, thus showing them their participation in the Spirit World. Today, experimentation shows that a derivative from this plant, *ibogaine*, so regulates dispersal of serotonin in the brain that the cravings of even heroin addicts are dramatically reduced. But that's a lot harder to come by than, say, a bottle of single malt.

An inadvertently funny scene in the film adaptation of James Michener's historical epoch, *Hawaii*, shows the aftermath of a Calvinist Church service by Reverend Abner Hale (Max von Sydow), who looks for all the world like a macabre Edward Gorey cartoon. One Native exiting the Church service wears a woven helmet sprouting what appear to be *magic mushrooms*. The sacred use of hallucinogens would definitely have made this New England Missionary's fire-and-brimstone sermon exceedingly dull in contrast. Fire and brimstone: raising Hell into this Pacific Paradise, in the name of Christ.

INITIATION VS. INEBRIATION

Humans are hard-wired for exploration of multi-dimensional, altered states of consciousness, something we experience every day with the mini-round of wakefulness, sleeping/dreaming, and reawakening. In a community with respect for mind-altering substances, ritual surrounds their use, and watchfulness on the part of Mentors protects the Protégés from "cooking" themselves too much or too little.

Shift from that world-view to the modern-day one of *control over* Nature, commodification and possession of it. Add to that the solitary, unguided individuals buying unlimited drugs and/or alcohol, and there's no measure of the damage being risked.

Something significant has to be factored into History lessons wherever we see Native cultures undermined by "firewater," such as via the state-endorsed breweries of *A Dry White Season* and *Once Were Warriors*, or the predatory liquor store owners setting up shop near reservations in *Skins*. And that "something" is the particular vulnerability that would arise for tribes subjected to addictive substances like alcohol, when they were used to ritualistically benefiting from the Spirits of mind-altering plants (botanical sacraments). I've never heard of someone addicted to Peyote or *Ayahuasca*, (aka "the Vine of Death/Vine of Souls" due to its transformative powers). The acutely purifying (read: *nauseating*) dimensions of these substances could hardly be categorized as "recreational."

Chronic use of a substance to provide no value other than a temporary high would have been a shocking and unheard of waste in old tribal cultures. No Sacred rite would aim at merely shifting one's consciousness toward oblivion. Even when rum is used in the context of a Voudon ceremony, the aim is to invite possession by a particular Loa, not mindless inebriation. Initiation always aims at greater assimilation of Spirit, not prolonged dependency on matter. In West Africa, adult drinkers are considered the equivalent of infantile, "wet behind the ears," unformed, uncooked. They're perceived as regressing to an amniotic haze in order to dream a better future, even while alcoholism erodes their capacity to achieve it.

TRUNCATED POTENTIAL

The other tragic element about addiction is the way it botches the Initiatory process. Despite attempts to romanticize male versions (Hemingway, F. Scott Fitzgerald, Dylan Thomas), addicts desperately seek out "spirits" in substances to help transcend a miserable existence. They go through the daily motions as best they can (zombies), while in actuality living for opportunities to have their drug or drink of choice shift their consciousness into something more pleasurable, whether greater stimulation or greater numbing out.

So addicts go from a *Living Death* to a temporary hit of *"Life"* only to crash into an even greater *Death* again: a downward spiral. Another way to perceive it is to say that addicts try to control and expand 'liminal space' which then becomes a chronic 'liminoid state' that is not reviving but savagely impotent, infertile. Addictive drink and drugs only contribute to psychic and physical death, without the regenerative rebirth of Initiation. And these death-dealing substances are what European conquerors, usurped from their pagan roots and bereft of the powers of their teaching plants, brought to Indigenous peoples world-wide.

A FINE MESS: *THUMBSUCKER*

This one tries to have its "drugs" and ignore them too. Sucking one's thumb at 17 years of age is a sure indication that stringy-haired Justin (the wonderfully adept Lou Pucci) hasn't managed the Initiatory round from infancy to youth, and is thus unable to enact an "appropriate" role for this stage of his life. They could have played this as a gifted outsider's crisis-of-identity, solvable through any number of viable venues. Instead *Thumbsucker* (based on Walter Kirn's semi-autobiographical novel) just churns Jason into a soggy familial and social backwater where everybody's always messed up, and tolerance of that fact is considered the greatest virtue.

The Chinese Book of Changes, the *I Ching*, was compiled to show the efficacy of right relationships, and the damage of inappropriate ones. The world is askew when, for example, the King is not the king, the Warrior not the warrior, the Parent not a parent, a Child not allowed to be a child, the person in a Superior position is Inferior to their followers, etc. In *Thumbsucker* all the life roles are ass-end-to and instead of painting this for the horror show it is, it sports the general attitude, "So what?"

Even before the plot proper begins, a cartoon comes up on screen with a hapless character spouting a balloon: "How can I be the parent when I'm the kid?" From an Indigenous perspective, you know it's OK for parents to be clueless as long as Mentors and Elders are on hand to guide the child. No such luck plays out here. More's the pity.

EVERYONE'S LOST: WHOOPEE!

Justin's parents don't want to be called Mom and Dad because it makes them feel old. Lack of initiation there. Mike (Vincent D'Onofrio) was a football star in his youth before an injury sidelined any hope for a pro career. Later revelations suggest that he actually may have sacrificed the game to win his sweetheart, Audrey (again, the ever pitch-perfect Tilda Swinton). This means that he erred by putting partnership ahead of Destiny, which, as *Anthony and Cleopatra* shows us, is a somewhat beautiful but ultimately tragic choice.

Justin is every bit as agog over Audrey as is his Dad (enmeshment), although he would prefer she act more like a Mom and doesn't appreciate it when she takes him along dress-shopping so she can "win a date" with a TV star (Benjamin Bratt). When that fails, she applies for a nursing position at a "celebrity detox clinic," where she ends up pulling stashed drugs out of her leading man's bloody ass. This woman seems doomed to serious disillusionment.

Since his thumb-sucking "habit" is misaligning Justin's teeth, he goes to see Perry (Keanu Reeves), a New Age orthodontist who tries to help the lad access a Power Animal's aid in overcoming his dependency. Of course this quasi-Shamanic overture is mocked, and instead of Perry helping Justin, we have Justin prompting Perry to take a more conventional career route, a miserable choice he compensates for with addictions to smoking and drinking. Everybody's doing it.

In school, Justin's Debate Coach (Vince Vaughn) sets him a healthy challenge, but blows it by buying booze for his under-age, on-the-road team and allowing them co-ed sleeping quarters (lack of proper boundaries all around). Besides, Justin's oratory skills only ignited after the School Counselor recommended Ritalin for his Attention Deficit Disorder. When he's accused of being "a speed freak" because the drug is just molecules away from cocaine, Justin "quits" the approved pharmaceutical and goes back on his thumb. Interesting choice.

But then it gets messier again. He gains admission into his College of choice by lying about his family on the application form, making himself out to be a victim while in actuality he's quite cherished. This is a false launching into a future horizon, where truth should always abide, in potential at least. Because Justin's acceptance wasn't honorably earned, it doesn't demand sacrifice, and our 'hero" is still digit-in-mouth as he flies off to the land of higher learning. Uninitiated.

INDIGENOUS VIEW

Sources of the word addict vary from "one sold into slavery" to "one who yields." When Audrey proclaims that "We're all addicted to something," she fails to distinguish between a healthy, inspired yielding and a slavish one.

That's the problem with *Thumbsucker*. While it raises important questions about why such an innocent, gooey, self-comforting act is less tolerated than more damaging compensatory activities, it fails to provide a Spiritual healing Domain Basin for all such compulsive dependencies. And when cast and crew buy into this theme that everybody's always at sea in a fog, it rings really false, disingenuous. After all, these are successful players in the highly competitive Filmmaking Industry who only reached their level of accomplishment via honing considerable skills, not laying back on the day-bed drawing on a hookah. And they know full well when they're *getting it right*, whether as scribe, shape-shifter, director, producer, technician or shooter, which is the responsibility and satisfaction of truly Initiated professionals.

One of the most wonderful teachings from the African Dagara tribe is that certain emotions are too much to be borne all by oneself, and need to be dealt with in a Sacred container. One example is grief, and we can all see how wakes and funerals provide social demarcations between life as usual and life that has been torn open to the Eternal realm via Death. Another emotion that the Dagara consider "sacred," dependent upon Divine intervention for healing, is *shame*.

If you're feeling shame, it's because you're suffering a judgment of inadequacy that you cannot manage to personally overcome. What if shame about thumb, beer-bottle, or joint sucking could be dealt with in a Shamanic chamber? What if an addict could find help in accessing yes, their Power Animal, *and* their higher Self (Grand Tete, Loa, Aumakua) in order to be reminded of a "blueprint" of their potential, how to get back on track?

In such a container, shame is not a judgment from a "sadistic Superego" amplified by a condemning society, which is what the addict usually endures. It's an urgent prompting from one's Higher Self that you have great work to do, in mortal time constraints, and are falling short of it. Thus shame has a Spiritual energetic, and to mute this wake-up call by encouraging people to *accept* their addictions (enabling) isn't doing anyone a favor. Depicting sucking one's thumb as temporarily healthier than turning to drugs or drink would work *if* it were emphasized that such a habit indicates self-stimulation, self-comfort, and thus awareness that the Self has the best answers. Anything less than providing this transcendent solution well and truly sucks (pun intended).

ATTEMPTED VENERATION: *RENEGADE*

Here is found a rare example of ceremonial use of plant substances. It should be contrasted with the likes of *Skins*, which manages some humor and much pathos in showing how genocidal decimation of American Indians via alcoholism has been every bit as insidious as the distribution of pox-laden blankets.

Adapted from a French cartoon, *Renegade* (aka *Blueberry*) is a somewhat clunky hybrid aiming to be a Supernatural Western. It involves a young Cajun man who runs tragically afoul of a thug interested in the same prostitute girlfriend. Years later, said Cajun has become a town Sheriff, with the nasty business from his past coming back to haunt him. (Note: in actuality, prostitutes of that age were desperate females who boarded trains to head West and service Indian-killer soldiers led by Major General Joseph Hooker. Thus they were originally referred to as "Hooker's Girls" and finally just plain "hookers." But, preposterously, the harlots of *Renegade* look like super-model beauties in their prime: perfectly coiffeured, made-up, attired and healthy. Uh-huh. Somebody's fantasy). Here's another quirk: *Renegade* is sincerely invested in Indigenous cultures, yet depicts them from a myopic eye across the Atlantic. The American Indians appear to be drawn on artifacts and garb ranging everywhere from Alaska to Patagonia. It's as if a North American artist wildly depicted Africans as a mix of every tribe from Ashanti to Zulu.

But director Jan Kounen probably had something more reverential in mind, since he attributes a hugely transformative (Initiatory) chapter in his life to time spent among the Shipibo-Kinobo tribe of South America, taking "strong journeys" via their "master plants." This biographical chapter is rendered in his documentary *Other Worlds*, in which the beauty and madness of his experience is addressed by artists, scientists and healers who endorse the *properly supervised* ingestion of hallucinogens, now known as "entheogens." (Shamanic sacraments, Sacred plants). *Renegade* is Kounen's fictional paeon to Nature's mind-enhancing potential.

The Sheriff had once been rescued from death by a Native family, and so has an American Indian "brother" (played by a Maori!) versed in the power of Peyote. And this is where the great value of this otherwise some-times logy, sometimes silly, story lies. While other Westerns would have the Sheriff and the Villain enact a good vs. bad, black vs. white show-down on Main Street at *High Noon*, *Renegade* serves up a much deeper encounter.

The thug from the past has been following a map to a Magic Mountain of gold, only to find that this is actually a Sanctuary for Sacred Peyote ceremony. The young sheriff ingests some and, laying alongside his "enemy," purges his past through a hellishly gorgeous kaleidoscope of snakes, scorpions, etc. His Shaman brother accompanies him "all over the Universe" through a death-and-birth canal, to a shattering revelation of truth. *Self-forgiveness* is found, the *inner* show-down complete, and he can finally avail himself of new life, all thanks to the powers of a sacred plant. *High Noon* indeed: the Shadow cast *internally*. Initiation accomplished.

PART IX

UNEXPECTED INITIATION

"What a necropolis the human heart is."
— *Gustave Flaubert*

DEATH AS RENT IN LIFE'S FABRIC

Especially when we're young and dependent on physical sustenance, our surrounding, established Domain Basins consume much of our attention just getting the lay of the land. When we are so absorbed in Middle World, it may take something as radical as Death to make us aware of being surrounded by Great Mystery, Deep Spirit, liminal space, the sacred, fertile Void.

Even if the Death involved is expected, some measure of disorientation results, and we need to reconfigure our identities before re-entering life without the earthly presence of the now Departed. Each person's grief has a shape and timing unique to them alone, although it is telling that the Haitians retrieve the Soul from the Watery Abyss after one year, and the Hawaiians gather together for a cleansing, celebratory "Feast of Tears" after the same passage of time. But when we're in the grip of grief, all familiar measures of security give way to thin black ice indeed.

A DARK & STORMY WOMB: *ORPHANS*

Scottish writer/director Peter Mullen tracks the different paths taken by four already fatherless siblings during the restless night following their mother's unexpected death and leading up to her funeral the next day. This rough and tumble, dismal, rainy, verbally-vulgar and physically-violent production won't win the city of Glasgow any five-star tourist points. But it does provide an assured cinematic destination for a Soul-scouring pilgrimage through bereavement at its most acute.

In our modern culture where the sunset, transformative, Western point of the Soul Compass is so strongly resisted in favor of the sunny, Eastern yang "values" of progress, permanence, greed and insurance, this gritty tale shows no man's consciousness going "gently into that good night." Absolutely everyone rages "against the dying of the light."

Storms figure strongly here, amplifying the emotional chaos these grown children are feeling at their sudden loss. There's a flashback to a time when the three boys cuddled and whimpered in their mother's bed, the lone wee sister in her crib, as they're comforted and assured that a thunderstorm wracking the house shall pass. That was *then*, and being orphans in a storm *now* is both the same *and* an entirely different matter.

If you open your Shamanic Spirit Eye, you can see that Death is the turbulence that enlivens the deep Heavens as the Mother moves from parental to Ancestral status. Think of how Native American Indians rattle in order to echo the dancing of the stars, of how Haitians believe the Loa animate the Cosmos. With this Mother's Soul moving into participation in the Cosmic Womb, she is able to remind her children of both their mortality and their *im*mortality, their need to sound out authentic Destiny. Abruptly made mindful that they must strive for fulfillment during their earthly round, these offspring are tossed into the arena of that challenge with the acute, singular loneliness Initiation entails. Once a source of human nurturance and consolation, the Mother is now a Source of Revelation. And that's no pabulum, Baby.

FOUR FATES

Thomas (Gary Lewis), the eldest, most conservative son, has clearly been the Mother's substitute consort, as shown via the love song he tearily sings in the pub the night of her death. When one of the patrons scoffs at Thomas' tears, the emotionally volatile middle son, Michael (Douglas Henshall), accosts him, only to receive a swift and burning stab to the gut, a wound which hemorrhages throughout the night. Youngest son John (Stephan McCole) vows to kill the assailant out of loyalty to family, even as Michael does his best to dissuade him. On hand in her wheelchair is the partially paralyzed, mildly retarded, but nonetheless scampish baby of the family, Sheila (Rosemarie Stevenson).

Being the youngest male, John is the most removed from thoughts of mortality, most inchoate in his resistance to this loss, and thus most apt to deal with Death in a clunky, concrete manner. Add the fact that he was only in College to please his Ma, and you can guess how disorienting his new "freedom" is. Lost and outraged, he thinks he can defeat Death's power by flipping into his Shadow and killing another. Brutal stuff, this.

Michael, with his wide, hooded eyes and longish wavy hair, is the most emotionally labile of the crew, most yin, most watery. He goes to his job at the docks hoping to wrangle Workman's Comp for his pub injury. But as he lists his demands, weaving on his feet, blood-drained to a whiter shade of pale, he dwindles from a bombastic litany of "I want compensation!" to a frail whine of "I want comp... I want my Mommy..." before collapsing on a pallet and launching out to sea like a corpse himself, an indelible image.

Sheila, tired of keeping an all-night vigil at Holy Cross Church with Thomas, revs up her motorized wheelchair and smashes him into a statue of the "Virgin Mother" before taking off solo for home. Derailed on a cobblestone street, she is rescued by a young girl wearing a coned princess hat, and welcomed into her sweet family. The fact that Sheila arrives on their scene the night of a *birthday* party and is attending a *funeral* the next day, makes their bonding seem not merely promising, but Archetypal and irrevocable.

SODDEN CEREMONY, NEW DAY

Thomas' resistance to his Ma's passing is shown by his patient, all night, candle-wax cobbling together of the Blessed Mother's shattered statue: "Don't worry, Ma. Everything'll be okay for your service; I'll see to that." Whereas John is earthy and concrete, Michael watery and emotional, and Sheila fiery and willful, the sanctimonious Thomas is principled and abstract. He needs the element air to provide the lesson that he should not continue as his Mother's Spirit Spouse. So a magnificently turbulent squall sweeps off the

Church's roof and wafts a candelabra into the beloved maternal statue for a final shattering. A potential Revelation.

Thomas is slow to learn, however, even insisting upon pall-bearing his mother's casket to her grave literally on his back alone, since John and Sheila have accompanied the by-now unconscious, anemic Michael to the hospital. It's too much of course, as it should be, and this all-too-dutiful son collapses under the weight. Hawaiians believe that when a body suddenly becomes too heavy to carry, it is resisting transport because someone is missing from the funeral procession whom the deceased Spirit wants to see: in this case, the Mother is likely awaiting her three other children.

All four siblings reunite in the Cemetery at a later date. It is a sign of Rebirth that finally we are shown much-needed sunlight after so much depressive, nocturnal, urban crampedness: the greenery is verdant and refreshing as grief's night weds Resurrection's day. Here we can imagine the funeral flowers providing bouquets for the mother's heavenly reunion with her husband, who died 23 years earlier.

Whereas Thomas had preached the imperishability of the Soul (Diamond-Cutting, Pearl-Spinning), his siblings are concerned about the implacability of his devotion suspending him from a return to Life. They invite him away from the Land of the Dead to join them at an Indian restaurant, an invitation which he initially resists, claiming not to be hungry (immortal). Then he agrees to go there "for a starter, 'cuz the Mushroom Paroka's not bad." A starter indeed, for cherishing mortal life in Middle World. Alleluia.

VISITATION: *TRULY, MADLY, DEEPLY*

Voudon practitioners can converse with the retrieved Souls of the Dead in *canaris*, water vessels lovingly preserved on venerable altars. In Old Hawaii, relatives retained a bone from the deceased to be used ritualistically for summoning back the Spirit whenever needed. In either culture, reports of visitations from the Beyond are considered natural and only rarely cross the line to be deemed pathological.

In the modern world, such encounters are common enough, but seldom discussed or expected, a negligence which surely diminishes their potential. Spirit Visitations are certainly not cultivated ritualistically: we have a busy, mutant Marketplace-driven culture given to ghost-busting rather than ghost-beckoning. And so it's wonderful that Anthony Minghella dared a Romantic Comedy winsomely and seamlessly bridging both worlds without trivializing the gut-wrenching grief process in the least: *Truly, Madly, Deeply*.

We don't know how long ago Jamie (Alan Rickman) died, only that his Spirit voice still accompanies his girlfriend Nina (Juliet Stevenson), giving helpful, albeit mundane advice: how to better traverse a nocturnal street, secure her flat, and brush her teeth.

At this particular stage of grief, Nina's yet to tap into her windy rage at Jamie's abrupt departure (he succumbed to a cold), but it's coming. In the meantime she's "gone to ground," hibernating when not putting in her hours at a small institute that teaches immigrants English as a second language. If it weren't for the fact that her problematic flat requires plumbers, carpenters and rodent removers, she'd have no social life at all.

NADIR POINT & REUNION

Nina is shown to be such an all-around affable person that we're caught up short when the wretchedness of her grief is revealed. This happens when her sister politely asks if Nina would be willing to sell or loan the late Jamie's cello for her son's music lessons, only to be harshly rebuked: "It's practically all I've got of him. 'Tis him — You might as well ask me for his body!" This acute dismay and Nina's subsequent isolation is reminiscent of how I heard Russian poet Peter Vierick describe desolation after his first wife's death: *"When I awake in darkness, without you by my side, I have to ask in anguish, which one of us has died."*

In a truly exquisite scene, Nina, alone and playing the piano, begins to hear Jamie accompanying her. As she's used to hearing his voice, this isn't discombobulating, until she turns 'round to see that he's actually, well and truly, returned! Half gasping, half sobbing in a melt-down of sheer incredulous joy, she is reunited with her Beloved. And if you don't emotionally melt down beholding that scene, check yourself for a pulse.

Foregoing friends, family, plumbers and work, these bi-dimensional lovers spend every moment together straight out for about a week, playing games of imagination, music, dance, words, relishing the best of their Love, until its Shadow intrudes. Nina's become a tad too independent for Jamie, and Jamie was always too judgmental for her. She remembers smuggling pieces of her life out to her car when he disapproved of them. They start to recall an affair as rife with pitfalls as promise, although they're still loathe to admit it.

Add to the usual relational challenges the fact that Jamie is a ghost, and therefore requires soaring room temperatures stifling for his human mate. He's also taken to inviting over a quirky cluster of male ghost buddies from many countries and historical epochs who like to bundle up and watch old videos in Nina's bedroom 24/7. When they begin redecorating, she finally snaps.

BIRTH & REBIRTH

One of her Spanish-speaking clients from work is very pregnant, and implores Nina to accompany her to the hospital to provide translation while attending the birth. Cradling the newborn child, Nina realizes she too longs for a fresh and immediate life, not that of regressive isolation with a chilly ghost, no matter how hauntingly he plays the cello. Rebirth.

A dynamic metaphor in *Truly, Madly, Deeply* involves an antique rug in Nina's flat. Jamie rolls it up, lauding the beauty of the oak floor beneath. Nina wants the rug. He protests: it's threadbare and full of mildew and silverfish. He wins, and so does she. As her faith in prolonging their relationship has unraveled, she too has reached a stronger bedrock of potential with a new-found beau, a loving and dramatic Art Therapist (Michael Maloney). It seems that Jamie and his motley crew only returned to help Nina better understand herself and move on, even at bittersweet cost to him. Most touching.

SUBMERGED HEARTS: *JINDABYNE*

As *Orphans* shows, the Void of Death can ultimately be maternal and regenerative. And *Truly, Madly, Deeply* illustrates the African teaching that tears provide the river of emotion connecting the Earthly realm to the Afterlife: I can't imagine viewer's hearts not flooding with empathy when Jamie's ghost reunites with the deeply bereft Nina.

And as more and more people we've loved die, we begin to sense how populated the pulsing Starscape becomes with their Souls. That overarching Domain Basin should become less and less alien and impersonal as we work our way Homeward toward it: our Death, the final Initiation, for which all others provide preparation and diminish the sting.

By now we're also catching on that Death provides layer after layer of variegated darkness as it pulls us toward its nadir point before Re-birth, the proverbial "darkest hour before the dawn." Depending upon what of ourselves we've disowned, repressed or suspended, Death can open us to heavenly and/or hellish realms. It can provide a slippery vortex, not so much fertile and formative as riddled with psychic land-mines, tempests and quicksand which feel like Death alone: annihilation. But this painful Soul-tumbling run, as shown via *Renegade's* Peyote-induced insights, is meant to provide something more empowering: reclamation or release, integration or purification, whichever the Soul needs. We must, must, must reclaim our experiences of Hell as empowering.

If we don't adapt to Death's ever-spiraling Initiatory processes as we mature, we risk awkwardness and desperation in its presence, hastening to avoid it altogether or trying to use it to destroy all we have not resolved. This even at the risk of throwing the proverbial baby out with the bathwater. To be (authentic), or not to be? Such is the challenge of Ray Lawrence's cultural character study, *Jindabyne*. Here Death provides a backdrop to a racially divided community as it takes a measure of unresolved grief, of four men's decency or lack thereof, and the faith of one already frayed and wounded marriage.

GONE FISHIN'

That troubled marriage is at the heart of the story, with all else rippling out from it. Stewart (Gabriel Byrne) and Claire (Laura Linney) are, respectively, Irish and American, a couple who've relocated to New South Wales, Australia. Much of the old Jindabyne township there was flooded to provide for a hydroelectric dam and encourage tourism. This image of submerged life plays out strongly, with nothing being as simple as it appears on the surface.

Stewart *seems* content enough. He's not. Having been a stock-car racing star in his glory days, he's now reduced to running an automotive service station, a drudge of a life compensated for by "the fuck and the beer" and an annual fishing trip to a river on the other side of Snowy Mountain, an area sacred to the local Aborigines. Claire also appears content, while in actuality her private awareness that she's pregnant again has cast her into crisis: after the birth of their son Tom, she sank into a severe post-partum depression that kept her away from hearth and home for a year and a half.

This revelation allows us some sympathy for Stewart's mother, who at first appears gossipy, meddling and too indulgent toward her grandson, until we realize she was imported from Ireland as the substitute mother-figure during what must have been a confusing lapse for the lad. And while pale, wee Tom seems as innocent and angelic as can be, he shares a darkly secret life with a spooky playmate from school, Caylin-Calandria. She's being raised by her grandparents after her mother's death, which none of them has yet accepted.

Demotion, depression, doubt, despair: among the many rigid masks of Death that haunt and stultify us but don't shift the paradigm to Rebirth until we dance them.

And then we face the genuine article full-bore. When Stewart and three of his mates go fishing, he discovers the body of a beautiful (of course) half-Aboriginal girl (Tatea Reilly) floating face-down in the water. While initially horrified, the boys are miles from nowhere, out of cell-phone reception, and don't want to interrupt their excursion to deal with the tragedy. So Stewart tethers the girl's ankle to a tree with fishing line and gets back to the business of netting trout. But Death cannot be so trifled with: displaying the duality of Archetypal realms, all is Paradisiacal for the fishermen until their return to town, where the callousness of their delayed report causes all Hell to break loose.

A LARGER DOMAIN

That's what Death does to the living: opens us up to all the chaos and glory of the Spirit Realm, measuring our covenant with it to date. In that larger realm can also be found the vibrational patterning of Stewart and Claire's marriage covenant. From this Shamanic perspective, an explosive fight they have, which spills over to the grandmother, is sad but potentially *very good* news. I say that not to endorse domestic rancor but to promote ongoing Soul disclosure between spouses, so falsehoods don't accrue to such density that only dynamite can shatter them. Love's Shadow knows what Love laments.

The elemental energetic of anger is heat and light, and thus can provide illumination. Claire is prodding Stewart to reveal "what kind of *man*" could continue fishing under such egregious circumstances, "what did it feel like?" She wants remorse of course, but gets more candor than she bargained for: "It felt *good!* It was a beautiful day, the river was beautiful, I felt so fuckin' *alive!*" Then he turns the tables and submits a topic long overdue: "What kind of *woman* runs away from...?" He's trashing her into the couch as he demands this: "We never talk about that...What about *that?*" Of course the audience realizes that Claire, while demanding painful disclosure, hasn't even been honest about her recent pregnancy. The old township isn't the only thing submerged in Jindabyne.

Black-white issues also surface, and with 19-year-old Susan O'Connor's murderer still on the loose, her Aboriginal kin vent their rage by accusing the four fishermen of hate crimes. In the midst of it all is the also mixed-blood Carmel (Leah Purcell), schoolmistress to the children and budding friend to Claire, who at times bridges the racial gap and at others reinforces it.

After much, much discord, the Whites are finally allowed to attend the Native ceremony to promote Susan's Spirit passage onward, a ritual as much for the living as the dead. Carmel encourages young Tom to walk with her through the smoke issuing from a tall purifying pyramid, "so the Spirits don't latch onto us." Caylin-Calandria and her quasi-racist grandparents also benefit from the Aborigines' generosity, as they are finally able to let their kin's Spirit shine on.

FINALLY, SUSAN'S SOUL

Jindabyne was submerged to acquire hydroelectric energy, and the psychopath who murdered Susan was an electrician. Make of that what you will. When he accosted her in her car on a deserted road wending through broad prairie grasslands, he exclaimed insanely, "It all comes down from the power station, electricity!" Egads. Her body/Spirit is found in a region including a wasp's nest, and in the final scene the killer, stalking fresh prey, is stung by a wasp. Lethally? A Clan Totemic animal? We don't know, but the message is clear: while some Trickster egos may fool themselves into thinking they can get away with murder this life, we ultimately must answer to a higher, vaster Law.

Speaking of the Law, there is one scene here that will truly wrench your gut if viewed from an Aboriginal perspective. (Even without that knowledge it's harrowing enough). The killer backs his truck up to the water to unceremoniously dump his victim's body. When he opens the flap on the back of his vehicle, we see that Susan has been stabbed in the heart, with a dark puddle of blood coagulating on her midriff.

The movie doesn't address this, but one Aboriginal ritual reserved only for Initiation and Death is the painting of a person's Clan Totem design on their torso, from below the heart to beneath the navel. This painting has a vibrational affinity with a Sky region that holds a starry pattern of the Ancestral Source to which one will return after Death. It supplies a binding resonance with the Eternal throughout life. As Jung says, maintaining such a living connection to the Infinite is our Soul's core mission.

To have the bloody issuance of lethal brutality on Susan's solar plexus, instead of a venerable Totemic painting, seems blasphemous. And to have her dumped face *down* in the water sets up an entirely different reverberation from the starry Skyward disposition she deserved: discord and desecration instead of reverence. Since she couldn't begin her Spirit journey without Ceremony, a gruesome resonance is animated in the days following her Death. We know what bloody trouble pulsated *down* the mountainside: dissonance between spouses, families, friends, neighbors, and community members.

But the beauty of Susan's Soul (she was a writer/singer of love songs) should have the final measure of this rocky tale. It was her Death, after all, that set all else in motion, and I like to think her opening the Spirit realm challenged horror by opening to Beauty itself. *Jindabyne* provides this sense in two most subtle, quietly-stunning visual strokes. At one point we are shown water rippling in the shape of a fish skeleton, below. And at another, we see that same bony framework floating in the clouds, above. A Cosmic embrace. *Gone fishin'* indeed, for more than they imagined: a Soul-sounding from the Dreamtime.

THE GRACE OF THE MARGINALIZED
OR "THIRTEEN THANK YOU'S"

The delightful Shaman/artist Martin Pretchell has a beautiful prayer which includes the litany of "Long life, Honey in the Heart, No Evil, Thirteen Thank You's." I once heard him teach that, while we may see "13" as unlucky, we must be grateful for how much we can benefit from what is pre-judged negatively in life. Think of the wheelchair-bound Ram Dass in *Hofmann's Potion* saying that his stroke, which most others would judge as merely debilitating, became a realm of insight and meaningfulness thanks to his LSD experiences.

That is what we are going to investigate here. And celebrate. Integrating the wounded and marginalized dimensions of our world/selves, is both similar to and different from integrating the Shadow. Sometimes they overlap. But the Shadow is usually cast by our clinging to a Persona catching a preferential light, and so often involves a moral judgment, a good vs. bad polarization. Dealing with the outcast is a more tender emotional matter. When it comes to the marginalized there can be fear and avoidance, since some don't want to deal with affliction, especially if it means sacrificing a life of relative privilege.

But suffering at its best, vs. masochistic suffering, has genuine virtue. The opposite of this is conformity to the very existing systems which wound (*The Conformist*). Admitting your pain and dissatisfaction means hanging in there long enough to find or shape an alternative Domain Basin to that which originally pained you. And besides, it's delusional to think we can avoid suffering, our own or others, and inhuman not to respond to it in some heartfelt way.

We can go further and actually begin to perceive personal pain as indicative of unlived aspects of our Soul, read inner turbulent weather as an indication that we've lost our Navigational way. But realizing that we have a Way (Destiny) to lose means it can be regained, that by taking a reading from our Soul Compass, we can sail forward on a wave of renewed hope.

Imagine the couple in *Jindabyne* living from a Shamanic marriage perspective: knowing they are always accompanied by a conjoined Spirit Guardian comprehending both their potential and their woundedness.

Imagine Stewart Kane saying he made love to Claire after the fishing trip because for him she was a warm source of Eros after a chilling encounter with Thanatos. Now *that* could have penetrated to a place of true intimacy, and bound them together throughout the ensuing community storm. If only their acrimonious fight could have awakened them both to profound aware-ness of what and why each had *suffered* by going through the conformist motions in their wedlock: he by becoming a garage owner, she by becoming a mother. So much could have been redeemed when their suffering was re-vealed, if only they believed the wake-up call came from their Marriage Spirit to serve their Destinies. Thirteen Thank You's.

Sometimes we are drawn to suffering in the world out of a sense of com-passion or a desire for justice. Think of Jennifer Connolly's journalist in *Blood Diamond*, Rachel Weisz' activist in *The Constant Gardener*. And sometimes an artist is drawn to the marginalized out of a sense of profound affinity that stems from an innermost dwelling-place which no externals indicate. Such was the case with a woman photographer, born and raised to be the social equivalent of a swan, who passionately and radically preferred the company of ugly ducklings.

BEAUTY IN THE BEAST:
FUR, AN IMAGINARY PORTRAIT OF DIANE ARBUS

I'm selecting this movie more for its subject matter than its production values, however fantasmagorically engaging. I'm looking at the woman here, within and beyond the film depiction, because there are three aspects of it that rubbed (my fur?) the wrong way. So I'll address them before getting down to what of it I valued.

First there's the matter of casting. Who could imagine electing the tall, pale, willowy, flawlessly pretty, red-headed Australian, Nicole Kidman, to play the short, brunette, broodingly intense, Jewish, suicidal New York photographer, Diane Arbus? Ouch. It's not only way off the mark on the surface elements, which Arbus recognized as determinative factors in society. It *absolutely* misses the true mark of Arbus' work, which was not to warp the real into the cosmetically perfect, but to jettison all of that for the love of bringing the most bizarre "freaks" of our society out of the Shadows and into the flash of her Rolleiflex.

Then there's *Fur's* fictional upstairs neighbor, Lionel, whose body sprouts head-to-toe excess hair, and who becomes Diane's totemic Wolfman escort away from an Upper West Side life of privilege into the city's Underworld dens for the aberrant. He's played by Robert Downey Jr., whom I imagine having the wherewithal to credibly plumb the emotional depths of society's discarded. But *Fur* doesn't allow him to go there. Instead, this character is preposterously conceived as George Clooney in Chewbacca's body: both suave and cartoonish. They could have learned something from *The Elephant Man*, where another extremely physically-distorted figure showed the genuine anguish of his condition as well as the grace required to transcend it.

And finally there's the well-known fact that Diane Arbus committed suicide in her late forties. By only addressing the start of her career, however compelling in its contrast to her former stylish Society life, this future Demon retroactively haunts the story, making us question the ultimate value of what appears to be good and compassionate artistry. Why did she not prevail? As creativity is so key to Deep Cinema, encouraging us to dare bring inspired work to the Marketplace, we have to face its destructive Shadow. Artists risk depression like no others, in that their work stems so radically and intimately from themselves. Identity, not mere Persona. We're not "working for the man"; we're working for the Muse, and that covenant is Sacred.

CANDID CAMERA

Where *Fur* does work wonderfully is in showing how the scope of Diane's Soul refused to be contained or constrained by her family, no matter how intimidating (parents), devoted (husband) or dependent on her safety and well-being (daughters). She lived her Destiny. Even as a child, Diane is shown to have had a native curiosity about, e.g., Shantytown dwellers, or dead animals. But both her mother and her nanny would shelter her eyes from such nasty facts of life.

As an adult, she couldn't get enough, traveling to nudist camps, asylums, mortuaries, circus sideshows. Among her more famous signature shots (not shown in this movie) can be found a *Jewish Giant at Home with his Parents*, a manic *Boy Clutching a Toy Grenade in Central Park*, and an *Albino Sword Swallower*. Transvestites, dwarves, the physically and mentally handicapped, bag ladies, tattooed derelicts, and risqué prostitutes, all were sought out and included in her distinctive black-and-white oeuvre, which at the time was truly avant garde. An elite Socialite's high life pales in contrast to this down and dirty real life. Which is precisely the point.

It's intriguing that Arbus' choice of camera was the Rolleiflex, held at waist level with the viewfinder on top. There was nothing hiding her face from her subjects', with Nicole Kidman exposing that vulnerability beautifully. And the fact that Diane often used a strong strobe meant that her figures were not merely brought out of scapegoated obscurity, but were actually so illuminated as to cast Dark Shadows themselves. Very humanizing.

This reminds me of a Hawaiian teaching that we should bless everything we are tempted to envy or judge, since their word for "Blessing," "*Pomakai*," translates to "Sending Light into the Darkness." Intriguing too the French word "to wound" is "*blesser*." The wound as blessing, as opening to potential grace: kissing "*cousines*."

Arbus once said of her subject matter, and her society: "*Most people go through life dreading they'll have a traumatic experience. Freaks were born with their trauma. They've already passed their test in life. They're our Aristocrats.*" Well, whether *they* would assess themselves that way or not, these Untouchables compensated for a stifling aristocratic life that didn't suit Diane: she certainly wasn't at ease in the skin she was born into. But this movie falls short of a Shamanic challenge by merely depicting the courageous outset of her career, prior to the death-rebirth-death spiral of divorce, celebrity, and suicide.

ARBUS IN UNDERWORLD

If you know Diane killed herself, it makes her outré career both laudable and suspect. As with Shadow work, there's a difference between integration of our woundedness (positive) and identification with it (negative). It seems Arbus may have identified with her marginalized subjects not for their aristocracy, but precisely for their *suffering*, a suffering she artfully catalogued but didn't actually provide with a healing Domain Basin. At least not for herself. Maybe that was too much to ask of one Artist in a conservative day and age, who nonetheless boldly began outreach to, and inclusion of, Society's most rejected outcasts.

One of Arbus' lesser known portraits is a carnivalesque shot of an ornately garbed *Headless Woman*. Ironically, psychological decapitation may have been precisely what Diane required. Having taken up permanent residency in a transitional Underworld, she needed a radical change of mind-set, ego constellation, in order to resurrect. *Heads must roll.* Sometimes Initiation comes to that.

We don't consciously go the psychic Soul distance when opting for literal Death instead. Jung appreciated the desperation that might push a Soul there: *"There are many human beings who throughout their lives and at the moment of death lag behind their own potentialities. Hence their demand to attain in death that. . . which they failed to win in life."* Alas! Had she lived, it would be really, *really* fascinating to view what this singular talent would be up to today. Film perhaps? Goth Cinema? Her own radical genre?

As a child Diane Arbus was fascinated with *Alice in Wonderland*. In *Fur*, this pampered daughter of a wealthy New York department store owner/ furrier finds a classic fairy tale object, a mysterious key, among the damp hairs clogging the apartment plumbing she shares with Lionel. When she later asks why he sent her such a curiously compelling implement, he replies, "I wanted to meet a real freak." How flattering!

Indeed. Diane Arbus was an anomaly in her familial and social circles. She had to risk a larger embrace than many, include more of the bizarre and/ or wounded, to make her Soul whole. If only someone brazen, adventurous, heartfelt and real (not merely fictionalized like Lionel) could have provided the same blessed mirroring for her that she did for so many others.

There's a Buddhist saying that we all are granted a key to the gate of Heaven, and the same key opens the gate to Hell. Thirteen thank yous, Diane, for unlocking so many lonely doors. Here's to your Heavenly homecoming.

PART X

ADULTHOOD: BECOMING THE INITIATOR

....

"The way we look to a distant constellation / That's dying in a corner of the sky.
These are the days of miracle and wonder / So don't cry baby, don't cry, don't cry."
— Paul Simon, *"Graceland"*

Aging, we begin to sense our mortality, that the constellation which blessed us at birth is melting into our bones, or not, blessing this earth, or not, that we are the stuff of the gods' First Intentions which can encourage those younger than us unto seven generations, or...

We've come a long way Navigating the Soul Compass: from sustaining, Womb-Weaving Nature up through Nest-dwelling passages of childhood and adolescence, onto negotiating Trickster temptations and Shadow dancing, addressing romance and marriage (inner and outer), the lacerations of unexpected Death and the grace of woundedness. And always, always, always sounding out the authenticity of our Destiny as we aim toward becoming genuinely adult.

At some point our formative work feels satisfactory or, at any rate, we have chronologically grown into the realm of responsibility. From the perspective of the mutant Marketplace, we can be successful and still fall far short of Initiatory maturity. See *Son of the Bride*, *The Devil and Daniel Johnston*, and *Kings and Queen* for examples of apparently successful men who are emotionally arrested eternal youth. Women suffer from the opposite agenda:

encouraged to stay forever girlish, voiceless and disempowered. But such are only society's dictates and the Soul, like the Cosmos which is its ultimate starry Domain Basin, never ceases to prompt us into more and more enriching and original participation in Life: men into their soul's enchantment, women into the World with mana.

In Hawaiian teachings our core identity is Spirit Greatness. If we identify with anything less our canoe is off keel. Imagine a lei of flowers or shells around your crown, indicating your Mind. Another lei around your shoulders dipping down to your heart: Emotions. And then one around your hips, indicating the Body. At the core of them all is your Deep Self, Spirit Greatness. If your mind or emotions or body is ailing, you say just that: "my mind is racing, my heart is anxious, my body is tense." Never say "*I* am distraught." "*I*" am always *Spirit Greatness*, and allowing that little buffer between your core, Deep Self and your mortal dimensions provides extraordinary healing and empowerment.

SPIRALING ABOVE: SOUL CLEANSING & RETRIEVAL

One of the keynotes of true maturity is that we've gotten the ego-self in perspective, have begun trusting the Deep Self's inspiration more than operating in a reactionary mode due to past conditioning. We may have had experiences of Divine navigation, or of womb-weaving the true Mysterium, hinting at our wondrous potential. Another profound signifier of Adulthood is when we begin to look back at the formative chapters of our lives, however deprived or turbulent, and begin to find *meaning* there. Patterns. Skillfulness. A sense of Karmic dues paid off. This is *hugely* important, but since it is inner work, subjectivity, it is too often passed over in film for the substitution of, say, a car chase instead. We can do much better, and gain Soul-esteem.

Often we experience ourselves as hobbled by our past and know that something's gotta give if we are to access the requisite mana to proceed. We sense the satisfaction provided if only we could invert our Domain Basins and begin feeding others from the cornucopia of our insights and giftedness. Sometimes the formally uninitiated find themselves making the quantum leap required to actually provide for others that which they themselves never enjoyed. This is because suffering has been endured (a mark of the Shaman) and not collapsed into resignation, keeping internal hope alive and prowling all along the watchtower on the look-out for opportunity.

We see several of these poignant signifiers of growth blossoming within a young woman returning to the scene of her violated youth in this excellent ensemble work.

SPANNING GENERATIONS: *MARION BRIDGE*

Certainly the experience of parenting your own offspring should organically progress you into Adulthood. But not all children are conceived equally, as this Nova Scotia film shows, with the surrounding social Domain Basins quicker to judge than to help a young pregnant woman. Fortunately one's Soul can find a way to navigate even the most entangled maze, given some cleansing, retrieval, and reorientation.

Agnes (Molly Parker) is in need of both cleansing and retrieval as she returns from the big city of Toronto to the small coastal hometown she left half a lifetime ago. The fact that she's the family's black sheep, striving to be clean and sober while joining her two older sisters at their divorced mother's deathbed, assures that Archetypal gears, however rusty, will be shifting.

German-Canadian director Wiebke von Carolsfeld beautifully fulfills the Initiatory mandate of submerging into the Underworld before emerging into Heaven with her opening and ending scenes of *Marion Bridge*. Opening: dozing in an airport, Agnes enters a liminal space of daydreaming a nightmare — finding herself drowning in cold seaweed-strewn waters, an exhausted castaway. Ending: picnicking on the shore with her newly cobbled-together family, Agnes looks vibrant and promising as the camera pans into the sky, a Domain Basin she can finally call her own after expunging her father's rancid Spirit from it.

Home is the scene of a crime in which Agnes was the victim, a fact the rest of the family seems to prefer suppressing. Having borne and given up her own father's child who is now a teenager herself, Agnes not only fled the outer provinces but dove headlong into alcohol and cocaine abuse. Newly clean, sober and fairly manic in the light of health, Agnes finds herself irresistibly stalking her daughter at the adoptive single mother's local Craft Shop, spying on her through wavy psychic seaweed, as it were.

Agnes is stymied: doubtless regressing into her youth at the sight of Joanie (whom she'd named Marion), she's also imploding with resentment toward her parents' combination of abuse and neglect. The teen daughter's wonderfully painful naiveté — she's impressed that her boyfriend "drives better" after drinking, "with *better* concentration" — must also impact Agnes with the atrocity of her father's exploitation when she was so young. His oppressive Spirit, albeit in absentia, looms large over the all-female household as the mother's health wanes.

OFFLOADING THE HAIR~SHIRT

A Scapegoat (or Sin-Eater) is a dualized Totemic creature. On the one hand scorned and exiled from the group, it's actually chosen because it's the only member with a strong enough back to carry the collective sins away into a realm of transformation. In the Wampanoag Nation of Cape Cod, the family Scapegoat is revered as the "Pot Carrier" the one conscious enough to peer into the darkness of the family's tarnished Domain Basin, cleanse it out and bring them all a new Dawn: a collective Soul-scanning.

Agnes is clearly tired of playing this role, and we see her detox some hostility onto her mother as the older woman approaches the Void, intuiting that this omnipotent Domain is Solution large enough for all this family's affliction. Plying her mother with drink and cigarettes (despite her lung cancer), Agnes shows little compassion when she's reduced to coughing spasms. On the other hand, when this dying parent writes a heartfelt apology for blindness in the face of her children's suffering, Agnes is the first forthcoming to forgive. Very touching. And transformative. Able to bury her mother with love, Agnes achieves a soulful connection to the warm heart of the Earth, rendering the cold seaweedy daydream prior to her homecoming innocuous. Now gravity pulls toward inner peace. On to reclaiming her Spirit in the sky.

The film's most indelible scene is the siblings' visit to dine at their long-lost father's home where he lives with his second spouse. In the ghostly realm of incest, pregnancy, sacrifice and adoption, the stage is always crowded with complex, echoing players: the false selves mere façade for the forbidden selves. Time to break through the masks.

Apprehensive, angry, and restless, Agnes awaits the appearance of the imposing dark King who so oppressed and corrupted her youth. What emerges on the scene instead is a senile, shuffling, crepey-skinned, drooling man-child who can barely feed himself. Psychologically such an absence of former self is called a "personality death," an unnerving, erratic, uncanny loss. So we see Agnes staring at this odd zombification of her father/rapist in quiet shock, and with increasing personal authority. Sitting in silence at the dining table, she actually blossoms.

As the three daughters and their hostess exit the house into brisk coastal winds, Agnes lingers behind at the liminal threshold for one last confrontation. The old man scrambles down the vestibule steps with the eagerness of a boy craving more attention from guests he doesn't even recognize. Agnes turns and steps deeply into his personal space, once again attaining the face-to-face intimacy of the "lovers" they should never have been. If looks of distain could kill, his paltry dust would have been scattered to the four winds.

The Monster disempowered, Agnes' Soul is re-empowered: its fled dimensions enter her body like a loving Loa. She turns and paces away in a stately, ever more confident stride, getting her sea-legs as a true and liberated Adult for the very first time. What a triumph!

DUELING SOULS: *THE SON*

This Belgian-French film by the Dardenne brothers brings a most original and excruciating moral dilemma to the screen. Here the Archetypal realm provides a hallowed but harrowing echo chamber which these mere human players navigate like the benighted Indigenous Souls they are, unaware that deep Spirits seek to mount and reconfigure them. One man, Olivier (Olivier Gourmet) is wrenched out of an overlong liminal passage by a bruised and needy, damaged and damaging young Trickster who provides the older man an inestimable source of both pain and promise.

If you haven't seen Gourmet act, you're in for a treat. He's the Euro equivalent of Philip Seymour Hoffman: a physically plain, hefty, singularly unremarkable figure whose reservoirs of interior references and outer skills nonetheless result in the most subtly galvanizing performances. Gourmet once said he'd enjoy the challenge of enacting an entire stage play with his back to the audience. And you can believe it: *The Son* shows that this quiet genius of a shape-shifter can act with the back of his ear.

A DRONING TENSION

The stars must have been in challenging alignment for Olivier's character (also named Olivier, the part having been conceived for him) on the day when three bits of disturbing news rock his placid, orderly universe.

The semester is already underway for this Carpentry Teacher in a Rehabilitation Center for parolees when he's requested to take on a new student. Scanning the boy's application, he initially refuses. But soon afterward, his sober, opaque demeanor shifts into agitated gear as he scurries down staircases, peers over transoms, and lunches standing behind the cafeteria servers, all with the avid intent of getting a glimpse of this boy. Mysterious.

We know next to nothing about this vocational mentor. Could Olivier be a sexual predator skulking a once and future prey? His solo trip home at the end of a day reveals little more. The apartment is merely utilitarian in décor, the messages on his answering machine all work-related. Even his bachelor's meal of canned soup is a sad and paltry repast. Then ex-wife Magali (Isabella Soupart) comes to the door with a one-two punch: she needs to get on with life so she's remarrying. And she's pregnant. Again, Olivier appears nonplussed at first, then rushes downstairs to the residential parking lot demanding, "Why did you tell me this *today*? Why *this* day?" Clearly the Cosmos is closing in on him with pressures we cannot fully appreciate.

In an abrupt turnaround, the obsessed teacher admits the sullen student into his class. Their first encounters are mildly intimate and do nothing to dispel any suspicions one may harbor as to the adult's possibly perverse motivation. He watches the boy curled up asleep in the washroom, an intimate perspective, before awakening him and providing an exact assessment as to what size overalls he'll require for class: also quite familiar. But it's clearly a one-way fixation: no notes of recognition glimmer in the tough little scrapper's vacuous eyes. Hmmm.

CONFLAGRATION

We're one-third into the story before we get to the heart of the matter, and what a pivotal shattering that supplies. Clearly a loner, Olivier has no one to turn to for disclosure other than his ex-wife, whom he seeks out at the gas station where she works. Magali is staggered to be told that "Francis Thirion (Morgan Marinne) got out" and came to the center. When she intuits that her former husband might actually be teaching the youth she explodes, "You're crazy! He killed our son and you'd teach him?"

Olivier denies this involvement, and the fact that he can lie so easily adds to both his inscrutability and unpredictability. This in a man so meticulous and precise in his work skills and personal discipline is surely a sign of Shadow intrusion. So much so that when he packs a tarp and a rope in the back of his car before driving Frances on a solo weekend trip to an isolated Lumber Yard, we don't know if he has revenge or redemption in mind.

The egregious loss of a child is commonly enough lamented as "unnatural," "out of order," and disruptive of Cosmic cycles. When a mother or father dies, a chapter of one's past is completed. A particular parental configuration of nurturing and discipline ends, and we can either continue living from it via introjection, or we can transform it.

In *Orphans*, when the youngest son, the "college boy" suddenly no longer had to live to please his widowed mother, all sorts of shadowy dragons emerged from suppression to challenge his angelic disposition. And Agnes of *Marion Bridge*, after distancing herself from addictions and challenging her mother, was rewarded with maternal remorse, and so gained the courage to face down her once monstrous father. Thus her familial past, her Soul's human source, was reconfigured from a cold, treacherous sea to a solid grounding of her own making.

When a parent dies, we see it is the Past which is addressed. But a child's birth is all about the promise of a new *Future* for all involved, one that the parents initially have a strong hand in determining. And when that child prematurely dies, the identity of the father as a virile, protective provider also dies. Bill Plotkin, author of *Soulcraft*, refers to the loss of such an early adult dream as the surrendering of the Summer House. In the case of *The Son*, Olivier's Summer House dream of shaping a loving family went up in flames.

CITY OF REFUGE

While this movie has built from an objectified droning tension to a ship-wreck of a revelation, the final scenes trap us in a much more engaged, claustrophobic emotional turmoil. The stakes are raised when, on the trip to the Lumber Yard, Frances asks Olivier to become his guardian. Making no commitment, the man uses this request as a leverage to make the boy confess why he'd done time. We learn that while Frances had been trying to steal a car radio, a boy he hadn't seen in the back seat surprised and tried to stop him.

When Olivier demands more details of what we know was an ensu-ing lethal struggle, he's daring to intimately enter the scene of a crime that cataclysmically annihilated not only his treasured son, but also his treasured identity as spouse and father. The tension of this scene is so amped up, you'll find yourself urgently fastening your seatbelt.

On a Soul level, these two have been approaching one another for some time, over the past five years: fully one-third of the boy's life and an ample tour of Hell for the bereaved parent. Olivier, who had once worked with his brother in the family enterprise, threw out that job, and his marriage, along with the baby. The next employment he sought, as a Carpentry Teacher of juvenile delinquents, allowed him to enact the stern, exacting, moral side of fatherhood, while the capacity for sweet, honeyed, visionary nurturance had been buried with his son.

The movie's climax comes at the isolated Lumber Yard, where Olivier quietly discloses, "The boy that you killed was my son," immediately triggering fright and flight in Frances. The panting man catches up to the youth in a wooded cluster of trees, leaves, humus, and roots, a swirling morass of the living, dying, and dead. Pinning the boy to the ground with those strong and most capable of hands around his throat, which option will he choose?

Life. Releasing the boy's neck and dropping his hands to either side of his face, Olivier off-loads a vast private reservoir of grief, tension, outrage and vengeful impulse into the only Domain Basin large enough to compas-sionately absorb it all: Mother Earth.

Back at the Lumber Yard, you see these two silently working together loading planks, the lad facing a full measure of potential atonement, the man finally free to move on into his Destiny, one more intriguingly complex than he could ever have imagined. They look like the only man and boy in the world, the only possible Father and Son: Archetypal puzzle pieces as repellent as they are attractive to one another. Mysterious.

As I looked at this vast collection of wood, I could imagine Olivier building a *Toltec Altar* to ritualize his *Exit out of Hell*. I also flashed onto a vision of Hawaii's *Sanctuary of Refuge*. This outdoor, seaside Temple of towering, wooden Totemic figures was built to offer protection and sovereignty to all, even fugitives desperate and wily enough to make their way to its shore. After a Parting of the Waters, one's suffering flowed into the past, and one's Soul was free to catch the opposite, refreshing wave of forgiveness and future. Such as we just witnessed in *The Son*. Mahalo.

MISSING OR MONSTROUS MATURE WOMEN

In terms of living via the Soul Compass, it's no less than atrocious that mature women's stories aren't being told on film. It's like global Corporations over-riding Natives, Nature, and everyone else in their path (*Koyaaniqatsi: Life out of Balance*). To have men dominating our cinematic storytelling circles, with young females acting as idealized accoutrements or becoming male-identified "Yangsters," puts holistic balance entirely out of whack. We may as well just tear out of orbit and career into the Sun, kissing off the Moon and sacred depths of the Galaxy/Deep Mystery, altogether.

It's especially dismaying when women, who in actuality are hugely successful actors and culturally-mindful adults, go the Bette Davis, *Notes on a Scandal*, *Mommy Dearest*, *Monster-in-Law* route of playing repellent, radioactive psycho-babes after they cross the mid-century mark. "Oooh, Meryl Streep plays the Boss (*The Devil Wears Prada*, *Rendition*): Be afraid, be very, very afraid." As if this peerless performer wouldn't be *any* young actor's real-life, *to-die-for* Mentor.

Having done some acting, I appreciate what a friend of mine meant when she said, "I'd rather play crazy-bitch any day than well-rounded and adjusted." To which I say, "Both are boring and predictable. Why not a third option, 'crazy like a fox' instead?" Have a woman shrewd enough to face down damaging Domain Basins and transfigure them to her uniquely realized values. Why not? Stories only pack a *wallop* of originality when they dare tell a story from a radically subjective perspective. It'd be good for Navigators to have their boats rocked, lured into foreign waters by Sirenes of strength.

But too often when a grown Womb-Weaver integrates her Navigator's skills enough to move and speak (Uhane) in the world with genuine authority, she's cast as the equivalent of that Medieval traveling minstrels' prop, "the Mouth of Hell." Even if it's true that the reproductive, feel-good hormones drop off at that stage, there must be a natural reason for that, like prompting women to become more discriminating about the world.

How come only curmudgeonly old men are considered endearing, discerning, and honorable? My own Shamanic journeying on this matter has shown me that at midlife women are invited beyond the nurturing Moon-Earth embrace into the vastness of the Milky Way, where we have light, darkness, stars, moons and meteorites at our creative, reflective, and destructive disposal.

ASSININE: *CHECKING OUT*

What's even worse than the movies' monster-crones are the mute, crippled and comatose contenders in the older women's field. In *Children of Man*, Michael Caine has the most humane, engaging role: a retired activist, living in a glorious woodland hideaway, growing multiple strains of marijuana and reminiscing while the world apocalyptically self-destructs around him. His wife, however, has about all the life of his potted pot, bound to a wheelchair and largely checked out.

Speaking of *Checking Out*, this comedy has got to be the worst variation on "old man surrounded by adoring young things with dead wife confined to pictures from her prime." Heaven forbid we should have to look at an *older* woman for any extended duration! Then the older guys in attendance might feel their mortality, something easy to dismiss when you're surrounded by the firm, fresh and dewy. How delusional!

In this case a retired Shakespearean actor (Peter Falk, b. 1927) is contemplating a "suicide party," since retirement and the death of his acting partner/wife have drained his life of its former juiciness. So we have the infuriating "noble widower" again. Only this time, he's devoted one whole chamber of his upscale apartment to his late beloved. Sounds sweet? Wait.

Since they were a famous couple who traveled in international artsy circles, the wife was always having her portrait painted by famous artists. Make that "portraits" of one particular part of her anatomy: her ass.

That's right: the Butt-Room. The Cheek Chamber. Derriere Den. Temple of Tushy. Unbelievable — new lows (pun intended). Does anyone even take a *second* to imagine how unphotogenic the personable Peter Falk's fanny might be? Ewwwwww! Double standards. His character's legacy is that of a *Great Thespian*, while his wife and co-star's legacy is that of a *great ass*. The same can be said of many young females who play the polarized puella roles in these ageist, sexist movies: they're too naïvely *assinine* to know that they're doing their culture, and their future careers, a disservice. Just say no, and insist upon better scripts.

In the words of the young, lovely Naomie Harris from *Pirates of the Caribbean*:

"Everything starts in the writing. And getting more and more women's perspective will have a huge impact on the quality of films we'll get. At the moment we don't see ourselves as we really are because it's only men writing for us. I've read a lot of films where I've thought, 'No woman would ever say that! No woman would ever behave like that!'"

Think of Marisa Tomai pathetically jiggling her boobs like a retro bimbo fantasy figure in *Before the Devil Knows You're Dead*. Naomie's complaining, and she got to play a Voudon Mambo *and* the Nature Goddess Calypso! Shows how deep the hunger runs for just plain human female Uhane. And it only gets worse in movie-land as women age.

STEERING ON HALF A COMPASS

While Julie Christie (b. 1941) did a laudable turn as a woman mentally atrophying due to Alzheimer's disease (*Away From Her*), again we have an older woman *drifting*, not all there. Christie herself is a passionately engaged spokes-woman, backing vital indigenous and ecological causes. A radical activist movie ("crazy like a fox") about the likes of her would be more inspirational for 60-something women, and those who will become them. To showcase the psychological demise of an aging woman, in a dramatic playing field devoid of mature women, is a tad redundant.

This is tragic from a Shamanic Soul Compass perspective, since Elders should not just fade out of the cultural picture (other than slowing down physically), but should enjoy honing their best, most enduring, authoritative qualities. Humans face death like fetuses face birth (*2001: A Space Odyssey*), only we're aiming for rebirth as Ancestors, Loa, Aumakua, where we take on a deeper role of sustaining Universal Order. No less. Unless we don't do our Diamond-Cutting, Pearl-Spinning, stellar, lunar work, in which case we just join "les morts." We need movies which teach Elders how to shine forth, and show adults worrying that they may not. And if Heaven is only shown suffused with the Spirits of dead *men*, then it can default to a harshly judgmental realm, lacking womanly attributes.

I personally boycott most May-December cinematic pairings where the male star is some three (or more) decades older than his female co-star for no reason other than providing titillation for the entitled old dudes. That's about as easy to do as avoiding land-mines in Cambodia, because they're everywhere. *Winter Passing* is the movie that prompted me to finally make that resolve. *Entrapment*'s Catherine Zeta-Jones (b. 1969), serving up her cat-woman curvy bod as eye candy to Sean Connery (b. 1930), also tried my patience. Oh, and Michael Caine with some anima-ideal, neo-natal, stereotypical Asian beauty in *The Quiet American*....

Don't get me started, the list is endless, and endlessly boring *if* you know better, which Caine and Connery should; their talented wives aren't ingénues. The ever-lovely actor/activist Audrey Hepburn was actually a year *older* than Connery, 47 to his 46, when they supplied a fine and credible middle-aged pairing in the Middle Ages (*Robin and Marian*). But how rare is that?

The young female who stays glued to the old man is too often copping out, cheating *Life*, hitching a ride, playing it safe, eternally staying home as a puella. And the older man with the *trophy* wife who won't *atrophy* in his day, is often cheating *Death*, playing it safe, and staying emotionally a puer.

A young woman looks at an older man with awe, alright (*Guinevere*), awe that anyone should live so long, and concern that she herself might not make it other than as a bag lady. Sorry to burst your bubble, gents, but that's often the appeal. At best she wants to admire and learn from your skills, and have you genuinely bless hers. At worst she's willing to sign on for the glow and security of being chosen by what the Australian Aboriginals call "an Initiated Man of Status." Only those young Tribal females are also allowed younger sweethearts, and also remain sexually active well into their Eldership.

I'm not saying there can't be genuine love across decades, but the personal needs to pay off publicly and politically, as well as privately, for this to mean anything: the couple needs to go toe-to-toe in Domain Basins larger than the boudoir to sustain true equality. Would viewers have flocked to see *The Girl in the Café* (Bill Nighy, b. 1949, with Kelly MacDonald, b. 1976) if it was *The Woman at the G8 Summit*? Nighy's *older* real-life partner, Diana Quick (b. 1946) could have played *that role* to a polish!

MAY~DECEMBER: REBIRTH OR DEATH?

Dreamkeeper includes the classic, universal story of a young Native man needing to "kiss" an old hag in order to learn her wisdom and save his life. The Shamanic teaching here is that if you really want to go the distance, die to a youthful chapter and enter a new level of consciousness, you have to age. And once you embrace this "old" age, you're opened to a truly new, expanded horizon, in the face of which you're youthful again. The young man lies with the old woman and she's transformed into a nubile beauty. Great!

Only in Viagra-saturated films such as *The Human Stain*, the young beauty (Nicole Kidman, b. 1967) beds down with the aging gent (Anthony Hopkins, b. 1937) and wakes up dead. Well, not immediately, but she *is* doomed. She's certainly not waking up with Johnny Depp after bedding down with Cronos, shall we say. Hardly an equal opportunity Mythic exchange. An old man's fantasy is a young woman's nightmare, if only because she's likely in for a long widowhood.

These May-December pairings usually involve a stealthy bargain on the part of the older man who, like the mythic Amor with Psyche, will only make love in the dark, so his true identity is hidden from judgment. (Wham, bam! Who *was* that masked man?) It's an opaque, blinding darkness he provides, like the ink squirted by a squid in subterfuge. Or it's a shallow darkness he wants: his girlish companion's cloud of unknowing. Because, you see, the young female is not so much stealthy as sadly naive, still ignorant of her depths, vulnerabilities and powers, about which she can best be taught by an older, wiser woman. If she can find one in Hollywood. As this chapter illustrates, mentoring the youth of our tribes is one vital gear-churning of our growth. But if older women are just asked to compete with younger ones, it messes up the Buddha field.

Women are human, *and* natural *and* divine, just as men are. And when men stop the schizoid splitting of the female into either demonic (because not indulgent) Monstrous Mothers, or adoring (because dependent) Puella Partners, we can all be restored to mutually enhancing, empowering and loving exchange. Which many of us have — now let's just bring it to the screen! In the old traveling tent revival shows, performers saved the more risqué acts for when the children had gone to bed. Now we have childishly fantasized female behavior extolled well past their bedtimes.

OLD DOG, NEW CHICKS: *WINTER PASSING*

You can't reference Shakespeare in a movie without paying some serious obei-sance to the Bard as a playwright. As a feminist even *he* was a bit of a victim of his age, but the fact that the movie *Winter Passing*, which makes reference to Will's stage play *The Winter's Tale*, is actually more sexist/ageist than he was centuries ago, says something about the sad state to which drama has devolved over the millennia regarding mature women.

This movie has some good players, some quirky, delightful elements, and even some genuine pathos, so I'm not dismissing it out of hand by any means. It provided my first sighting of Ms. Dechanel, who looks promising. And a scene with Ed Harris' character waking up from a nightmare on an outdoor bed is wrenchingly wonderful: it shows how our Souls best sound out their true wildness at home in Nature. But on this issue of preserving older men in a youthful estrogen solution, while killing off their female chronological peers, *Winter Passing* is downright appalling.

Reese Holden (Zooey Deschanel, b. 1980) plays a struggling New York actress with a dual alcohol-and-coke habit, a dying kitten, and bad taste in lovers. So she's easy game when a book agent comes along offering her $100,000 for the publication of old love letters she'd recently inherited from her mother, a famous novelist. Problem is, they're back in the Midwest at

Dad's house (Ed Harris, b. 1950), also a famous novelist, also an alcoholic, also a long-estranged parent.

So Reese cops an advance, drowns the ailing kitty, boards a bus, and shows up at the door of her currently not-so-reclusive father's house where she's met by Corbit (Will Ferrel) and Shelley (Amelia Warner, b. 1982), not a couple, just a couple of Dad's devotees. Seems like he's created his own little Utopia since his wife's demise, with these quasi-servants tending to his every eccentric need 24/7.

SKEWING SHAKESPEARE

Before dieseling out of the Big Apple, Reese was part of a production of Shakepeare's *The Winter's Tale*, a play within this plot that requires a nod of serious recognition, especially since they highlight the final, climatic scene. It is here that King Leontes, after some 16 years of mourning, comes upon a chapel with a statue of his late wife, Queen Hermione. He'd driven her into exile when she was young and pregnant, believing the child to be the fruit of the Queen's affair with the Bohemian King. Too late, an Oracle was consulted, who assessed Leontes' suspicions as mad, jealous delusions, and he's been mournfully in search of his daughter and only heir ever since.

The Queen didn't actually die, but since that was widely rumored, she'd taken advantage of the tales to remain safely encapsulated until she learned her husband's wrath had subsided. Now, in the face of his grief, her "statue" magically comes to life, the King and Queen embrace and renew their vows just in time to celebrate their daughter's wedding. Fright, flight, and freeze, followed by atonement and thaw: Winter passes.

Only in *Winter Passing*, "King" Don Holden stays put, with his sole heir, Reese, coming to him. She's navigating, he's holed up drinking. Nature is corrupted. Like the child "Perdita" in Shakespeare's play, Reese is well and truly "lost," and deserved more than her self-absorbed, career-driven parents had provided her. Only instead of Father doing the requisite regal atonement, (like the Mother lovingly managed in *Marion Bridge*), he has a total precious melt-down when Reese so much as swears (angry Uhane = bad girl). So she is dutifully reduced to taking a page from his worshipful caregivers' book, becoming teary, simpering and apologetic *to him*. (Ugh.)

Mom's not around to buffer the narcissistic sink-hole of Dad's ego. Besides, it's not enough that she's dead, but they really go to work making her the villain. ("Don't seem right, sir, whipping a dead (wo)man.") Her subject matter for writing is dissed as more bourgeois than Don's. And she largely ignored Reese too, *really* nasty behavior in a *mother*. Her death's revealed to have been a suicide, not *because* of her husband by any measure, but *despite* his long-suffering loyalty to her (the noble widower again). Old love letters disclose that she'd harbored self-destructive ideation from the beginning of their affair, and he was *always there for her.*

How about a little "Show, don't tell" here? But then we'd have to (shudder) actually *look at* and *listen to* a woman as old as, say, Ed Harris. Instead we have the 20-something former-student-turned-maid presumptuously and obnoxiously filling in the dead woman's back-story. And we see the old photos along the stairwell of when the wife/mother was alive, young, swan-necked and handsome. But somber, you know: suicidal. At least it's better than *Checking Out*'s rump room. Or is it?

Although Don emotes anguishingly, it's all about *his* feelings, with little revealed about the woman he purportedly grieves. And she's certainly not welcome to thaw and come back to life either, in any way, shape or form, since she's in a crypt rather than a Shakespearean chapel or coma. Ono. That resurrection's reserved for the King, with his perky young princesses prompting publication of his new novel, and thus the promise of Spring.

Not only did this movie fail to *Save the Cat*, it also killed off the Queen, permanently, when a little more plagiarizing from *The Winter's Tale* would have offered a much better option for everybody. Tragedy cloaked in semi-Comedy.

RESTORING THE DAZZLING DEPTHS

Note bene: Culturally we can point to someone as soulful, savvy and spiritually disciplined as Leonard Cohen (b. 1934) opting for a May-December partnership, with the jazz chanteuse Anjani Thomas (b. 1959). So we have to accept that even grown men apparently capable of seriously relating to older women may still go in for the youthful erotic quota. Think of Cohen's lyrics: "Had a dream about you baby, just the other night: most of you was naked, but some of you was light." *Some* of you.

As for older women, growing more and more knowing about our inner light (and darkling depths), and less apt to lounge around in thongs: we just have to create and endorse films that make wisdom erotic and necessary for the later years — the essential oxygen mixture to swim the Unknown, dare the *Mysterium Tremons*, ignite the awe of truly going beyond. It has been scientifically proven that intrigue with Mystery ignites our brains' production of dopamine. Consider Sophie B. Hawkins' song entitled, "Mysteries We Understand." Older women *get* that, and if lucky, over time are both suffused and surrounded by it. Think of the children's song about the Old Woman ascending over the Moon, with youngsters then clustering around her, begging to learn how to fly. Her loving response? "Well, yes, by-and-by." Over time. Get grounded first, then your sea-legs... Flight? You *earn* it.

I'm sick of *not seeing* adult females "fly" on screen. Whenever I witness older women's faces glaze over in movie theatres at yet another trivializing depiction of their lot, I always think of the wonderful Susan Traherne line from *Plenty*: "You don't know how much it costs me to pretend to be this stupid." Wouldn't that make a wonderful bumper sticker in L.A.?

Deep Cinema talks a lot about the Law, Nature's ways. And while that differs in different tribes, with coastal peoples needing navigational lore (Astronomy, etc.) vs. the hunting skills (Botany, etc.) of the forests, at bottom the Law begins as the Universal spiraling of entwined opposites. Sometimes this is depicted as two snakes, one white, one black, one ascending, one descending, one yang, one yin. If this represented the majority of Hollywood's male-female pairings, the female snake would be cut off in midlife, leaving the male doubling back, the whole Spirit of the infrastructure gone awry, DNA spliced.

Recall the perception of the yang, male model as "the Word made Flesh," and the yin, female model as "the Flesh finding Voice." This requires a whole re-orientation to appreciate where women could be coming from: instinctual inner/under-standing power vs. abstract, cerebral "power over." Both are needed, both male and female values and voices. And venues: an even playing field on which to consolidate these power bases. "Men's Business and Women's Business," as the Aborigines call it. THAT's what's missing, and has been for so long that the loss is hard to measure: it bleeds off into a Cosmic squall of grief which, if attended to, could paradoxically get our Soul ships back on course.

BUTTERFLY BUDS

It's understandable how both men and women may initially resist the call to integrate their contra-sexual skills. Navigators don't want their richly laden galleons to sink in what appears to them as a treacherous, womb-woven whirlpool: "Beyond this point, there be demons!" And Womb-Weavers don't want the spangled light of their richly dark depths eclipsed by what they perceive as some Navigator's solar ego glare. We resist what we ultimately need to integrate because, at first, it seems threatening to our uni-lateral gender-identity's Comfort Zone.

As it so often is the case, *Love* is the answer to the fear we face. Just as loving those who have died makes the inhabited Cosmos more personal an overarching Domain, so does loving a partner give us a chance to negotiate a fertile dance with the Archetypal Other. A woman must learn the glow of her own light in order to move it into the world: is she lunar, dawn, high noon, candle-light, the Aurora Borealis, or a flashing opal sunset? And a man must abide with the vortex long enough to see it as providing a classic, natural Initiatory Domain: spiraling down and gushing forth, enfolding and un-folding, teaching him to trust his emotional authenticity and inner knowing, death and rebirth: the pirate's Black Pearl surviving the maelstrom.

Ultimately, resistance to the best of our gender opposite aborts our growth. We can look to butterfly cells for an answer to this conundrum, as they provide an overview of the requisite process.

Yes, butterfly cells. In their metamorphosis from caterpillar to chrysalis to winged wonder, these beings undergo an Initiation of gruel-ing proportions. Yet their outcome is so beautiful and delicate that we rarely look to them as guides for courage, risk, and triumph. But harken to this: inside of the caterpillar is a cluster of cells called "imaginal buds" which already promise its Destiny as Butterfly. While the wee wormlike, spiky, furry creature crawls the earth, is a part of it already imagining, say, flight through the vast canopy of the rain forest, or even thousands of miles beyond?

Well, the trouble is, at this stage of the game, the immune system of the caterpillar actually experiences vertigo at the prospect of such a quantum leap, sensing these visionary buds as alien, something to be destroyed. Only after the immune system itself is mulched out in the soupy, liminal womb of the chrysalis do these cells have their say, igniting and fashioning the last, most stupendous stage of life: winged bliss (remember those photon cells ~ "eyes" ~ on their genitals)!

This is a great metaphor for male-female discord. Some men, in their paranoid resistance to women's power, have organized the social equivalent of overwrought immune systems, literally wiping women out like so many millions of threatening, imaginal cells. Whether an East Indian woman dies on a pyre or in a purposely set kitchen fire is even money in my book. *The Lady's Not for Burning*, as playwright Christopher Fry avers. But we're so in denial about the extent of such damage that I'm going to turn back to the Inquisitional Age in Europe, the scene of the cultural crime as illustrated in *The Burning Times*, so we can see the woman's wisdom lost, which must be regained.

WOMB WITH A VIEW: *ANCHORESS*

Here's a unique log-line for you: "Ecstasy and Orthodoxy in the 14th Century!" You can guess on which side of that divide most of the empowered men could be found. The wonder of this story is that one young woman, Christine Carpenter (Natalie Morse), stays true to her Earth-sourced capacity for ecstasy despite oppression by church, state, the military, and even her own cowardly father (Pete Postlewaite). It probably helped that her mother (Toyah Willcox) was a firebrand, although *she* meets a tragic end. Of course.

The keynote here for Shamanic consciousness is *respect for interiority*. Two of the few staunch rules of Huna are that you never use your mana to control the life of another, and you never willfully do another harm. We shouldn't need veils and chastity belts to be reminded that the interiority of the female needs reverence and ripening before she can move in the world confidently and safely. But young women desperately do need modeling on how to shun premature, exploitative penetration. Not only by men but by peer and mutant Marketplace-driven images of themselves (*Thirteen*). Movies like *Whale Rider* and *Anchoress* point beyond the youthful surface to burgeoning spiritual lives, providing much, much better options.

Where does a fledgling Medieval woman turn when her mother, an herbalist, is unhappily wed, and her only suitors are a boorish soldier and a secretly uncelibate, decidedly randy priest? To Our Lady, of course, making beautifully-designed offerings of apples (uh-oh, Eve!) to her statue in a church alcove, to be blessed in return with voices and visions.

So fulfilling is her accord with the Blessed Mother, or "God, our Mother," as the peasants call her, that Christine vows herself to the life-long devotion of being an Anchoress: a walled-in recluse whose inner companionship is Divine and whose only access to the outer world is a window through which pilgrims beseech her advice and healing. This young woman's alignment to a deeper world, with the wisdom of her flesh and of the earth, is evident from the start, and only grows stronger via her Mystical communications.

The sinister minister is a sadly predictable piece of work, impregnating a local woman, only to dismiss her. He then complains when Christine's Mother, Pauline, as midwife, delivers a stillborn: "Another soul condemned to everlasting Hell and you'll pay the price!" He doesn't want the child, evidence of his broken vow of chastity, but isn't beyond using its death as part of a litany of sins with which to condemn the older woman as a Witch. The more obvious reasons were that she knew of his sexual indulgences, resented his 'burying' her daughter alive, and was always cursing the church hierarchy ("I piss on the lot of them!") literally squatting down to angrily pee in his presence when he commands that she stay away from "his" Anchoress.

EMOTIONAL BUDS

Follow the feelings. The Unihipili holds them, occasionally flooding our more rational Uhane. But remember all our mana starts from our "lower" Nature Spirit and we can't ignore its truth, its programming, its inherent disposition toward pleasure and away from pain. And the truth of the matter here was that Pauline angered and frightened the priest, and he pretended to be above all that, condemning her from an elevated churchly posture. After whipping the villagers into a condemnatory frenzy, he joins them, along with her flaccid dunce of a husband, to greedily watch Pauline drown in a well.

I see emotions as part of those imaginal buds which men too often resist in their personal, Initiatory evolution. Huna teaches that emotions fuel the efficacy of our prayer-actions: "If you're not on the floor laughing or crying, you're not praying." So emotions provide the connective tissue between our human and Divine selves, and are supplied by our Nature spirit. Thank God(dess) scientists are starting to catch up with Indigenous wisdom in this regard, asserting that *emotions and consciousness tend to be present or absent together.*

Men have been acculturated toward an impossibly objectifying, rational posture, and thus feel weakened or overwhelmed, swamped from below, when admitting to emotions. So they often project or repress them. In T. S. Eliot's words, consciousness is "music heard so deeply/That it is not heard at all." By some, since it plays out in the luscious, treacherous feeling zone. Time to tune in and listen up, men. And begin to express yourself (Uhane) from this essential realm.

Christine certainly has her Uhane mojo running, and verbally holds her own when the cleric wants her artwork to depict Mother Mary in innocuously pure, heavenly sky-blue robes. The young visionary counters that Mary wears red (blood, fire, passion) and emotions certainly flare as they engage in a verbal sparring match of "Red, *blue*, red, *Blue*, RED!" Christine continues to sound out the theme of interiority by saying her "visions" extend to the everyday mundane: "I smelt Her when I broke my bread, I saw Her in my cup." She also confirms the Divine Mother's love of Her manifest world by saying Her Voice is "like milk, like bird's wings." But when the priest asks what that divine Voice discloses, Christine bleeds away into mysterious Kapu territory upon which he cannot trespass, answering "It calls me." (pause) Invitation only.

INNER WORLDS: SACRED AND PROFANED

Certainly her earthly mother's Spirit-voice must have called out from the watery grave to Christine, adding to increasing promptings that the young woman escape confinement. She does so by burrowing under the church alcove's walls, emerging from the Earth fingers first, like a human flower blossoming. Descent before Ascent, from Lower to Upper Worlds: she climbs into a ship-shaped tree-house, thus also claiming the Heavenly vistas as her purview. Integrating the Navigator.

In Middle World, Christine becomes the prey of all who would destroy her independence. (Even our Aumakua doesn't transgress our free will so!) She must go to the city, seeking out church leaders in order to be officially released from her Anchoress vows. The local priest had already become apoplectic when her artistic work conflated the sexual and the sacred: "The Devil likes women's bodies better because it is easier for him to find an entrance there... to conceal himself in their snaky, changing shapes, their foul smells, their loose and flagrant forms." One word: "Projection," you horny devil, you.

While *Anchoress* is, for the most part, as earthy and unadorned as a peasant's frugal bowl of soup, it starts shifting into the fantastic with that tree-ship scene. Perhaps director Chris Newby wanted to imply that anything above the bodily and the enclosed, the alcoves and watery wells, were realms far-fetched, suspect. Surely this message is reinforced when Christine strides into the city cathedral to confront the bishop, the would-be sublime becoming decidedly surreal, the edifice walls blasted, pitted and crumbling.

The equally crumbling old bishop is the most ungrounded of all the players in this Medieval morality tale, sitting atop a rickety scaffolding with a ladder attached, two candles on either side of him in all their dripping, flaccid, phallic impotence. Christine accosts him, insisting her vows be rendered null and void because, "You lied! The Church is not Her house! Her house is the ground!" His response, "I cannot see you! I cannot hear you!" And to his minions, "She must be re-interred!"

So our holy Uhane, who *can* see and hear and speak for the Sacred in juicy Nature, bolts. She slithers fabulously between the more predictable roles of heroine or victim, scrambling onward like a stealthy anaconda to become something more unique and unpredictable. Down the ladder and through a trap-door she goes into the cavernous Underworld, with the fluttering of bird's wings providing Annunciation of the Goddess' realm. Christine's face is beatific as she makes her way through the amorphous cavernous forms, semi-human, animal and Divine, toward an inner Light. We the audience spelunk right down after her into this concealed grotto, trusting in a darkling, glowing Maternal Presence that lives to see, hear, and lovingly liberate us, Eternally.

HEALER OR HERETIC: *SORCERESS*

Anchoress does a wonderful job sounding out the value of the earthy and the inner as Sacred, the natural as Numinous. It also shows that such "mystical" awareness, even when confined to a walled-in chamber, has significant political consequences. Consciousness influences Manifestation, in fact is the first wave of it. This provides good counter-balance to the false belief that Mysticism only flourishes apart from "real" life to provide personal consolation, and evaporates once in public realms. Oh no.

I like to think that after Christine escaped, she was able to become a wise Woodland Woman, such as featured in this splendid tale of the *Sorceress*, whom we also find in the cross-hairs of church and state.

Medievalist, Art Historian, co-Producer and co-Screenwriter, Pamela Berger was inspired to write this story by 13th-century accounts of a Dominican monk who was a part of the early Inquisition in France. His treatise shows adequate cause for this pious predator to have brought a certain healer, herbalist and "Mistress of the Beasts" to trial and probable death as a heretic. But ultimately he did not. This curious gap between evidence documented and execution denied ignited Berger's imagination. So she created a story which shows the monk's condemnatory eyes being turned inward for a personal reckoning instead.

One of the key teachings of Deep Cinema is the poetic note "the world is too much with us, late and soon." Middle World, that is. And Middle Self. The mutant Marketplace and the distended Ego. Recall that church and state worked together in the Middle Ages as negative Tricksters to deprive the peasantry of their landholdings. So the solution to be provided for this abysmal distortion can be found in celebrating characters with Shamanic consciousness, claiming all three dimensions of world and self. Those characters with *lesser* awareness would surely be the ones who have to grow, as is the theme here.

INDIGENOUS FOLK

Of course the Dominican friar, Etienne de Bourbon (Tcheky Karyo), with his Aristocratic family roots and Theological education, strides into this isolated village with an innate sense of superiority and entitlement, however arrogantly he protests his humility. He tries to enlist the support of the local cleric (Jean Carmet) in routing out enemies of the Faith, a pursuit the good, older, wiser priest dismisses as absurd: "There are no heretics in my parish. My people are as pious as they are poor." But the intruder remains as rabid in his quest as a dog with a bone.

Speaking of canines, *Sorceress* begins with, and repeatedly spirals back to, the tale of an elegantly speckled greyhound, Guineford, who (back in the ninth century) rescued a Count's baby from death by snakebite. The Count returned home to misread the aftermath of the struggle — a tipped cradle, a bloodied Guineford — and impetuously killed the loyal dog. Over the years the peasants' reverence for this beautiful creature elevated him to the rank of a saint, as in the instance of a Haitian Ancestor becoming a Loa, an animal becoming a Hawaiian family's Aumakua. Guineford's burial site was marked with a Celtic triskele, an emblem of power, and became a site of healing for ailing babies. The current Count of the region is shown to be as brutish as his predecessor, flooding the people's land for his personal gain.

This latter issue provides a subplot for this morality tale. A saboteur, a young family man, comes under arrest for vandalizing the Count's dam, and is imprisoned in a tower to waste away. But his visiting wife, her breasts ripe with mother's milk, suckles him, as well as smuggling in a rope of hemp by which he makes his eventual escape.

An aside: a popular performance by Shamans of old was 'the Rope Trick,' a conjurer's performance in which a hemp cord was cast upward to a nether region into which the Shaman would scramble to perform great feats. Hemp was used for these ropes not only because the fibrous vegetation was indigenous to the regions, but also to credit the Spirit of a power plant with altering consciousness: traveling up and down from Middle World.

It comes across as subtle tribute to Mother Earth, the Feminine Divine, that in *Sorceress* the rope is used for *descent*, indicating Spirit as inherent. The phrase used among the Chuckechee for a Shaman falling into a journeying trance was "Na naarkin": "He sinks." Think "inner knowing," faith as fidelity to the *in*sights you gain. A yin-yin situation.

TOE TO TOE, BRO'

The good Trickster priest has already confided to his housekeeper (and probable life companion) his assessment of the Inquisitor's eyes: "like a bat's — fierce, unblinking, and blind." When the monk wanders into the sorceress' woodland domain with his nose in his breviary, he obviously only has eyes for his abstract, sky-based God. As Theologian Mary Daly noted in *Beyond God the Father*, "The new space has a kind of invisibility to those who have not entered it."

The eyes of the woods-woman, Elda (Christine Boisson), are anything but distracted, with her first request to the friar — that he move his *Shadow* off her collection of drying leaves — resonating on levels physical and psychological. He needs a gravitational Shadow blessing to get real. Etienne's avid gathering of evidence against Elda as a "vetula" using crafts of the Devil, is prompted as much by his sexual conundrums as by church dictates. Elda is a very comely woman who was widowed immediately after her youthful wedding, and so is a bit of a Loa already. Torn between worlds, the wonders of the woods and the grief of her loss, she nonetheless tirelessly serves the more complete family lives of the villagers.

The priest obviously respects Elda, working right alongside her when those dying need attendance, and all of this infuriates Etienne de Bourbon. Sainted dogs, tamed wolves, plants for divination, serpents for fertilization, nocturnal pagan rituals, all whip the monk into a sanctimonious frenzy, culminating in his condemnation of Elda as a Witch. But her unwavering articulation (Uhane) of her knowing is more than a match for the monk. And even as he pronounces her a fatal judgment, a lurid chapter from his past comes back to bite him with a serpent's acuity. Saint Guineford would surely have approved.

Curious? I'm sure. But as restoration of Deep Mystery is part of the task of Deep Cinema, I find myself disinclined to reveal any more particulars of this delicious fable. Please enjoy it for yourself. Suffice it to say that the peasants outwit the monk. And, like the Voudon and Hula dancers, Elda knew how to "raise and spread the light" from within the Earth. In other words: she had the ballast to hold her own. And that kind of truly grounded Womb-Weaver can go toe-to-toe with a sky-based "Brother" anyday. A sublime lesson for the uprooted everywhere: profound liberation for all takes place when women are also seen and recognized; have no doubt about it!

Third Interlude

CREATIVITY
AS SOLUTION

"The goal of life is not to possess power but to radiate it."
— Henry Miller

By now the creative among you — writers, actors (shape-shifters), directors, etc.— should have a sense of what needs to be navigated and negotiated if you are to engage in Deep Cinema. When Middle World is *too much* or *too little* for the realization of your Destiny, then you must descend to shake up "Hell" and ascend to recreate "Heaven" in order to contend with Middle World satisfactorily. Heeding, healing and harmonizing the Spiritual powers of all three dimensions is Shamans' work at its most essential. Just look at their sacred regalia: with every bone, quill, shell, fur and feather, they gain another "eye" into the layered realms, with bio-spiritual savvy.

The last chapter was vital for acquiring such an orientation. By restoring grace to grottos, dignity to dogs, power to plants and faith in females, we have gained restoration of a much more Indigenous world-view. With all of this in mind — the damage of the Inquisition, the interiority of the *Anchoress*, and the powers of the *Sorceress* — I'm suggesting that we break through the bedrock of *any* misogynistic systems, be they religious, social or economic, and change our attitude towards what's cooking beneath — from an idea of "Hell," to that of the Cosmic Cauldron, Chalice, or Holy Grail.

195

We must "re-cognize" the much-feared Underworld as an ultimately loving Domain Basin that won't forget or forsake so much as a hair of our heads. Yes, a region which is certainly grueling at times is actually a Womb woven lovingly enough to contain all our injured, repressed and rejected Soul dimensions. All our impassioned, unlived dreams dwell there, until we have the courage and consciousness to enact the required scannings, retrievals, eliminations, resurrections. Which isn't to say it doesn't absolutely feel like Hell at times. But if Kali and Pele roam those infernal depths as our fiercely-loyal Mothers. . . .

Even Freud caught on that imploring Upper World without passionate guts and gospel from Below leaves us in a state of abstraction, feeling lost and abandoned. Acheron is the Greek Underworld river, timelessly flowing beneath Middle World consciousness, circulating through our bloodstreams in varying states from polluted to pristine. Freud was fond of this line from Virgil's Aeneid: *"If I cannot bend the gods, then I shall stir up Acheron."*

The Hawaiians know you *cannot* bend the ears of Aumakua *without* stirring up Unihipili. When someone asks, in exasperation, "What the Hell's the matter with you?" they're acknowledging that your lower self/Nature Spirit is looping toxic negative programming that impedes graceful, effective exchange in the present. You need a *kala* — a cleansing.

My own Shamanic experience in the darker realms has shown me that they are inhabited by as many valiant totemic Spirit guides as Demons. Yes, disguised Angelic beings swim (dog-paddle?) the sulphuric ethers awaiting our descent to help us reclaim whatever treasures have been lost. Jesus descended into "Hell" before ascending into Heaven. Who's to say He wasn't restored to the best of Himself below? That the fires of Hell aren't displaced, suffering, flaming spirits fallen from Heaven?

The philosopher Nietzsche has said it most powerfully: "Whoever has built the new Heaven has found strength for it in his own Hell."

WORLD WEAVERS & MAP MAKERS

Recognizing the Death and Rebirth round of Initiation in life affords the Artist a gem of a gift — perspective. After a few distinctive chapters play out, you begin to get some genuine understanding of the *shape* of your life-map:

the contours of its peaks and valleys, water sources and weather systems, its Totemic Creatures, and solar, lunar, Cosmic cycles. Try to name your life's originating and repeating themes. Shamanic consciousness always includes the Creation Story, asking where in it humanity can best participate. In creating a movie, you must ask yourself what World you are composing (present), how it came about (past), and where its evolution tends (future).

Lacking formal Initiation, can you say when your life truly began? *Your* life? Some people's Creation Story does begin with a wonderful childhood to which they can return (via memory) for renewed blessing whenever needed. For others there is no nostalgia whatsoever, as they were born with Paradise ahead, the one they will create. For them Creation begins with the discovery of their vocations. Others find bedrock in partnership, marriage, or in Nature. For still others, life purpose is revealed in catastrophe, a point they never would have *consciously* chosen. When and where did your real life initiate?

Deep Cinema paints Middle, Lower and Upper Worlds, usually in that order: present, past, and future. Some mild nudge, increasing awareness, or outright panic in the *Now* demands that you make the descent for purging or reclamation. Ask yourself the nature of your key players' discontent or torment, what Hell they endure along the spectrum from stoically to hysterically. Ask yourself what they await, desire, or need in order to exit their particular Soul incarceration. The flutter of a dove's wings, a flash of inspiration, or an embodied god striding right towards them? (How about Sean Connery's brief guise as Shaman in *The Man Who Would be King*? Delicious! The musical group, October Project, sings of a similar sensual "god who dances in the rain.") Then go the distance to gain ascent, re-scribing the books of "Heaven" in order to create a New World. Or show the tragedy of failing to do so.

True Artists' need to be authentic makes their biographical works more fascinating than most. How do they stay alive? How much of themselves comes to bear on their productions? How Shamanically do they manage to dissolve the veils between "actor" and "audience" (those who listen), so the Souls of the "seers" are able to genuinely journey into depths and heights along with them? It should not be a conscious matter of politesse that those watching a film suspend their disbelief, like removing one's shoes at the door. Rather the world unfolding before their eyes should be so compelling that credulous engagement is the *only* option. The Shamanic artist knows the three-dimensional map and leads the way such that we can't help but follow.

The first question any artists should ask themselves is "Where do you currently default on the Shamanic Templates?" Where are you usually found? Do you often feel like a Holy Fool? Do you tend to drift and dream in Liminal Space? Are you more at home in the Underworld struggling with the Demonic Shamanic? Do you come into your stride in the Marketplace, where a strong ego may find effective voice and successful exchange? Or do you find that you tend to float to the top, gaining an overarching view? Remember, balance is needed, and only by entering the realm(s) you'd rather avoid can you gain a Wounded Healer's Shamanic perspective.

Simply put: Are you mainly kinesthetic and embodied, grounded in the Nature Spirit, the Manifest? Playing the Market? Or Spirit-aligned and visionary, concerned with creating a new future? Let's look at examples of artists who fill these three bills, working from the bottom up.

DEATH VALLEY RESURRECTION: *AMARGOSA*

As with most of us, it seems that the first imprint of Divine parentage for Marta Becket came from her experience of human parents, with her father too absented from her life and her mother too smothering. The result: thin, airy, judgmental Upper World, supportive yet exploitative Lower World. But, bless the child, she was gifted with her own multiple, redemptive, artistic talents from the start: dancing, singing, painting, choreography, and piano playing.

In midlife, a fortune-teller's unlikely prophesy for her came true: Marta took those talents from the teeming metropolis of New York City to the wind-scrubbed, sage-dotted desert sands of Death Valley Junction, California. There she restored a decaying theatre to a splendor beyond the imaginings of the grateful townspeople (all ten of them, not counting the ghosts): the Amargosa Opera House.

This film opens with a meandering, dreamy prologue, invitation to enter Marta's equally meandering dreamscape: "It begins with a distant notion, a plaintive whisper of the heart. It comes in the flash of an epiphany, or through a deeper, unexplainable longing, that it has always been present: it is the recognition of conception... In a place abandoned by hard men and harder gods she makes a path by walking in a state of mind called *Amargosa*."

Marta Becket reminds one of dancer/choreographer Martha Graham in that she's gained her deserved reputation in part by dint of sheer endurance. You just *know* she's going to drop with her ballet slippers on. At 76 years of age, when documentary filmmaker Todd Robinson captured her unique life in the badlands, she was still dancing on toe and staging comedic cabaret performances alongside her unlikely partner, local handyman Tom Willet. With his Jimmy Durante nose, hefty Buddha belly and handle-bar moustache, Tom makes an incongruous figure donning a baloney-curl wig, bonnet and tutu, flirting demurely from behind a fluttering fan.

AGING CHILDREN

Both these players have that Lower World/self aura of aging children, despite Marta's yeoman-like, physical self-discipline. Tom's physique and demeanor indicate no such inclination for attempted exercise, never mind punishing routine. He's shown delightfully playing on a three-wheeler, raising dust with manic glee, visually compared to a frantic ostrich. And then there's the matter of his elaborate train set, running through one empty house symbolizing America, soon to cross over into the next door edifice: Europe.

But such child-like "Make Believe" is truly at the start of any creative endeavor. Let's make believe we can fly to the moon, "fly" to the Underworld, fly into the hearts of others via culturally enthralling media. The dream world of the Amargosa Opera House eventually accrued the requisite gravitational "mana," to exert a pull on a busload of former dance professionals from New York City, including colleagues Marta hadn't seen for 45 years. The performance before them was a winsome triumph, and the high point of this film biography.

When very grounded in the manifest physical, one often carries the weight of the past, and indeed, tradition weighs strongly in Marta's world, both familial and cultural. Her parents divorced when she was young, and their subsequent appearance together at a school performance filled this lonely daughter with hope that her stage skills could reunite them. So when we see that central to her elaborate audience mural in the Opera House is an attentive Spanish King and Queen, you have to ask if she's created a solution, or is still beseeching one. Defaulting to Lower World/Self has its advantages, but can leave one feeling at a sad remove from Upper World/Self. Tri-part balance of the Shamanic Templates is everything. If only the Unihipili-oriented knew that blessing from the benevolent, parental Aumakua was just a heartfelt prayer away.

While a skit she designed about the cost of being too dutiful a daughter indicates resolution of her mother issues, Marta's pain is still acute when relating a tale about her father: he died mere days before an article about her came out in *National Geographic*, for which she'd purchased him a subscription. "He says, '*Ha-ha!* You can't win me over.'"

Such woundedness, along with divorce from a philandering husband (despite her seeking love tips from a local bordello's Madam) has somewhat soured Marta on humans. Perhaps we have here her personal life's "hard man and harder Gods," as referenced in *Amargosa*'s prologue. She blatantly prefers the company of animals, again Unihipili territory. Part of her property is dedicated as a wild burro Sanctuary, and she wants to be interred out back in the wild horse Cemetery. Bury her galloping.

One may as well. Because if she has her way, even death won't be the end of Marta's love affair with Death Valley Junction. She has every intention of coming back as one of the shimmering balls and ectoplasmic entities that haunt the oft' empty Hotel. And you don't doubt she well might. Also in Marta's elaborate murals can be found Native American Indians in various states of public exhibition, such as juggling. This indicates the point when the Trickster Shaman crosses over into the "performer" in order to distract the critics in the audience, to entertain the uninitiated. But a showman Shaman can juggle all three worlds, and when the time comes, Marta will surely show that the *Dead Can Dance*.

The Upper World of her theatre space has a god blowing wind ~ storm or blessing? It is also festooned with cherubs, reminiscent of Marta's birth, which she recalls witnessing from outside and above her mother, "waiting for something." Via her next Death and Rebirth, Marta Becket won't be *Waiting for Godot* (Samuel Becket), but has every intention of returning to the beloved earthly, Middle World Paradise she herself created: *Amargosa*. We should all be so fulfilled that the best of our heritage is Heavenly to us.

BURIED GHOST: *THIS SO~CALLED DISASTER*

Artist Sam Shepard is my nomination for a fine example of creative Middle World/Self denizen. His theatrical career began in his youth and has met with evolutionary success for several decades. So he has certainly been able to cultivate a healthy ego in a competitive Marketplace.

Less successful have been his ongoing attempts to make peace with his real-life alcoholic father. But this is one of the comforts of the Soul Spiral: knowing that even if your efforts miss their first mark, they may go on and succeed in a larger Domain. By giving voice to his Father-Son struggle on stage, Sam must have provided many other children of addicts considerable catharsis and solace. But finally here, in frank disclosure, you can find this aging Prince offloading the oppression of his errant King. Enjoy Shepard's ruminations about the play within the film, *This So-Called Disaster*. Shaman, it looks like you've healed thyself.

Like choreographer/painter/musician Marta Becket, Sam Shepard has access to the Shamanic multi-dimensional orientation via his multiple skills: playwright, actor, and director. The playwright has an *under*-standing of the plot, the director has the *over*-view, and the shape-shifting actors provide the horizontal verbal flow or dissonance required to illumine and transform all worlds.

Actor James Gammon is among the players shown here in rehearsal of Shepard's play *The Late Henry Moss*, which enjoyed a sold-out run at the Magic Theatre in San Francisco. Over the years Gammon has played Shepard's father figure in a number of plays, leading him to ponder the ghostly liminality of the task: "Who am I supposed to be? Are you an echo? Are you a shadow? Who exactly are you supposed to be?" The play focuses upon Gammon's character whose girlfriend has pronounced him dead, much to his shock and denial, and the effect that supposed death has on his sons, a neighbor, and a naïve cab driver.

Another oft-repeated element in Sam's plays is that of two brothers contrasting, fighting, and longing for one another, in various measure. In this production, they're played by Nick Nolte and Sean Penn. As midwife to Henry Moss' Underworld journey, we have Sheila Tousey (of Menominee & Stockbridge-Munsee Indian Tribal blood.)

CANDID CONFESSIONS

While voyeuristically eavesdropping on the rehearsal is both vastly instructive and entertaining, it is the candid confessions of the players that has the more stirring impact.

Nick Nolte is shown seated in a somewhat garish theatrical setting, sharing a bare-bones admission of an early life breakdown that became a breakthrough (Initiation) to his Destiny as an actor. He also tells how he recently blew his knee out in rage over his mother's death, and how sitting alongside her in her final days provided his life's most important lesson: how to die. When he phoned Shepard to inform him of his grievous condition, just when he was due in San Francisco for rehearsal, Sam responded, "Why don't we just pretend none of it happened?"

That sounds callous, but that's what the Middle World Marketplace can do to people, catch them in a vice-grip of monetary concerns and deadlines. A better response might have been for Sam to invite Nick to bring his mother's Spirit as an aide to the stage of his father's Ghost. Shamans are famous for making such daring interventions into Cosmic play — in this case the psychic grave-robbing of a probably willing Soul.

Sam's personal disclosures during *This So-Called Disaster* come from what looks like a rustic-chic Ralph Lauren catalogue set — an elegant, primitive style rocking chair outside a cabin. He ponders the Walking Dead state of the Hungry Ghost he's depicted in the play: "It's an amazing dilemma when one begins to discover that you've been living your life as a somnambulist... in a trance, in a dream. When that occurs, amazing things take place. One is despair. The other is a sudden awakening, you know, to another way of being."

You have to wonder if that wasn't his personal experience when, three weeks before his father's death, the older man asked his son to hire him on as a farm hand at Sam's ranch in northern California: *"Well, he was in no condition to... he'd burn the fuckin' place down!"* Sensing rejection and flipping into alcoholic rage, Sam's father verbally and physically attacked him, against which no retaliation whatsoever was taken. That was their last encounter. To have had a life of longing for paternal blessing shattered by realization — that the living ghost implored can only be a source of curse and destruction — must have provided a profoundly bittersweet wake-up call.

An archival, timeless image of Sam walking the shore with his child shows a measure of himself in the very role his father failed to lovingly embody. Watching it, I thought back to the lines he'd written for Sheila Tousey's character in the play: "It takes courage now. I give him courage. The drowned man, he comes up for air, he gasps. Now he begins to go back home. Now he begins to return... you will see." Welcome home, Sam. You've earned it.

NEW DAWN: *A MOMENT OF INNOCENCE*

Unlike Marta Becket and Sam Shepard, Iranian writer/director/actor Mohsen Makhmalbaf does not seem to have his adulthood encumbered by unresolved parental issues. So his over-arching personal, cultural and political world-views make him my chosen candidate for Upper World/Self consciousness. He moves beyond mere Marketplace concerns when assessing that he sees two kinds of cinema — as business and as culture — and counts himself as contributing to the latter. Hollywood he perceives as a commercial hurricane that would gladly uproot any Indie plant in its path. Having gained full height and stride as a moral and responsible creative figure, he can be truly nurturing of those younger than himself. Rare.

Initiation has to do with successfully navigating the cycles of life, getting our past in perspective as regards our Destiny, and launching into the future with every intention to fulfill our purpose. One of the key elements has to do with dissolving any negative ties with our familial Domain Basin and finding Mentors who can help cultivate our truest gifts, which are then acknowledged (ideally) by both family and larger social Domains. In *Amargosa* and *This So-Called Disaster*, homage is paid to influential teachers who barely manage to eclipse the parental damage which dragged on for decades in both Artists' lives.

Even when Shepard's father, working in a book warehouse, came across one of Sam's published collections of plays, he denied it could have been written by his son. Witnessed ritualization is needed to move beyond the nest. This may be why Sam wished he'd attended a production of *Buried Child* in Santa Fe, during which his drunken father flung slings and arrows of protest at the stage. The wounded son may have wished for public reckoning to put closure on their overlong, crippled dance.

THE SUN ALSO SHIFTS

A Moment of Innocence is an illuminating example of the classic Initiatory paradox: closure that opens to the future. That shimmering slice of life between Death and Rebirth. It was inspired by two incidents in Makhmalbaf's life, which he layers in a parfait of fact, fiction, and fable.

Firstly: When he was a 17-year-old activist, he and his female cousin "wanted to save mankind." They attempted to steal a policeman's gun for use in a robbery supporting their cause during the Iranian Revolution. The attempted theft went awry, Makhmalbaf stabbed the policeman, and for a time they went their separate ways. Explains the director in an interview with David Walsh: "He was sent to a hospital and I was sent to a torture chamber."

Secondly: 20 years later, Makhmalbaf, having chosen filmmaking as the best means to influence culture, was having a casting call for his latest work, *Salaam Cinema!*. To his astonishment, the police officer from his past appeared, seeking a role: "Since I had been disappointed in politics I didn't need his weapon any longer. Now he needed mine — the weapon of movies."

A Moment of Innocence conflates the two encounters, with the stated intention being that the two older men direct younger actors as versions of themselves, recreating the violent encounter of their youth. If this film within a film sounds a simple matter, it isn't, since even the truth of the past gets morphed for the sake of the current climactic focus. What rings most true is that the element of youthful idealism comes to us refreshed every generation. The men find in their past collision elements of love and vision now given a second, better chance. But the process isn't without pain.

Only during the making of the film does the officer (Miradi Tayedi) learn that the young female, "the lost love of his life," was not genuinely drawn to him, but was an activist who betrayed him. He who once wanted to keep the peace now instructs his younger self (Ammar Tafti) to shoot the girl he'd so desired. In the words of T. S. Eliot, "Too long a sacrifice makes a stone of the heart."

Both the older men are humble enough to depict themselves in some regards as relatively benighted compared with their youthful counterparts. And yet Makhmalbaf is orchestrating the whole picture! Even as the political Domain Basin failed his past ideals, so does Makhmalbaf have the adults' directions appall the current-day youth of the picture.

At one point the younger cop has left a potted plant bathed in a ray of sunlight which penetrated the enclosed marketplace. He then runs along the corridor crying, "Have you seen a ray of sunlight?" to which a man responds, "The sun doesn't stay in one place."

THE MOMENT

Indeed. As idealism finds similar, and somewhat different, enactment generation to generation. The young version of the director (Ali Bakhshi) *also* wants to save mankind, also wants to feed the hungry, help the poor and, along with his female comrade (Maryam Mohamadamini), be Mother and Father to *all the world*. It is made clear that the role of women in Iran has devolved and diminished in the director's assessment. Times have changed both for the better and the worse.

While joining a militia might have been an option for the actual Makhmalbaf, it's the last thing his youthful counterpart would want to do. The sun-ray has shifted since the Revolution. When the time comes to enact the film's climatic, violent encounter, the actor breaks down crying that he doesn't want to stab *anybody*, not even with a harmless retractable blade: "Isn't there another way to save mankind?"

Although the girl has been directed to be stealthy, the young men to be violent with knife and gun, at the film's finale they are true to their highest values. Instead of an exchange of deceit and violence, we are shown something amazing: the young woman's lovely face disclosed (out from behind the veil and all that implies), the policeman proffering the flower in love, and the activist offering the flat-bread beneath which he'd hidden his now-discarded knife.

205

For a *Moment* we are all caught in a splendid ray of their idealism, a high noon of light so pure as to cast no shadow, as it needs every iota of its warmth to fulfill such enormous, compassionate longing. Stunning. And none of this would have been possible had not Makhmalbaf inverted the Domain Basin of his youth and offered a new and more benign firmament for the young of his day. Bless him. And may he keep up the Shamanic, Initiatory work, for *all the world's* sake.

PART XI

ELDERSHIP
DIAMOND~CUTTING &
PEARL~SPINNING

"*The splendor of Heaven's shore will not be unfamiliar to me. I will have known of it from the beauty of Nature and the joy of my Beloved.*"

— Tagore

APPROACHING THE VOID

There is a term gaining popularity in circles psychological and cultural: "Elderquest." Like the Hero's Quest, Vision Quest, or Midlife Crisis, it has its own sense of what comprises accomplishment and integrity, but in this case for the end of our life-span. Especially as longevity increases, and we face a new chapter between the usual retirement age and the final farewell, we need stories that distinguish those trials and rewards from prior ones. Can you imagine looking at aging from an Indigenous Soul perspective, not as a period of inevitable decline (again, with blessed allowance for slowing down), but as a Soul pinnacle of life?

As the once-young, questing Prince or Princess matures to the status of King or Queen, values shift towards what in life is vouchsafed most enduring. Straddling a rusty lawn mower is a far cry from straddling a trusty steed, but it's perfect for the old gent in *The Straight Story*. Traveling three hundred miles at three miles per hour gives this lead character time to ponder life.

Our Eldership is always with us, even in youth, like the proverbial oak tree encoded in the humble acorn. And we carry our youth into our

Eldership, sometimes kicking and screaming, sometimes gladly willing. That vertical Soul Compass connection knows full well, as we approach the final, fertile Void, whether or not we've been true to our initial promise. A Diamond-Cutter/Pearl-Spinner should be an old hand with the winnowing rake — the farming tool used to separate wheat from chaff. When the small, ego-defined self gains greater and greater confluence with the larger Soul Self, when the small head gets reeled in by the Grand Tete, surely this looming transcendence prompts a series of nudging (or panicky) "final judgments."

We've all encountered children who appear to be Old Souls, who astonish grown-ups with their sobriety and thoughtful demeanor. And we've all known older folks who are Elders in chronological age alone: still child-like, self-absorbed, and grasping, for whatever sad reasons. Deep Cinema allows that we can always regard one another Soul-to Soul across the age divide, as was shown in *A Moment of Innocence.*

That title alone acknowledges that youth are allowed to be more naïve than knowing, and move into their worldly authority organically, over time. At some point, however, they should find themselves standing toe-to-toe with their parents or mentors, the light of their burgeoning inner authority providing discernment, insight and blessing where once they knew only hunger and dependence. Such an inner shift embodies an Initiation, as when Sam Shepard held his reserve in the face of his father's final verbal and physical onslaught, realizing he'd outgrown the old man on so many levels: an awakening. The fact that the senior Shepard was dead in three weeks possibly says something about how he felt his mortal standing collapse when his famous son withdrew. Left to his own devices, Shepard Sr. left. "The (old) King is dead, long live the (new) King!"

And sometimes it requires review of an apparently successful life to take a measure of its gaps and fill them with grace:

WHERE THE RUBBER HITS THE SKY: *MEN WITH GUNS*

John Sayles again, spinning a number of Domain Basins in an unspecified Meso-American country: familial, social, medical, military, *turista*, anarchist, multi-cultural. At the center of this modulated maelstrom is a recent widower, Dr. Fuentes (Federico Luppi), taking a vacation from his teaching post in a

Medical School. He plans to visit seven former students whom he trained three years ago to be "Ambassadors of Health" among the impoverished mountain Natives. The problem is, there's a lot of nasty business happening at ground level which this well-meaning but naïve Doctor hasn't perceived from the privileged vantage point of his Ivory Tower.

Among other deft balancing elements, the film book-ends with two anal references, which should be noted. At the outset, Dr. Fuentes is examining a growth on the posterior of a military man, a growth which is neither growing nor diminishing: "We'll have to watch it." The much-decorated soldier is mildly amused: "What a thought — watching my ass." Clearly he's more used to covering it. Double-checking on the matter of doctor-client confidentiality, he also warns about the guerrillas waging terror in the mountains: "You are like a child, Humberto. The world is a savage place."

At least the military man *knows* he's a part of the world's savagery. Fuentes doesn't. He doesn't realize that he's sent his medical graduates into the jaws of the Jaguar, or, more specifically, the cross-hairs of various "*Men with Guns.*"

By the end of the film, the doctor will have acquainted himself with a number of mythic-sounding Indigenous folk — the Salt People, Sugar People, Banana People, the Gum People, Corn People, and finally, the Sky People. As for his students, at least one has fled his medical post under atrocious conditions, another has been shot by the *army* for treating guerrillas, yet another killed by *guerrillas* for healing army members. Altogether those who have vowed to "First, do no harm" have proven no match for soldiers, anarchists, deserters, and thieves whose capacity to do *deadly* harm is facilitated by firearms.

The elegant doctor has already been humbled by the loss of his wife, and yet undergoes ever more chastisement as he spirals up the mountain, lured by the Higher Self, Aumakua. His expensive luggage is rifled, his camera stolen, then his hub-caps, next his tires, finally his cash. All petty privations compared with the grueling death toll of his students.

As his Diamond-Cutting/Pearl-Spinning legacy loses ever more of its sheen with the loss of medic after medic, Dr. Fuentes endures an unexpected shattering of Shadow. While his faith in science has heretofore gone untested, he picks up a Hungry Ghost of a former priest who's been deeply disillusioned in his vocation: having once dreamt of being a martyr, he fled/betrayed his parishioners when the opportunity presented itself. While the doctor has known comfort and education, he becomes "adopted" by a starving, illiterate orphan. Where he is genteel and cultured, he is joined by an angry military deserter. Where his wife and daughter were provided an upper-class urban lifestyle, he takes on a mute rape victim (Uhane) from a refugee camp for villagers.

A DEEPER ENDOWMENT

Also threaded through the film are conversational snippets from an Indigenous mother and daughter who live at the highest altitudes and await a medico to remove shrapnel from the woman's leg. And just when you think the doctor and his motley crew have waded into the most thickly overgrown of Rain Forest outposts, they re-encounter an American tourist couple (Mandy Patinkin and Kathryn Goody) whom they first met at a restaurant. Well-versed in the dangers of the region, this pair is nonetheless avid in their quest for Native ceremonial ruins: "The concept of sacrifice is a tough one to sell in the States." Amen.

There was one female doctor among Fuentes' students, and his investment in her provides his final hope. Something in his debonair appearance tells you that this old gent would want the woman protected, and certainly our culture expects women to manage to somehow be civilizing agents even in the face of armed mayhem. This final student is rumored to be healing at Circa de Cielo, a high and hidden village, a Latin Shambala. But this turns out to be a heavenly place of Upper World truth, the place that allows for no illusions, the place "where rumors come to die."

Here too we have the second anal reference: "The Sky People live here. They eat air and shit clouds." With his lack of knowing, his criminally overweening innocence, his ignorance of the world's dark side and his own, Dr. Humberto Fuentes senses his legacy to be as insubstantial as celestial gas. But wait. By risking the trip at all, and taking on his life's Shadow components, he has actually cultivated an endowment that "matters," one that has the stuff of endurance.

Where the doctor feels despair over his Summer House's ravagement by firing squad, we're shown that "in a twinkling" he's engendered a more essential and enduring Heritage than his more naïve self could have dreamed. Thanks due to (and from) the orphan, the soldier, and the maiden. Bravo!

ABIDING CONSCIOUSNESS

As we age, both imagination and memory should get a nonpareil work-out. What lies beyond that final threshold? And what lies before it, in terms of our life's accomplishments? When we see ourselves as Indigenous Souls, we may imagine ourselves becoming a pearl or diamond among Indra's heavenly net of gems. We can become a lens to the Divine map, enfolded into the Cosmos as a benign, blessing, consolidating or transforming power. Some of us get a premature taste of what it means to touch the Infinite during this finite passage, via near-death experiences. As we shall see next.

If "all the world's a stage," we're lucky to get to see a true Shaman walk these boards. Most observe such rituals from the side of the audience, little knowing how much our faith contributes to the efficacy of their "performances." As the curtain opens, those watching bring to the experience a unique configuration of hopes, wounds, beliefs, expectations, doubts and willingness. The Shaman sees the curtain open from another side altogether, with his or her spine aligned to the Spirit World, and all it can bestow. Their desire is to uplift those ailing into a Remembrance of health, to be sustained henceforth by Love. They lift the negatively-entrained Unihipili up to the Aumakua realm of original potential, invoking a shattering of impediments. Such is the wished-for legacy of those who walk between Worlds.

NEAR~LIFE EXPERIENCE: *RESURRECTION*

In *Resurrection*, lead character Edna McCauley (Ellen Burstyn) exhibits many characteristics of a Shamanic Healer, with her one great misfortune being that she lives in an age where patriarchal and scientific viewpoints make little room for a Shamanka (one name for female Shaman). As ever, we must appreciate these gifted practitioners from the specific locale of their Soul Compass, which includes earth, body, sexuality, family, education, skills, faith, etc. Persons raised in Guatemala vs., say, the Land of the Midnight Sun, or Sri Lanka, are going to draw on different powers and meet different resistances than does this modern-day American.

Edna was happily married and comfortably well-off when she and her husband met with a car accident at the liminal site of the seashore, fatal for him and life-altering for her. As in *Sorceress* and *Men with Guns*, the loss of a spouse here provides a deep and high vertical resonance for the bereaved, opening a proverbial stairway to Hell and Heaven.

Wheelchair-bound and moving back to her childhood home to recuperate, Edna is embraced by sympathetic kin, to varying degrees. Her greatest blessing lies in having Grandma Pearl (Eva Le Gallienne, a Pearl-Spinner indeed!), in her simple and straightforward manner, be the first to recognize that her grandchild has come back from the accident with healing gifts. Also on hand for support is a sweet dog, witness to Edna healing herself from paralysis. (I love that this is a real pooch and not a Totem animal, as in Shamanic circles *all* of life is sacred, the Animal Kingdom often in cahoots with our best efforts, if only we have eyes and ears to discern their loving signs).

One of Edna's earliest tests comes when a local, Cal (Sam Shepard) is brought to her in the back of a pick-up truck, hemorrhaging from a bar brawl knife wound. Soon he is courting her, looking for some "hands-on healing" of the most intimate variety, and eventually she succumbs. Trouble is, Cal's father is the neighborhood fire-and-brimstone preacher, and it turns out this apple didn't fall as far from the tree as it first appears. Opposition also comes from the intimate quarter of immediate family, with Edna's Father throwing her out due to her unwed sexual activity. Too holy for some, not enough for others, we have men left, right, and center assuming the authority to judge and control an exceptionally gifted woman. Hellfire vs. Heavenly fire indeed.

EXPANDING WEB OF LIFE

The beauty of *Resurrection* is that Edna and Grandma Pearl resolutely keep things simple, and simply about Love, even as Edna's healing sessions expand from pick-up trucks to living rooms to revival tents to outdoor arenas. Her humility is typical of the best of Shamanic healers, who attribute their successes to participation in the Divine web of life, and accept failures as part of their own deficiency. Or the patient's choice. We are also shown how the faith of the local audience contributes to healings when, by contrast, Edna is invited to have her skills tested at a university medical center in southern California. Here the possible skepticism of the onlookers requires that she take on the full brunt of the patient's ailment solo, a task which wipes her out for days.

Edna awakens with an awareness that her father is dying and she needs to return home. Again, as with the truest Indigenous healers, she is most human, not holier-than-Thou, and addresses how painfully her father has wounded her before inviting him into the Light of the Hereafter. A lot of family pain is contextualized in negativity between them, what we might call a "psychic invasion" or "curse" from the Shamanic perspective. But as soon as she is able, this loving daughter returns to the "First things," in this case the first impulse of a child to love a parent and to restore the two of them to Ohana.

Attending to her dreams, her *intuition*, and *inner* knowing, Edna refuses to acknowledge any transcendent Source other than Love. This Womb-Weaving ballast is naturally womanly, and an orientation Deep Cinema encourages most enthusiastically. While the movie ends with dogmatic persecution driving this modern-day "Witch" into isolation where she continues her practice on the sly, matters hardly ended there.

Ironically, this 1980 film about halting a "Heretic" continues to find appreciative viewers today, and Ellen Burstyn lauds it in her biography, *Lessons in Becoming Myself*. A healer/consultant on the set successfully tended to a cast member's injury. And many people have approached Ellen to say they only began living out their psychic, spiritual gifts after viewing the film. Why not? Once you've touched onto the Mother-lode as Mother, what's to hold back a cornucopia of effulgent outpouring? Like a Loa walking the earth, thrilled to transform all those open to her, such a woman can (as with *Anchoress* and *Sorceress*) Trickster-slip between the roles of victim and heroine to something more enduring.

EGO TRICKSTER: *AFTER THE WEDDING*

(I want to note here that I've become recently aware of cinema from Denmark, with all the enthusiasm of a sommelier discovering a new wine source: Australia, South Africa, or New Zealand. Several Danish films are truly wonderful, perfectly aged, mature, delivering a resonant aftertaste. Others of course are downright silly. But do check them out — highly recommended.)

While most people, if they think of their personal demise at all, probably imagine it occurring at the last possible mortal knell, Death does come for some earlier than expected or desired. And while the story of *After The Wedding* belongs most centrally to the humanitarian Jacob (Mads Mikkelsen), I want to also focus here on his Antagonist/Shadow, Jørgen (Rolf Lassgård). Jørgen is the one terminally ill and attempting to deal with that fate with all the imperial control of the successful CEO he has become.

Early on in the plot, Jørgen's son-in-law to-be mentions how the billionaire came from nothing, and it doesn't show. In deft repartee, Jacob asks what it is exactly that '*doesn't show*' — that he came from nothing? Because, obviously, all the evidence this aid worker from an Indian orphanage has seen only demonstrates opulence to the nth degree.

That's the first warning that the dying man may be resisting the dissolving thin ice of his mortality. Folks who are ashamed of their humble beginnings tend to pile up the subterfuge between themselves and those origins, including, at times, buffeting the gap with Shadow scapegoating. But dying dissolves all such masks. To date, Jacob would have fit that Shadow/Scapegoat bill nicely. But now, as Jørgen faces his final exit, he wants to plug the penurious idealist into the most unlikely of roles: that of his posthumous surrogate.

CRASHING WEDDING

Jacob has no idea of this elaborate scheme at first, and neither do we. All we know is that he's been called back to Denmark from India in order to meet with a potential benefactor who could save the orphanage from financial collapse. Upon arrival, he's baited and switched by Jørgen, dangled without secure economic promise, asked to stay on longer, even to come to the tycoon's manorial country estate to attend the wedding of his daughter the very next day. The younger man hesitates, the older one parries, Jacob resists again, and his host insists. It's our first awareness that the one has a will of steel and the other is malleable.

You know by now that this book needs be full of spoilers to round out the requisite information illustrating Deep Cinema. But there's a revelation at this wedding that is so original, so emotionally tumultuous for all concerned, and so subtly rendered, that I must suggest you see it before reading on. Director Susanne Bier's signature close-ups of eyes and lips at times open up interior worlds, and at times become so detailed as to be abstract. Jacob's eyes speak volumes in this pivotal scene.

Okay? Here it is, disclosure: Once at the wedding, Jacob recognizes a woman, Helene (Sidse Babett Knudsen), who was his lover two decades earlier. It turns out that she's now Jørgen's wife, which indicates that her taste in men underwent a radical shift, from pauper to prince. While Jacob seemingly resigns himself to that revelation gracefully enough, he's certainly not prepared for the next one: as the young bride, Anna (Stine Fischer Christensen) toasts her "parents," she notes that Jørgen is not her biological father. Gazes between Helene and Jacob hint at a stunning truth: the young bride is a daughter he never knew he had.

SIGNING THE PACT

Tempest in a tuxedo! During the ensuing explosive exchanges between the former lovers, we learn that Jacob and Helene were together in India when she became pregnant. But she'd broken off with him due to his alcoholic and sexual indulgences, and only learned of her condition once back home in Denmark. Given that debauched description of the humanitarian worker as a youth, it's interesting to note how he's matured: He was seated next to a sexually predatory beauty at the reception, and Jacob treats him to a largely liquid lunch soon afterwards. Was he being tested by the CEO? If so, he passed with flying colours, showing decided restraint in both instances.

But you just know *these* two unlikely business partners are going to come to loggerheads at some point. A part of the final contract, a very generous trust fund, demands that Jacob administer it from Denmark year round, with only the occasional trip back to India. One man is controlling via his wealth, and the other resisting out of legitimate pride. Then comes the CEO's confession of imminent death, complete with his breaking down in Jacob's arms.

And here is a missed opportunity in the plot, for these Shadows to temper one another. Jacob and Jørgen are clearly complementary. And while the mogul's big bucks certainly fill in the blank in Jacob's life, the story could have benefited immensely by making theirs a *mutual* exchange. Jørgen is a materialistic man having a spiritual crisis in the face of death, Jacob, an idealistic man having a material crisis in the face of life. Each possesses what the other lacks. When the dying man rushes downstairs and throws himself into Jacob's arms, something beautiful could have passed between them.

After all, in India Jacob must have passed by dead and dying bodies every day, must have looked into their eyes and possibly seen some evidence of the Afterlife playing out there. He could have broken open inwardly and recognized what a richness of awareness he was carrying, and comforted Jørgen with it. Given him some measure of peace beyond the prey-predator nightmare he'd tried drinking away in his estate's ominous "trophy" room of animal heads. But just as he didn't know he had a child, this man-child doesn't know his own other-worldly wisdom in the face of worldly wealth. And thus this insane, imbalanced system threatens to make Spiritual paupers of us all.

Alas, we have a successful mutant Marketplace player making the Middle World over in his image and likeness: controlling wife, adopted daughter and stranger like so many pawns. This is the ego as Trickster, trying to absorb elements into its willful purview that belong to Nature and Spirit. Good intentions, maybe, from his benighted standpoint, but intentions that deprive everyone else involved of their own passages through grief, growth and free will. What we have here is largely a quiet mystery of Soul Tragedy, a "gift" from the Marketplace wrapped in glittering, false gold.

ENDURING DECADES: *LEONARD COHEN: I'M YOUR MAN*

If you were introduced to Canadian singer/songwriter Leonard Cohen's poetic lyrics in the '60s, the era of Joni Mitchell, Bob Dylan, Joan Baez, Carly Simon, and Crosby, Stills, Nash & Young, you may have been lulled into thinking that the musical world would always provide such an embarrassment of riches. But to watch the engaging bio/concert/tribute that is *Leonard Cohen: I'm Your Man* is to agree with Irish musician Bono's assessment: *"Let's face it: Very few people walk the ground on which he treads. There's humility in the way he waits for just the right word to come. The rest of us would be humbled by the things he throws away."* Here's an Elder with a considerable *oeuvre* to celebrate, who's entered the Marketplace mainly on his own terms, and shows few signs of creative diminishment.

In addition to Bono and his U2 band are a collection of varied musicians who covered Cohen's songs in a 2005 concert in Sydney, out-takes from which provide the bulk of the film. There's Nick Cave, Kate and Anna McGarrigle, Beth Orton, Teddy Thompson, Antony (who *is* this fabulously bizarre creature with the angelic voice — a visual cross between Joe Cocker and Tiny Tim?), etc. Cohen family friend, Rufus Wainwright, does the lion's share of performances, largely to good effect, except for his oddly effeminate, overly precious rendition of the incisive anthem, "Everybody Knows."

All the singers interviewed speak of this indubitable Diamond-Cutter in the most reverential terms, as well they might, one even comparing him to the likes of poets Byron and Shelley. This is nicely countered by Cohen's own oft-demonstrated humility: "I'm not nostalgic by nature. I have neither regrets nor occasion for self-congratulation." At the same time, he doesn't deny his talents, seeing them as gifts for which he's indebted: "I'm just paying my rent in the Tower of Song." Watching Bono sing "do-whop" back-up for this number in a New York City club is both a hoot and touching. The scarlet beaded curtain from this set is hauntingly morphed into a transitional wash of red platelets throughout the film, a liminal threshold veil that reminds us of this living treasure's mortality.

The music is augmented by archival photos, Cohen's artwork, and delightful interviews with the man himself. Such a synesthetic blending of visuals, memory, prayer and song gives us privileged entrée into the well-polished neural Dream-time of this wonderful Artist. What a Mentor figure! Now in his '70s, the poet-philosopher sings of the losses incurred by aging and shows some physical, but very little mental diminution since his heyday: "I ache in the places where I used to play." But he's still soulful as a folk singer, savvy as a beat poet, and suave as a cabaret performer.

There is always such a comely, seasoned intelligence in his eyes, such a bemused knowing and true sensitivity there, that you want to know what he's pondering. And if he'll just sing it, all the better.

FROM MENACING TO MELLOW

Over the decades, some audiences were repelled by what they deemed the too-dark, depressive, suicidal elements of Cohen's work, for which he made no apologies. At the time of his album, *Songs of Love and Hate,* he drolly noted, "People are wrong to call me a pessimist. A pessimist worries that it might rain, and I'm already soaked to the bone." Aha! Probably not. He most likely had the good sense to don his "Famous Blue Raincoat," one of the more in-delible of his oldies, along with "Bird on a Wire," which doesn't get coverage here, although the popular "Suzanne" is featured.

Angelica Huston once shrewdly summed Cohen up as "part angel, part wolf," and that duality plays out thoroughly. In "Chelsea Hotel #2" he writes of "getting head on an unmade bed" while a limo waits outside (his one-night stand with Janis Joplin). Then his melodious "Hallelujah," gives substance to The Edge's glowing assessment that he's got the dignity of a Biblical prophet. Upper, Lower and Middle selves/worlds harmonize. He can enfold the sacred and the profane into one, with facility.

The title song "I'm Your Man" is a lover's litany of offerings, a willing-ness to Shamanically shape-shift into whatever may be desirable, including invisibility: "If you want to work the street alone, I'll disappear for you." And disappear Cohen did, heading off to California's Mount Baldy to become an ordained Zen Buddhist monk for five years, where his chosen name translated to "the Silent one."

Even such an atmosphere of Spartan discipline (beatings with sticks, walking in sandals through snow) couldn't quell his humor: "The Roshi of the monastery was Japanese, the head monk German: I think it was revenge for WWII." But love for and from his Mentor provided just what Cohen as Protégé needed: " He deeply cared for me… or perhaps it was that he so deeply *didn't* care for who I was, that who I was began to wither and something deeper was free to emerge." Dissolution made way for the Initiation into Deep-Self beyond ego-self.

Fortunately for us, Cohen emerged from that spiritual sabbatical, and suffered through economic travails and acerbic litigation to consider resuming what he refers to as his writing career: "It's not a bad idea. It's becoming more and more attractive the more we drink." Then Bono notes the Initiatory wisdom of the man: *"He has you in your youthful idealism. He has you when you can't face the world. He has you at all the stages of your life."* A Bard for all seasons and cycles of Death and Rebirth.

How wonderful that this devil who wears Armani and sings with a wild angel's grace will continue gifting us. Not everyone can orchestrate God's Illumination and Shadow so seamlessly, challenging us all to embrace the largest Domain Basins. A sexy, diabolical "Halleluiah!" indeed.

BEYOND THE FINAL THRESHOLD: DEEP SELF~POSSESSION

There is that famous German woodcut, *The Vision of Ezekiel*, which depicts a Medieval monk thrusting his head beyond the starry firmament into the deeper, vaster prophetic workings of the Cosmos: over-arching gears, clouds, and planets. In Indigenous cultures such as the Australian Aboriginal, he would be expected to carry some comprehension of these realms, to have aligned himself with them, begun to know and embody his part in sustaining them.

Stones, stars and humans are all of interconnected, woven accord for Hawaiians. The starry belt of the Zodiac constellates merger of animal and human forms. Taoists have discerned alignment between our bodily organs and the North Star and Big Dipper, with their rotating, harmonizing, glowing lights echoing in the "Crystal Room" of our cranium and along our neck and jawline. And so it goes: "As above, so below."

We can begin by asking which element we most enact, and to what end. Are we largely Fire in its destructive appetite, and/or its glowing enthusiasm? Air in its inspiration and/or fleetingness? Water as enchanting, as destructive? Earth in its opacity, its venerability?

I suspect we all gain some radiant insight into this awareness upon facing Death. Whenever spindrift flies off the wave that has been its body, a leaf falls from a tree, a human exits mortal life, there comes a Sacred opportunity to open up to the larger space of containment: the nova-nesting, cosmically woven, verdant Void embracing all. From such a containment, the froth cannot entirely take leave of the ocean, the leaf fully forget the tree, nor the human depart its beloved Earthly source, any more than the valley can take leave of the mountain. Identities vast and minute begin to eternally sustain one another, through Love.

A reversal of sorts must take place. As once we viewed the Heavens through human eyes, we shall come to view the Earth through our Shamanic Spirit Eye. Upon leaving Earth, and thus seeing it as the "wave"-length we once rode, the tree of life on which we blossomed, our Natural Domain Basin, we can then recognize this home planet as the Heavenly body it is. In that rare flash of insight, we realize our body and all of Creation as Spiritual. Our skills sharpen to name what we value most and what, in exquisite anguish of Love, we shall henceforth brand as Everlasting. And thus we contribute to that which even Death cannot annihilate.

EVERY THIRD THOUGHT: *PROSPERO'S BOOKS*

Possibly the last play written by Shakespeare, *The Tempest* is given most opulent, visually intoxicating treatment in Peter Greenaway's rendition, *Prospero's Books*, starring Sir John Gielgud. Here we have that 16th century genius of a playwright composing in his final years, so considerable insight into Eldership should be culled from this spectacle.

In short: A literary man of the world has been exiled by his more politically ambitious brother to an island, with only his infant daughter and his books to accompany him. There he amplifies his learning to the point of honing Sorcerer's skills, creating an astounding but illusory world and, via a Tempest, bringing his brother's ship to wreck upon these shores. Only then can this Magician, via counsel from an airy sprite (Unihipili), offload the bile of two decades spent seeking justice from his sibling. He can return to the fraternal, loving impulse of "First things." By working Shamanically *with* the powers of Nature, he awakens his brother to the wrongs he's done. Prospero also awakens himself to his own imbalance: the need to return to worldly responsibilities as Duke of Milan if his daughter is to wed and have her own chance to "prosper."

Like a good Elder, Prospero makes way for the next generation by marrying off the now-grown Miranda. Like a skilled Shaman, he strips off his masks (some more beloved than others) offloading his life of magic for a final chapter more real. He liberates his "monstrous" Shadow, Caliban, frees his blithe Sprite, Ariel, destroys his implements of magic, drowns his books. And prepares return to the mainland where, he proclaims, "My every third thought shall be of Death." Aha!

What becomes of Life when one's *every third thought* turns to its ending, and thus to both review and Afterlife? This is the stuff of Initiation writ large. While it is often hard to over-ride life's distractions truly enough to invoke the liminal, numinous Womb of Deep Mystery, there comes a time when we have no choice. Some, like the mogul in *After the Wedding*, evoke Jesus' teaching that "it is easier for a camel to pass through the eye of a needle than for a rich man to enter the Kingdom of Heaven." But I suspect a heightened sense of mortality burns off the dross for most. Shakespeare's *Propero* leads the way.

FEMALE SHOOTING STARS

It's not that women don't die in films, they die left and right, they die singularly and they die in mundane droves, but usually at the hands of men and as catalysts for more male action. Seldom do we cinematically sound out a woman's subjective depths enough to really mourn her passing. And this deprives too many of us of something essential: a sense of the afterlife, of "Heaven," as suffused with womanly qualities.

Even spiritually evolved people who know, for example, that heartfelt empathy trumps final judgment, and inclusiveness is kinder than condemnation, still flash onto a sere, bearded, judgmental White Male as the major player "Above." This is the stuff of childhood programming, a child's punitive god, something to be outgrown. We need to balance out the Yang oppression of that ultimate Domain Basin with considerably more Yin sensuality, softness, soulfulness, splendor — which is actually what most Shamanic voyages to the Afterworld reveal. Such "judgment" as is found there is compassionate, rendering how we may have missed the mark, failed in our intended life mission.

OUR MOTHER, WHO "AREN'T" IN HEAVEN

In 1986, I witnessed the explosion of the U.S. space shuttle *Challenger* upon its take-off in Florida. The white, thrusting vapor trail from the launch suddenly expanded into a fuller vessel-shaped cloud with two curving handles, like ibex horns (elegant even in death) curving left and right beyond.

Because this was the first launching that included women passengers, this disaster (dis-aster: against the stars) impacted me strongly. And what I saw, as I sank into grief before that smoke-plume after-image, was the shape of a womb and fallopian tubes. The Shamanic message was all too clear: the modern-day Upper World in its outer altitudes, tainted by militaristic Star Wars' programming, had become as inhospitable to women as it had for displaced goddesses (from Calypso to the Flying Vagina).

I was mildly obsessed by what I saw as this symbolism, and everything about that space mission confirmed my suspicions. The number "one" is the ultimate masculine digit, and this had been the *tenth* ($10 = 1 + 0 = 1$ again) launching of that workhorse of a space shuttle, *Challenger*. It disintegrated 73 seconds into take-off, another ten, on the 28th day of the *first* month of the year. Disintegration: back to the Void, Zero, the hungry Goddess, starving for recognition (sacrifice?) from the stratosphere. Back to Mother Earth, scattering remains into the depths of the Ocean Womb. The craft had been named after the *HMS Challenger*, a British *warship* from the 19th century. Ronald Reagan capped off the male litany of factors by mourning the Astronauts with a quote from poet Jon Gillepsie Magee Jr., saying they'd *"slipped the surly bonds of earth to touch the face of God."* Double whammy: *bad* Mother earth, BIG head-trip of a male sky-God.

In this next film we do have a woman dying and, although her screen time pales in relation to that of her spouse, at least she doesn't have to shape-shift into a vacuous Barbie for his heavenly gratification, is actually allowed dark swaths of grief and madness. And I'm grateful for that.

TO HELL AND BACK: *WHAT DREAMS MAY COME*

This lush, painterly-saturated extravaganza dares to explore Life after Death, and with methods both conventional and daring. Conventional are the constructs of Heaven and Hell. Unconventional is the tempering of this polarity by the more radical teaching that we create our After-Life via longing, will, and self-judgment. The film's palette is dominated by the jacaranda tree's purplish-blues from the New Zealand homeland of director Vincent Ward (*The Navigator: A Medieval Odyssey*). All the better to open our third eye.

It should also be noted that this film was produced by Stephen Simon, whose loss of his father at a very young age must have opened him early on to familiarization with Other realms. And, indeed, he has gone on to found the Spiritual Cinema Circle. Simon earlier produced *Somewhere in Time*, also involving lovers and reincarnation. That starred Christopher Reeve who, along with Robin Williams, the lead in *What Dreams May Come*, transferred the same year from Cornell to the Julliard School for Performing Arts. And the touching fact that Reeve and his loyal wife Dana died a mere two years apart, both prematurely, also resonates with the Soul-mate theme here. All of which gives substance to Dr. Michael Newton's research (*Journey of Souls, Life Between Lives*) and the knowing of the Fon tribal people, that we move through incarnations in Soul groups, families, pods.

COMPOUNDED TRAGEDIES

The comfortable and fulfilling life of Medical Doctor Chris Nielsen (Robin Williams) and his Artist/Curator wife Annie (Annabella Sciorra) is torn asunder when their two children are suddenly lost to them via a violent car accident. Mere years later, Chris dies in another vehicular tragedy, leaving his wife too bereft to carry on. So now all the family are on the Other Side, three in varying domains of Heaven ("In my Father's house there are many mansions" — Jesus) and the one suicide, Annie, in her grey, dismal, isolated Hell: the former family home now rotting in the inverted dome of an upended Cathedral.

Via a Spirit Guide (Cuba Gooding Jr.), Chris is reunited with his pet Dalmation and together they bound and splatter through a Paradisiacal-sized version of one of Annie's paintings. With those fabulous jacaranda blues.

All is pretty blissful until Chris learns that Annie has killed herself and is now Eternally lost to him. But he dares descend into Hell to retrieve her, a spectacular Odyssey that includes walking over a vast, murky Underworld landscape cobbled with the miserable faces of the damned. German director Werner Herzog pulls off what might well be cinema's most minute cameo, as a fervent face wishing that Chris was his son come to visit. Alas!

REUNION AND REBIRTH

As he's been warned (by Max von Sydow's character no less: a classic Western patriarchal god-figure), Chris is tempted to get caught in Annie's domain of doom. The film's title derives from Shakespeare, and this scene reminds me of a classically Initiatory line from his *Richard II*: "Through the hollow eyes of Death, I spy life peering." If we conflate this Lower World with Lower Self, our Nature spirit, the realm of physicality, emotion and memory, then we see that grief-work is required to cleanse us out in order to make way for eternal Love.

The liminal gap between human and Divine natures turns into a child's game of "hide-and-seek." Hidden, Annie is found by Chris, and together they manage to generate enough mana, cultivate enough loving focus, or vibrant intent, or Eros, or *je ne sais quois*, to catapult up to their children's (and Dalmatian's) Heaven for a joyous reunion!

But not for long. *What Dreams May Come* never does penetrate beyond the considerably wonderful state of loosening mortal coils and giving imagination free reign enough to create whatever one desires. It doesn't touch onto Loa and Aumakua strata beyond that liberating note. What Chris and Annie discover together is that what they valued most in life was each other: finding one another, falling in love and making a life together. And so they decide to be reborn as Soul-mates once again, only meeting much earlier (closer to the age when Stephen Simon lost his Father, hmmm). Their idea of Heaven is being together again, only sooner this time, and longer.

This romantically expresses the teaching that, in the best of ongoing Death and Rebirth cycles, we evolve to live ever more truly, more quickly. Some Indigenous Elders add lotus seed cakes to their diet in their final years, meditating on a branch continually blossoming, so that in their next reincarnation they'll have to deal with less opaque karmic mud. Thus we hope to gain a longer measure of time to bring our share of Heaven to bear on Earth. How sweetly Divine!

SHADOW CULTURE: *DEAD MAN*

Director Jim Jarmusch wonderfully manages to turn the iconic Western on its head, showing the Euro-Americans' continental expansion for the Indigenous tragedy it was, without ever once sounding a preachy note. With elements quirky, droll, mystical, gruesome, and at times downright deranged, this elegantly black-and-white buddy-on-horseback movie manages to give weight to the Native man's perspective merely by making the white man's so "lite." And that starts with the sheer physicality of the two key players: Johnny Depp as William Blake and Gary Farmer as Nobody.

Blake starts out as a recently orphaned young man (telling: no Ancestry) from Cleveland, riding westward on a train to "the end of the line," a town called Machine, where he's been promised a job as an accountant. Drifting in and out of consciousness (liminal passages) between games of solitaire, Blake awakens to find his fellow passengers devolving from some measure of urban sophistication to prairie-dwelling homesteaders, to rough-hewn, fur-draped trappers literally shooting buffalo from the train windows for wasteful sport.

His only conversation is with the train's darkly prophetic, sooty-faced engine fire-tender (Crispin Glover) who enigmatically launches into, "and doesn't it remind you of when you were in the boat?" Ultimately this book-ends with Blake's final transport in a totemically festooned Death Canoe at the end of the tale, his own face having been painted with dark lightning bolts. But for now it's merely unnerving in its sheer in-your-face eccentricity. Get used to it. Such bizarre notes will sound as often as Neil Young's twangy, haunting score.

DOWNWARD SPIRAL

Blake's destination turns out to be a mix of hard-scrabble squalor and disillusioned dreams, with the nearly penniless lad being told in no uncertain terms that he's unneeded and unwanted at what he thought would be his place of employment. He drowns his sorrows in whiskey and then takes to bed with a semi-reformed prostitute-turned-flower girl named Thel. (Her name is reference to one of the English poet/painter/mystic William Blake's creations). They are interrupted in their post-coital conversation by Thel's former beau (Gabrielle Byrne), whose jealousy turns homicidal. Thel takes a bullet for Blake, but it pummels right through her and lodges near his heart, deep enough to be debilitating but not immediately lethal.

After initially-awkward failed shooting attempts, this wimpy accountant manages to kill the assailant, who happens to be the son of the wacko who owns the town (Robert Mitchum camping it up in his final role). Stealing a pinto under a shooting star, Blake goes on the lam and soon has three hit-men on his tail. Lucky for this nebbishy city slicker (yes, Johnny Depp attempting nerd), he is rescued by a savvy, multi-lingual Indian named Nobody (Farmer).

Nobody's wonderfully blunt in his assessment of what he initially perceives to be another "stupid white man," until he learns William Blake's name. Then this well-traveled, self-educated Indian becomes enraptured by the conviction that he beholds the actual Spirit of the dead English poet, with his honorable duty being to help him cross over.

One could debate the meaning of the film's title, and at what point it actually applies to Depp's character. Of course this is ingenious because many Indigenous peoples saw whites as literal harbingers of Death, associating their pale skin with skeletal bones. And indeed, after ingesting sacred Peyote by campfire, the Indian sees his companion's face as an eerie skull. "Nobody" is nonplussed, happy to accept Blake as a wandering Spirit, and happier still that the great visionary is writing his poetry in blood now, killing "stupid white men."

WANTED: DEAD *AND* ALIVE

"Wanted" signs start springing up on every other tree, with the hunted doing his best to tear them all down. When two new bounty hunters come upon their prey and ask if he's indeed William Blake, he answers, "Yes I am. Do you know my poetry?" followed by a staccato haiku of bullets. His flip from humble accountant to violent outlaw is one Shadow thread here. Another is cultural. By projecting the best of a poetic genius onto this innocuous lad, Nobody is seeing *more* than meets the eye. Blake, on the other hand, is seeing less, clueless about any of his rescuer's witticisms, whether from the heart or from the scribe. One such Blakean quote could well apply to far too many Native-Euro exchanges: "The eagle never lost so much time as when he stooped to learn from the crow."

If Blake is clueless, other whites he encounters are truly bizarre: Billy Bob Thorton, Iggy Pop and Jared Harris play sexually ambivalent (one cross-dressing), Bible-quoting trappers, hysterically obsessed with the softness of Blake's hair. Alfred Molina portrays a "Christian," racist trading-post operator who attempts to sell smallpox-tainted blankets to Nobody. And then there's the matter of one decidedly sociopathic hit-man who kills off his competition and tracks Blake to the literal end of his line.

The contrast between this gorgeous Olympic Peninsula Makah Indian village and the wanton town of Machine is blatant, with mothers, children and artisans where before there were engineers, prostitutes and gunslingers. The stunningly-carved portal to their Meeting House is a Totemic animal's head: Unihipili leading the way to Aumakua. Classic thresholds. (When "active doors," these are threatening gauntlets to be run, with wheels or blades or rocks clashing from left and right. In an Inuit myth, a Shaman in a kayak must manage a narrow passage between two heaving, colliding icebergs.)

Nobody has escorted his weakening companion to the Bridge made of Waters. The Mirror. "There you will be taken up to the next level of the world. The place where William Blake is from, where his Spirit belongs." Decked out in venerable attire, laid to rest in a cedar bough-laden canoe, Blake is launched to sea on his final voyage. The last thing he beholds is his would-be killer catching up with Nobody, the one garbed in dark raiment, the other in light, and these two opposites fatally shooting one another. At the end of the line is the end of duality. And Blake, with an amulet at his unifying third eye, sails into an immeasurable peace.

Despite our choices, trite or meaningful, benighted or insightful, we are all generously brought to this final Initiation: a *Dead Man* (or *Woman*) sailing the glassy mirror "between sea and sky." Upper and Lower Worlds. All will face that exquisite moment when we'll gaze into the mirror of Nature and, in an illuminating, transformative flash, see nothing and Nobody. We can then hope that transport into the vaster, inner Sea will allot us a deeper reflection of our Soul.

PART XII

AFTERWORD
TOWARD A DEEPER
SHAMANIC CINEMA

E homai… Return me to the Wisdoms of the Ages
Return me to everything I knew. Return me to what is
known above. Return me to what is hidden below
Return me to the turnings of time. Return me
to everything I know. Return me to
my birthright. Return me to
my strength.
Return me
Return me
Return me
~ Aunty Edith of Hawaii

The End (of Deep Cinema) is near. And thus, given the Soul's swimmingly Eternal resilience in the round of Initiation, Rebirth will dawn soon-after. The tasks remaining for me as author are some measure of Recapitulation & Encouragement before Passing the Torch.

I began this book with a brief reference to a movie I *didn't* see, *Elvira Madigan*, in which star-crossed lovers (she poor, he aristocratic) were driven by their society to commit suicide, their departing Spirits symbolized by ascending butterflies. Much more recently I watched *The Illusionist*, another historical romance, in which iridescent royal blue butterflies figure strongly.

But here the two beleaguered European sweethearts (*he* poor, *she* aristocratic) are able to deftly shape-shift in and out of Death's realm (metamorphosize). They secure connubial bliss 'far from the madding crowd' in the blessed solitude of Nature: a triumph for Indigenous Soul-mates!!

Watching this lush, magical tale showed me that I'd grown considerably from youthful preoccupation with the Domain Basin of **Romance** to Weaving/Navigating the mature Ship of **Creativity**, which demands all directions of the Soul Compass be ignited. Where are *you* currently sailing, bobbing and weaving? What are your co-ordinates in the Web of Nature, deep Harmonics, Astrology, Sacred geometry, body and spirit? Do you feel truly, madly, deeply ALIVE?

Can you sense what it means to make your task of Initiation, of sounding out and fulfilling your Destiny, paramount? Whatever virtues (powers) you have, bring them to bear on this essential task. If you have Faith, have faith in the necessity of your life. If you have Courage, use it to proclaim your Fate. If you have patience, don't squander it on a life of "quiet desperation." If you have Love, love your life so that it resonates from the mundane (sunrise, sunset) to the exotic, the abstract to the erotic, the mysterious depths to the shattering heights...

Think of the bold faith of Voudon practitioners, slicing the air of the peristyle with machetes to open the pathways for the Loa. Let's play with those prospects here. What if, instead of imagining *possession by* a god, you realized you already *possessed* one: your Aumakua, Deep Soul-Self, Spirit Greatness. What if that Divinity were subjected to you, your awareness, your care and feeding, your expression? What if you knew it dwelt at your deepest layer of Subjectivity, longing to be revealed, and you that demi-god(dess)' only portal into Life? *You are.* Don't shut the door. In fact, grab your psychic machete, author's pen, or Bardic sword of light, and lacerate a pathway to usher in your uniquely vibrant frequency! Where is your Inner Light on the spectrum from Divinity to Zombie?

Has Deep Cinema given you a sense of Shamanic Soul? Is your wine-glass this Life one-, two-, or three-thirds full of Spiritual intoxication? Can you stretch your consciousness beyond the glitz and glare of the Market-place to Upper and Lower Worlds, and thus transform Middle World? To do so we must perceive this Earth-Water-Heavenly Planet as more than mere resource: as ensouled, and we sharing in that Life. We're only locked into the Manifest as much as we choose. Restorative Mystery is as near at hand as the Sea, the Wilderness, the "vasty" Heavens, the next enfolding Nightfall.

Know too that if you trust in the ever-expanding Domain Basins of your Soul, a vaster Order always lies beckoning you beyond any Season of Chaos. So don't ignore your roiling magma, your shifting tectonic plates. Don't tame your Hurricane. Don't turn a deaf ear to the profound strum of your ancient inner Whalesong. Let your heart become a Tibetan singing bowl attuned to anything and everything you love, from the infinitesimal to the Infinite. What is the Music of your Spheres? I'm listening... and the World awaits.

The End/Rebirth is near. How about looking to 2012 to give us a sense of mortal urgency? Study up on it (recommended reading: books by Daniel Pinchbeck and Barbara Hand Clow) as potential for a Collective Initiation. If nothing else, research will evoke your respect for the stupendous scientific, mathematical, and aesthetic articulation that is the Mayan Calendar. The Earth is currently undergoing an escalation of its hertz level (electrical influx) from 7.2 (1986) to 9.9 (1997), estimated to reach 13 hertz by that prophesized year. Native American Indians describe this "time between worlds" as a "wobble." We can all prepare to be wired for 220 in 2012, if we so choose.

Are you game to contribute to a New Vision, to join my imagined "Artists' G7 Conference": creating Screenplay, Song and Story-lines which sustain Souls unto 7 Generations? The prayer "All my Relations" must encompass the pleas of endangered plants and animals whose only home Planet we share. Can we become as eco-sacred-conscious as the ancient Irish story-tellers (Shanachie) and challenge the cinematic hub of Hollywood to become a Holy Wood? Ahhhhh!

Living Shamanically, are you in balance? Too yin, too yang? Here's your challenge:

Overly Yin: claim the East, the Sunrise. You've been carving out the dark Mystery of the West all your life, reflecting others' lights. Perhaps you've been long-pinioned with grief and loss, rejection and marginalization, in efforts to express yourself (Uhane). Be assured that your litany of loss is not a devastating and irreversible crop failure, precursor to starvation and grief. Each prayer you've planted and sent aloft has carved out another groove in the Labyrinthine passages of the Galaxy, where your Higher Self can Walkabout with the Loa, the Po'e Aumakua, accruing the means to realize those dreams.

Here on Earth, contemplate your Water-womb capacity for reflection, allowing your unique, unpredictable, irregular, singular constellation of lights to be reflected there. Soft dreams: lunar lights, passionate dreams: solar flares, dancing dreams: Aurora Borealis. Now let them all coalesce into ONE orb at your solar plexus. And tomorrow morning let your Orb rise in the East, blessing, composing, healing, inspiring, galvanizing the world with your warmth, the glow of your glorious, life-sustaining Sun, second to none.

Overly Yang: claim the West, your Holy Grail. An Eastern-born Navigator often resists the possible dissolution found in this direction, as when the daytime Ego fears morphing into something less manageable in nocturnal dreams ~ Hamlet's lament: "To sleep, perchance to dream!" Men and "Yangsters" are ultimately asked to "break on through to the other side," and integrate the initially disorienting but ultimately enchanting Dark as Source and Destiny, until their Souls resonate with these depths.

For enduring partnership: Only a man grounded enough in body and emotion can transport a woman to Celestial realms. Only a mature woman, a serene Sirene, who has accrued enough familiarity with Darkness via the likes of Shadow dancing, Sacred seduction, loss, Mystery, *intuition*, dream-work and grief, can provide adequate measure of a man in the reflective depths of her waters. (Puellas need not apply). She's built up a wedding bed of seaweed, Jamaican pearls and black sea-coral ~ a man needs a tough hide for that ravishing. Sleeping in the "vasty deep" with such a woman is a whole different kettle of kelp. She won't allow for escape, but will saturate you in deep, genuinely seductive, velvety dark *knowing* instead. Which, let's face it, is intimately more pleasurable for a *real* man.

So, dear reader, gaze into the Dark, and dare to whisper your name across those waters. **Your name.** You can trust that such a call will stir the depths of your Inland Sea, and strong currents will issue forth to cleanse you of all but your Eternal nature. "Who are you" who comes out of the blanching light of High Noon into this unfathomable place of "Mysteries we understand"?

Pray, and trust, that you will not return empty-handed, but encoded with the means to be "the music (movie?) maker and dreamer of dreams" your time requires. I leave you with this poignant, blessed encouragement, in the words of Ireland's Arthur O'Shaughnessey:

"We are the music makers, We are the dreamers of dreams.
Wandering by lone sea-breakers, And sitting by desolate streams;
World-losers and world-forsakers, On whom the pale moon gleams:
Yet we are the movers and shakers
Of the world forever it seems."

FILM INDEX

ABOUT THE AUTHOR

Photo courtesy of Ciarán Trainor-Brigham

MARY TRAINOR~BRIGHAM was born in Massachusetts and raised from earliest childhood with a foot in both canoes: that of Western culture and arts, and that of Indigenous cultures with their Nature-based wisdom. Her passion for Initiation, and helping modern people recognize their inevitable participation in it, has only deepened over her adulthood.

A graduate of both the New England Art Therapy Institute and the University of Creation Spirituality, Mary also has training in theatre (Boston Actors' Group), documentary filmmaking (with Mimi Edmunds of *60 Minutes* and *Discovery*), and feature film directing (with Richard Pearse of *The Long Walk Home, Threshold, Heartland*, etc.). Along the way she has continually sought out teaching by Native Spiritual leaders from North, South and Meso-America, Haiti, Hawaii, Australia, Bali, New Zealand and Africa, many of whom are referenced in *Deep Cinema*.

Professionally, Mary has acted in a number of productions, including the Boston Opera Company's *Montezuma*, has developed and taught drama and film classes for the United Way of Massachusetts, and was a long-standing member of the Harvard Square Script-Writers' Group. She also worked for Interlock Media of Cambridge, including a Smithsonian documentary project protecting the Rain Forest, and provided still shots for a BBC production. Via freelance work, she's had the deep honor of interviewing and photographing the Dalai Lama. And during her 15 years as a

Film Critic, her column was submitted into Pulitzer Prize competition for Distinquished Criticism.

In her work as a Therapist, both in residential treatment centers and her private practice, "Spa~for~the~Soul," Mary has integrated the healing potency of movies, developing *Film as Biography*, *Film as Initiation* and *Dreaming Beyond Demons*. She has also presented workshops nationally and internationally on Cross-Cultural Spirituality, most recently with the aid of her husband, Ciarán Trainor-Brigham, who has experience as an Actor in film and on the boards of the Taos Center for the Arts, New Mexico.

Mary is available to bring the tenets of *Deep Cinema* to bear on your screenplays (Scribe~for~Hire), on-site during film productions (Deep Cinema Consulting and Counseling), as well as via her Spa~for~the~Soul~Compass Workshops, Lectures, and Teleseminars. Please feel free to check in on DeepCinema.com and to contact her via *soulsoundings@gmail.com*.

All fulfillment in your Creative endeavors — May you flourish!

FILM & VIDEO BOOKS

Archetypes for Writers: *Using the Power of Your Subconscious*
Jennifer Van Bergen / $22.95

Art of Film Funding, The: *Alternate Financing Concepts*
Carole lee Dean / $26.95

Cinematic Storytelling: *The 100 Most Powerful Film Conventions Every Filmmaker*
Must Know / Jennifer Van Sijll / $24.95

Complete Independent Movie Marketing Handbook, The: *Promote, Distribute & Sell*
Your Film or Video / Mark Steven Bosko / $39.95

Creating Characters: *Let Them Whisper Their Secrets*
Marisa D'Vari / $26.95

Crime Writer's Reference Guide, The: *1001 Tips for Writing the Perfect Crime*
Martin Roth / $20.95

Cut by Cut: *Editing Your Film or Video*
Gael Chandler / $35.95

Digital Filmmaking 101, 2nd Edition: *An Essential Guide to Producing Low-Budget*
Movies / Dale Newton and John Gaspard / $26.95

Directing Actors: *Creating Memorable Performances for Film and Television*
Judith Weston / $26.95

Directing Feature Films: *The Creative Collaboration Between Directors, Writers, and*
Actors / Mark Travis / $26.95

Elephant Bucks: *An Insider's Guide to Writing for TV Sitcoms*
Sheldon Bull / $24.95

Eye is Quicker, The: *Film Editing; Making a Good Film Better*
Richard D. Pepperman / $27.95

Fast, Cheap & Under Control: *Lessons Learned from the Greatest Low-Budget Movies*
of All Time / John Gaspard / $26.95

Fast, Cheap & Written That Way: *Top Screenwriters on Writing for Low-Budget Movies*
John Gaspard / $26.95

Film & Video Budgets, *4th Updated Edition*
Deke Simon and Michael Wiese / $26.95

Film Directing: *Cinematic Motion, 2nd Edition*
Steven D. Katz / $27.95

Film Directing: *Shot by Shot, Visualizing from Concept to Screen*
Steven D. Katz / $27.95

Film Director's Intuition, The: *Script Analysis and Rehearsal Techniques*
Judith Weston / $26.95

Film Production Management 101: *The Ultimate Guide for Film and Television*
Production Management and Coordination / Deborah S. Patz / $39.95

Filmmaking for Teens: *Pulling Off Your Shorts*
Troy Lanier and Clay Nichols / $18.95

First Time Director: *How to Make Your Breakthrough Movie*
Gil Bettman / $27.95

From Word to Image: *Storyboarding and the Filmmaking Process*
Marcie Begleiter / $26.95

Hollywood Standard, The: *The Complete and Authoritative Guide to Script Format and*
Style / Christopher Riley / $18.95

Independent Film Distribution: *How to Make a Successful End Run Around the Big*
Guys / Phil Hall / $26.95

Independent Film and Videomakers Guide – 2nd Edition, The: *Expanded and Updated*
Michael Wiese / $29.95

Inner Drives: *How to Write and Create Characters Using the Eight Classic Centers of*
Motivation / Pamela Jaye Smith / $26.95

I'll Be in My Trailer!: *The Creative Wars Between Directors & Actors*
John Badham and Craig Modderno / $26.95

Moral Premise, The: *Harnessing Virtue & Vice for Box Office Success*
Stanley D. Williams, Ph.D. / $24.95

Myth and the Movies: *Discovering the Mythic Structure of 50 Unforgettable Films*
Stuart Voytilla / $26.95

On the Edge of a Dream: *Magic and Madness in Bali*
Michael Wiese / $16.95

Perfect Pitch, The: *How to Sell Yourself and Your Movie Idea to Hollywood*
Ken Rotcop / $16.95

Power of Film, The
Howard Suber / $27.95

Psychology for Screenwriters: *Building Conflict in your Script*
William Indick, Ph.D. / $26.95

Save the Cat!: *The Last Book on Screenwriting You'll Ever Need*
Blake Snyder / $19.95

Save the Cat! Goes to the Movies: *The Screenwriter's Guide to Every Story Ever Told*
Blake Snyder / $24.95

Screenwriting 101: *The Essential Craft of Feature Film Writing*
Neill D. Hicks / $16.95

Screenwriting for Teens: *The 100 Principles of Screenwriting Every Budding Writer*
Must Know / Christina Hamlett / $18.95

Script-Selling Game, The: *A Hollywood Insider's Look at Getting Your Script Sold and*
Produced / Kathie Fong Yoneda / $16.95

Selling Your Story in 60 Seconds: *The Guaranteed Way to get Your Screenplay or*
Novel Read / Michael Hauge / $12.95

Setting Up Your Scenes: *The Inner Workings of Great Films*
Richard D. Pepperman / $24.95

Setting Up Your Shots: *Great Camera Moves Every Filmmaker Should Know*
Jeremy Vineyard / $19.95

Shaking the Money Tree, 2nd Edition: *The Art of Getting Grants and Donations for*
Film and Video Projects / Morrie Warshawski / $26.95

Sound Design: *The Expressive Power of Music, Voice, and Sound Effects in Cinema*
David Sonnenschein / $19.95

Special Effects: *How to Create a Hollywood Film Look on a Home Studio Budget* /
Michael Slone / $31.95

Stealing Fire From the Gods, 2nd Edition: *The Complete Guide to Story for Writers &*
Filmmakers / James Bonnet / $26.95

Ultimate Filmmaker's Guide to Short Films, The: *Making It Big in Shorts*
Kim Adelman / $16.95

Way of Story, The: *The Craft & Soul of Writing*
Catherine Anne Jones / $22.95

Working Director, The: *How to Arrive, Thrive & Survive in the Director's Chair*
Charles Wilkinson / $22.95

Writer's Journey, – 3rd Edition, The: *Mythic Structure for Writers*
Christopher Vogler / $26.95

Writing the Action Adventure: *The Moment of Truth*
Neill D. Hicks / $14.95

Writing the Comedy Film: *Make 'Em Laugh*
Stuart Voytilla and Scott Petri / $14.95

Writing the Killer Treatment: *Selling Your Story Without a Script*
Michael Halperin / $14.95

Writing the Second Act: *Building Conflict and Tension in Your Film Script*
Michael Halperin / $19.95

Writing the Thriller Film: *The Terror Within*
Neill D. Hicks / $14.95

Writing the TV Drama Series – 2nd Edition: *How to Succeed as a Professional Writer*
in TV / Pamela Douglas / $26.95

DVD & VIDEOS

Field of Fish: *VHS Video*
Directed by Steve Tanner and Michael Wiese, Written by Annamaria Murphy / $9.95

Hardware Wars: DVD / Written and Directed by Ernie Fosselius / $14.95

Sacred Sites of the Dalai Lamas– DVD, The: *A Pilgrimage to Oracle Lake*
A Documentary by Michael Wiese / $24.95